Change or Decay

Final Report of the Liverpool Inner Area Study

Hugh Wilson & Lewis Womersley
Chartered Architects & Town Planners

Roger Tym and Associates
Urban and Land Economists

Jamieson Mackay and Partners
Consulting Civil and Transportation Engineers

LONDON   HER MAJESTY'S STATIONERY OFFICE

Designed by HMSO Graphic Design

Cover photograph by Peter Leeson

ISBN 0 11 751143 9

Foreword

by the Minister of Housing and Construction

This report is the outcome of one of the three studies undertaken by consultants for the Department of the Environment in the inner areas of major cities – Birmingham, Liverpool and London.

For over four years the consultants, in collaboration with the local authority, worked in a part of Liverpool's inner area which includes Smithdown, Granby and Edge Hill carrying out research into a wide range of issues. At the same time they have carried out action projects which in addition to shedding light on the issues have brought some practical benefits to the residents of the study area. Reports on many of the action projects have been published and are available from the Inner Cities Directorate of the Department, together with reports of particular research studies done by the consultants.

It is well over a decade since some of us started to advocate a 'total' approach to urban renewal, urging that this should be brought to the centre of politics rather than continue as a peripheral issue. During these last four years, while the studies continued, concern about the multiple problems and challenges of inner urban areas has grown. Peter Shore's statement in the House of Commons on 6 April 1977 made this a central issue of the Government's social, economic and planning policies. The work of the inner area studies has contributed much to our understanding of these problems. The Summary Reports published in January of this year have already stimulated many valuable comments as to the future directions of urban policy and have contributed to the discussions which led to the Commons statement and then to the preparation of the Government's White Paper. But the Summary Reports could only set out the consultants' arguments and conclusions in outline. The present report sets them out in full, with their supporting evidence, and contains a great deal of additional material.

It has been my privilege during the greater part of the consultants' study to serve as Chairman of the Joint Steering Committee which has guided their work. I am grateful to the members and officers of the Liverpool City Council for their help and co-operation. These studies will prove to be of lasting value to everyone concerned with renewing the conditions and opportunities for life in the old urban areas which lie at the hearts of our cities. I hope this report, and those from the other two studies, will be read widely and closely. They certainly deserve to be.

Reg Freeson

Chairman of the Steering Committee

June 1977

Preface

We were invited by the Secretary of State for the Environment in September 1972 to carry out a pilot study of Liverpool's inner area. Later, we were appointed to carry out the full Inner Area Study of Liverpool, starting work in July 1973 and finishing three years later.

During our time in Liverpool we worked on many problems of the inner area through action projects and more formal study and research. We wrote numerous reports on the different pieces of work. A full list, and copies of individual reports, may be obtained from the Department of the Environment. Now, at the end of the study, we make our final report. It does not attempt to recapitulate or summarise the earlier, detailed reports. Rather, it is a synthesis of the whole study, placing its various elements in their correct perspective. It sets out what we did, what we found out, our conclusions, and our recommendations for action by Government.

The study has been directed by a Steering Committee of members of the Liverpool City Council and Merseyside County Council under the chairmanship of a Minister of the Department of the Environment. Its membership has fluctuated with changes in Government, changes in political control of the local authority, and local government reorganisation. We acknowledge our debt to the Committee and are grateful for its support. Nevertheless the conclusions in this report are our sole responsibility.

We acknowledge our indebtedness, also, to the members and officers of Liverpool City Council and Merseyside County Council without whose help the study would not have been possible. We are equally grateful for the cooperation we have received from government officials, industrialists, voluntary organisations and community groups.

Finally, our remit was 'to look at the needs of the (inner) areas from the point of view of the people living in them'. We trust we have not failed in this duty for, in the end, it is for their benefit that the study has been mounted and it is to their future well being that responsible government action must be directed.

January 1977

The Consultants' Study Team

Hugh Wilson & Lewis Womersley

Sir Hugh Wilson OBE
Lyn Davies (associate in charge)
Colin Watts (team leader in Liverpool)

Joan Bischoff   Eileen French
David Cullingford   Robin Little
Daphne Davies   George Morton
Pat Eccles

Roger Tym and Associates

Roger Tym   David Chambers
Ian McDonald   Roy Brockman
Rupert Nabarro   Chris Gethin
Kenneth Wren   Rachel Tingle

Jamieson Mackay and Partners

David Pickering   Simon Burton

Contents

List of illustrations

An impression of inner Liverpool
photographic section between pages 61 and 80.

1 Introduction

Care homes

The inner areas

The inner areas of our large cities have been the focus of an increasing concern during the past ten years, highlighted by particular events and places. The litany of place names is long and growing: Notting Hill in London, St. Anne's in Nottingham, Maryhill in Glasgow, Moss Side and Hulme in Manchester and Liverpool 8. But these are only the well known places, dramatised by events or documented in careful study. There are many other, still anonymous areas where similar conditions prevail.

What images do these inner areas conjure up? They are of long terraces of small, bye-law houses built for the working classes a hundred years ago in the industrial areas, many still unimproved and long past affording adequate living conditions for the last quarter of the twentieth century. They are of substantial town houses built in the nineteenth century for the wealthy middle classes but now split up into flats and furnished rooms for a varied and changing population. They are of overcrowded blocks of council flats, ravaged by vandalism. The inner areas have become the homes of the unskilled, the unemployed, the socially disadvantaged and, increasingly, of dense concentrations of black people, not only new immigrants but also those whose families have been living in Britain for two or three generations. They live their lives amid derelict industrial sites, abandoned docks, disused railway sidings, boarded up shops, empty warehouses and factories and vacant land. This is the visible image; rundown slums, almost ghettos, sandwiched between redeveloped city centres and the suburbs, seen by many people only on their journey to work as they look down from the railway across the backs of terraces, or across the vacant land from main roads.

Nearly four million people live in the inner areas of London and Glasgow, of Newcastle, Leeds, Manchester, Nottingham, Birmingham and Liverpool. The neglect and decay is suffered by all who live there. But the extremes of poverty and social stress on which so much of the reputation of the inner city is based, is experienced only by a small minority. For them it has become a trap, restricting their opportunities to find good housing and secure employment. But for many it provides a strong community, proximity to the city centre, good public transport, and a variety of activities and services.

The inner areas are not a cause of deprivation found within them; responsibility for this must lie in the structure of our society, its economic relationships and institutions. They do not even contain a majority of those who are deprived. But they do contain the greatest concentrations of deprivation in Britain today. One in fifteen of the country's population live in these inner city areas yet in 1971 they contained one seventh of its unskilled workers, a fifth of its households living in some form of housing stress, and a third of its new commonwealth immigrants. The main reasons for this degree of concentration lie in the economic fortunes and housing conditions of the cities themselves.

The problems which the inner areas now pose for government were not seen clearly for many years. Increasing personal affluence after the Second World War led to an explosive growth in new private house building. Right up until the late 1960s, this new construction was being planned in the expectation that population and national wealth would continue to grow rapidly for the rest of the century. The emphasis lay on the creation of new suburbs, and the expansion of villages and small country towns around the big conurbations. At the same time, the major housing effort in the public sector was directed to making good the backlog of waiting lists which had accumulated during and after the war and to rehousing the population from slum clearance areas. The new towns were a significant feature in this post-war expansion outside the main cities, particularly in capturing the imagination of so many different interests. They aimed at, and achieved, a high standard of community planning which brought together good housing in an attractive environment, new schools and social welfare services integrated with jobs, shopping centres and recreational activities. Together with the new suburbs, they housed most of the additional households resulting from the growth of population and affluence and many of those who left the inner areas of their own accord.

But now national economic depression and the reappearance of mass unemployment have brought to the surface the economic decline of the inner areas which had been masked by regional growth. A series of studies and the activities of national pressure groups have drawn attention to the persistence of poverty. More explosively, the debate about race and immigration has inevitably focussed on the inner areas where so many of the black population live.

An increasing awareness can be traced through a series of special projects. The starting point can be found in the Plowden Report[1] which in 1966 argued that 'the principle that special need calls for special help should be given a new cutting edge'. It introduced the concept of positive discrimination in favour of schools which had exceptionally large numbers of children who were considered to be handicapped. Schools in deprived areas were to be given priority far beyond an attempt to equalise resources. The justification put forward was that the homes and neighbourhoods from which many of the children came provided little support and stimulus for learning. Thus the schools were to supply a compensating environment.

Although a number of the basic assumptions underlying this approach have been called into question through subsequent research, the Plowden Report remains the single most easily identifiable landmark in this evolution of concern with areas of deprivation. Its immediate outcome was the introduction of higher capital allocations, equipment grants, teacher quotas and high salaries for staff in

(1) Central Advisory Council for Education (England), *Children and their Primary Schools* (1967).

2

designated schools. The chosen criteria were such that inevitably many of the schools were in inner city areas.

Following the Plowden Report, educational priority projects were set up by the Department of Education and Science in four widely differing areas; Deptford in London, the West Riding, and parts of inner Birmingham and Liverpool. Apart from their lessons for education policy, these projects had a further, even more influential outcome. They legitimised an approach to the formulation and evaluation of social policy through action research. Halsey defined action research as 'small-scale interventions in the functioning of the real world, usually in administrative systems, and the close examination of the effects of such interventions'.[1] This approach became the recognised method for community development projects under the Home Office, later to be taken up by the inner area studies and area management trials of the Department of the Environment. The approach involved the selection of study areas, the setting up of teams for each study, and the implementation of action projects within each study area.

The next major initiative was the Urban Programme, announced by the Prime Minister in a speech in May 1968. Enoch Powell's notorious 'rivers of blood' speech which focussed so much attention on racial issues in the inner areas was no doubt a contributing factor.[2] The following July, the then Home Secretary (James Callaghan) said 'there remain areas of severe social deprivation in a number of our cities and towns, often scattered in relatively small pockets. They require special help to meet their social needs and to bring their physical services to an adequate level'.[3]

The Urban Programme has comprised grants to local authorities and voluntary organisations for work in deprived areas. It 'is not intended to do the work of the major social services like education or health; it does not build primary schools, houses or hospitals. It tries rather to encourage projects which have a reasonably quick effect and which go directly to the roots of special social need (ie multiple deprivation)'.[4] It could well be argued that these aims are mutually exclusive. Nevertheless the Urban Programme has contributed much to the growing awareness of inner area problems particularly in aiding the work of community groups.

Two neighbourhood projects were started under the Urban Programme, in Teesside and the Brunswick area of Liverpool. They were attempts at devising comprehensive programmes of capital expenditure on improving the social provision and quality of environment in small areas of special need.

(1) Halsey A H (editor), *Educational Priority, Vol 1: EPA Problems and Policies* (HMSO 1972).

(2) Speech on immigration to West Midlands Area Conservative Political Centre, Birmingham, 20 April 1968, reported in *The Times*, 22 April 1968.

(3) Statement to the House of Commons, 22 July 1968 (*Hansard*, col. 40).

(4) Home Office Notes on the Urban Programme (April 1972), quoted in Glennester H and Hatch S, *Positive Discrimination and Inequality*, Fabian Research Series 314 (March 1974).

The Home Office announced its community development projects in July 1969, to be financed partly from the Urban Programme and partly by the local authorities taking part. Their aims were 'to discover how far the social problems experienced by people in a local community can be better understood and resolved through closer coordination of all the agencies in the social welfare field ... together with local residents themselves. There is a special emphasis on citizen involvement and community self help.'[1]

Twelve projects were started, each to last five years. The first four, in Coventry, Southwark, Liverpool and Glyncorrwg (West Glamorgan), started in 1970. Each was intended to be autonomous, with a separate research team from a suitable university. The project teams worked largely independently of the local authorities and often came into direct conflict with them over policies affecting their areas. Despite this independence each project developed along very similar lines. Each responded to perceived local issues by setting up information and law centres, playgrounds, traffic management schemes, youth work, employment projects or community centres. But many of the teams felt that this work was achieving few results and turned to putting pressure on the local authorities to adjust their policies.

As the programme entered its final stages, the surviving projects decided to pool their experiences by setting up the CDP Information and Intelligence Unit as a co-operative venture, with the hesitant support of the Home Office. They carried their disaffection with the CDP approach and values a stage further. In their proposal for the final stages of work for the remaining CDPs they drew a number of conclusions about their work to date.[2]

Not only did they reject the original thesis on which the CDPs were set up, namely that a community development approach could achieve significant social change, but they also rejected their own interim conclusions that changes in local authority administration would have the desired effects. They argued that the problems they were supposed to be solving were a result of inequalities in society and that their eventual solution would require fundamental changes in the distribution of wealth and power, through a programme of political education.

The last two links in the direct line from Plowden to the Inner Area Studies curiously came from Liverpool itself. Liverpool City Council was one of the first in the country to investigate seriously its internal organisation and methods. Management consultants (McKinsey & Co) recommended a radical restructuring of the local authority's committees and departments on principles which later became standard practice in, for instance, the Bains report.[3] They included a reduction in the number of committees and departments, the creation of a policy

(1) Home Office Notes, 1972, quoted in Glennester and Hatch, *op. cit.*

(2) The National Community Development Project, *Forward Plan 1975–76* (CDP Information and Intelligence Unit, London, 1975).

(3) *The New Local Authorities, Management and Structure* (HMSO, 1972).

and finance committee, and the appointment of a chief executive.[1] The main outcome of these reforms was to simplify the decision making machinery of the local authority. But they also laid the ground for innovations such as the Inner Area Plan Reviews by the City Planning Department, interdepartmental working on projects such as the Brunswick Neighbourhood Project, and changes in budgeting techniques.

The final link in the chain had a more direct influence. The Shelter Neighbourhood Action Project (SNAP) was carried out in part of the Granby ward of Liverpool 8; a rundown area of a thousand Victorian terraced houses, many of them in multiple occupation. It was an area long renowned for its social problems but also for its community strength. The SNAP team set up office in the area in 1970 and tried to generate a common sense of purpose towards housing improvement in perhaps one of the most socially and racially diverse neighbourhoods in the whole country.

The direct results of SNAP were tenuous. It failed in its own chief objective, for a community-based general improvement area founded on a truly cooperative effort between local community and local authority. Nevertheless it left behind a housing aid centre, a housing cooperative and a residents' association and eventually Granby became a statutory general improvement area with some real achievements to its credit.

But the experience of SNAP led its director to the view that something more radical would be needed in order to achieve a lasting improvement in the social conditions, housing and environment of the inner area of Liverpool. A system of government was needed which would 'combine sensitive communication with effective action'. To that end SNAP recommended a number of changes in the institutions and priorities of government, amounting to a 'new urban programme'.[2]

The impact of SNAP on thinking about inner areas was more substantial. Peter Walker, when Opposition spokesman for environmental affairs, was only one of many influential visitors to SNAP. Other links were forged with the Liverpool City Planning Department and with McKinsey & Co whose time at Liverpool overlapped with that of SNAP. McKinsey & Co wrote a paper on the need for a new understanding of inner area issues.[3] The former director of SNAP was invited to become a special advisor to the Department of the Environment following the appointment of Peter Walker as Secretary of State.

The Inner Area Studies

By 1972 there was growing anxiety in government about the conditions in which many people were living in inner city areas; about the persistence of pockets of

(1) McKinsey & Co Inc, *A New Management System for the City of Liverpool* (May 1969).
(2) Shelter Neighbourhood Action Project, *Another Chance for the Cities, SNAP 69/72* (Liverpool 1972).
(3) McKinsey & Co Inc, *A New Approach to the Problems of the Cities* (1972).

poverty and social stress; about increasing crime rates and racial tension; about high levels of unemployment irrespective of changes in the national economy. It was becoming clear, too, that local authorities, despite strenuous efforts, particularly in slum clearance, had not succeeded in eradicating urban deprivation.

So, in reply to a question in the House of Commons on 26 July 1972 Peter Walker, the Secretary of State for the Environment, announced the commissioning of two groups of studies. The first was to comprise three fairly brief studies into the management of cities, the so called urban guidelines studies.[1] For the other group, he said that

'three studies should be (made) into the environmental problems of inner city areas. I am inviting the Birmingham City Council, the Liverpool City Council and the Council of the London Borough of Lambeth to join with us in these studies.

In these studies we shall be looking for possible courses of action on the environmental problems of inner city areas. This will involve practical work on the ground, of which my Department will bear the major part of the cost. We shall try to look at the needs of the study areas as a whole from the point of view of the people living in them, and to derive lessons on powers, resources and techniques. The work would extend over several years. The first stage will be to commission project reports which will set our proposals for the practical work in the main studies. We should have these project reports by about the end of the year.'[2]

The brief given to each of the firms of planning consultants appointed to carry out the studies contained four instructions

'to discover by study a better definition of inner areas and their problems

to investigate by experiments on the ground the actions affecting the physical environment of these areas which could usefully be undertaken for social and environmental purposes

to examine whether the concept of area management can usefully be developed and what the practical implications would be for the local authority

to provide the base for general conclusions on statutory powers, finance and resource questions, and techniques.'[3]

Each of the firms of consultants was invited, in September 1972, to prepare a project report setting out its interpretation of the brief and the programme of work which it proposed should be carried out. These reports were prepared in close consultation with officials of the Department of the Environment and the relevant local authority. The project reports were completed by March 1973 and the

(1) Department of the Environment, *Making Towns Better: The Sunderland Study* (HMSO 1973); *The Rotherham Study* (HMSO 1973); *The Oldham Study* (HMSO 1973)'

(2) Written answer to a Parliamentary Question, 26 July 1972 (*Hansard*, col. 319–20).

(3) Letter to the consultants from the Department of the Environment, 2 August 1972

consultants were appointed to carry out the full studies in July 1973. The three studies thereafter followed different paths, depending on how each study team interpreted the common brief, how each was received locally and, above all, on the variation in local circumstances found in each city.

Outline of the report

In the report which follows we devote the next two chapters to a brief account of the study itself. Chapter two describes the evolution of the study during its three years. A study area of some sixty thousand population was chosen and a programme of action research started. An experiment in area management was set up in a part of inner Liverpool and we analysed the allocation of resources to this area by the local authority. We commissioned an analysis of Census data by the Planning Research Applications Group of the Centre for Environmental Studies. Later, we widened the scope of the study to include more formal research into economic issues in Liverpool and Merseyside and reviews of housing, education and planning policies. We wrote a series of reports on the action projects and research during the course of the study. These have subsequently been published by the Department of the Environment from whom a complete list and copies of the reports may be obtained.

Chapter three describes each of the action projects and comes to certain conclusions about the usefulness of the programme as a whole and the problems of innovation in the provision of local authority services. The results of the individual projects are described more fully in the separately published reports, but they also contribute to the later chapters in this report.

Chapter four contains a description of inner Liverpool, identifying a complex pattern of three principal types of area, the older terraced areas, the rooming house areas and the inner council estates. The inner areas thus defined contained two hundred and eighty thousand people in 1971, about half of the city's population. They contrasted with the two principal types of area in the rest of Liverpool, the high status areas and the outer council estates. The contrasts lay in their social status, the nature and tenure of their housing stock and above all in the loss of population from inner Liverpool during the last half century.

The following six chapters describe different facets of inner Liverpool though at all times having regard to its wider context in the city and county. Chapter five picks on groups of people at risk of poverty, the unskilled; untrained young people; large families; single parent families; the elderly and single people living alone; and the black population. It shows the extent to which concentrations of these groups of people are found in certain parts of inner Liverpool and that these areas coincide with the worst incidence of social malaise. But it shows, too, that concentrations of people at risk and social malaise are to be found in some of Liverpool's outer council estates though not to the same intensity as in the worst parts of the inner area.

Chapter six charts the impact of Liverpool's economic decline on its inner areas, the resulting high unemployment and lack of new industrial investment. Chapters seven and eight look at different aspects of housing. The former describes the different tenures and the problems of those at greatest disadvantage in gaining access to housing. The latter concentrates on the problems of maintaining and improving the housing stock, using case studies based on action projects in an area of two thousand older private houses needing improvement and in the management of a similar number of council tenancies. Chapter nine examines growing up in the inner city. It does so from the standpoint of the difficulties which young people encounter at the end of their schooling, when they try to find a job and acquire work skills. From this, it goes on to ask questions about their education and the problems of vandalism.

Chapter ten brings the descriptive chapters to an end by a selective look at the workings of the local authority in the context of the inner areas. Three particular aspects are considered. The ability of the local authority to gain a comprehensive understanding of the needs of small areas; its impact as a developer on the inner areas; and the response by small communities to the actions of government. The chapter concludes by asking questions about the workings of representative local government in the inner areas.

The last three chapters in the report present our conclusions. Chapter eleven brings together the results of our descriptions of the inner areas of Liverpool. It shows that although they comprise about a half of the city, the real problems of social and economic deprivation are to be found in quite small parts of the rooming house areas and in much of the inner council estates whose population in 1971 was about seventy thousand. The rest of the inner areas, with a population of about two hundred thousand, comprise the better rooming house areas and older terraced areas, which have no more than average proportions of those most at risk of poverty in the city. However, the analysis shows that problems of a similar character to those encountered in the worst inner council estates also face people living in some of the outer council estates, although to a less intense degree.

Thus far, the analysis has focussed on the city of Liverpool. Widening its scope to the rest of Merseyside shows that the worst social and economic deprivation in 1971 was largely confined to the core city of Liverpool. Conditions similar to those in the older terraced areas of Liverpool were to be found in other parts of the county, notably Bootle and Birkenhead; and examples of the worst outer council estates were concentrated in Knowsley, notably in Kirkby. Extending the analysis still further afield, similar concentrations of deprivation were to be found in 1971 in the inner areas of London, Glasgow and most of the larger English conurbations, with local variations in character.

The chapter goes on to discuss the accumulated disadvantages of the inner areas which both bring about the concentrations of deprivation and add to their impact: the economic decline, the housing stock, the environmental dereliction, the reputation of the area and the unequal provision of government services in relation to needs. The long term trend for decline is described and a case made for a change in the direction of policy towards the inner area. The current changes in government policies are referred to and the aims and arguments described for a policy of regeneration for the inner area of Liverpool and, by extension, the inner areas of other major British conurbations.

Chapter twelve lists four programmes to implement a policy of regenerating inner Liverpool. The programmes would be to halt the economic decline of the inner area through various forms of industrial promotion and economic enterprise; to raise levels of skill through the training and placement of adults and young people and through work preparation schemes; to improve housing opportunities for those at greatest disadvantage in finding accommodation; and to channel additional resources into the areas of greatest social need, through improved council housing management, private housing improvement, environmental care and community development.

The recommendations are summarised in this chapter. Some of them have been worked out more fully than can be given here; further details may be found in separately published reports to which we refer. Others are akin to new policies currently being worked out by Liverpool City Council or Merseyside County Council, though with changes in emphasis. Nevertheless, we present all four programmes in this chapter as they need to be seen as a closely integrated group and indicate the range of tasks to be undertaken for the first priority, the regeneration of Liverpool's inner areas. But if they are successful in this, they will have a wider impact on the rest of the city and county and would provide valuable experience for application elsewhere.

Chapter thirteen turns to the final, crucial questions of how these programmes may be implemented in a way which offers hope of success. It discusses the institutional questions: the attitudes within central and local government to the problems of inner areas; the tasks for central government; and the necessity for a total approach by which we mean a political commitment to giving real priority to the areas in greatest need and an administration capable of identifying, and responding sensitively to, their needs. We consider briefly the question of resources for the inner area. Some would come through redistribution of resources currently being used elsewhere in Liverpool or Merseyside through a reorientation of priorities. Others would require additional resources from central government. But we conclude that resources are not the key question; that lies in the political will and administrative attitudes with which the total approach for the regeneration of inner areas is pursued.

This final report of our study comes after ten years of activity by central government departments designed to develop their understanding of the issues and the policies and institutions needed to respond to them. In 1973 the Home Secretary was made responsible for coordinating the government's urban social policies. An Urban Deprivation Unit was set up in the Home Office with responsibility for the Urban Programme and CDPs and out of its work, in cooperation with other government departments, came the proposal for comprehensive community programmes, though at the time of writing, only one has been announced.

More recently, Peter Shore, the Secretary of State for the Environment, made a major speech in Manchester on urban policy.[1] After reviewing inner area issues he concluded that their causes lay primarily 'in their relative economic decline, in a major migration of people, often the most skilled, and in a massive reduction in the number of jobs which are left.' He noted the significant change in projections of future population growth since the 1960s, as a result of which planning policy can 'no longer be based so much on the search for new space to house our growing families by dispersal from our major cities.' He promised a review of future policies on dispersal and the future of the inner areas, saying that 'if cities fail, so to a large extent does our society; that is the urgency of tackling the problem.'

Understanding about the inner areas is growing both in Liverpool and nationally. The close connection between economic decline, housing policy and social attitudes is gaining official acceptance and few would now advocate that the problems of the inner areas can be solved simply by slum clearance or planned dispersal. But other dangers threaten. One is an attitude which says that as the root causes of deprivation lie in society and its institutions, any inner area policy is doomed to failure in the absence of more fundamental social reform. But this is to misunderstand the purpose of the inner area policies we advocate. They are not a substitute for more far reaching reforms but an essential component of urban policy in this country.

An equally dangerous assumption is that lasting solutions can be achieved simply by the application of more resources to the inner areas through the unchanged machinery of government. Certainly, the scale of problems is such that many more resources will be needed. But fundamental to a change in policy must be a change in attitude reflected in the machinery of both central and local government which allows them to see and approach the total needs of inner areas in an integrated way, yet at the same time pay regard to the special circumstances of individual areas.

(1) Speech at Manchester Town Hall, 17 September 1976.

2 The Liverpool Study

The choice of Liverpool

In retrospect, it appears inevitable that Liverpool City Council should have participated in the inner area studies. Post-war central government policy consisted mainly of an attempt to stem the decline of the Merseyside economy by attracting new industry. At the same time, the local authority was pursuing a massive slum clearance and redevelopment programme requiring a large overspill of population from the inner area of the city to new sites on the periphery. Yet by the early 1970s both programmes were in difficulties. Unemployment rates in Merseyside remained

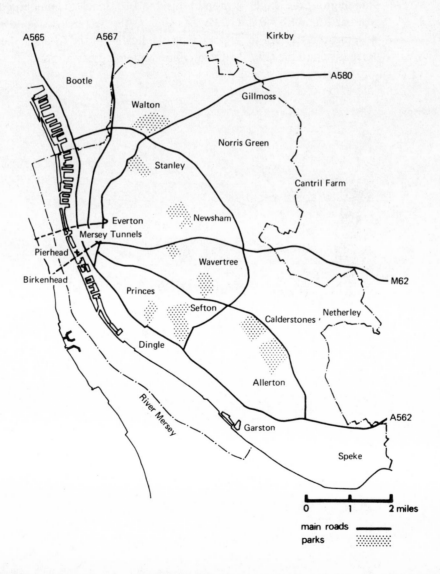

**Figure 1
City of Liverpool**

much higher than in the rest of the country while the end of the first stage of the slum clearance programme brought a reassessment of housing policy.

Furthermore, other changes were occurring. We have already referred to the McKinsey report and its effect on the structure of the Corporation. But from the middle 1960s onwards, no less dramatic changes were being experienced in political control of the Council with massive swings between Labour and Conservative. At the same time community action was intensifying and the rise of community politics brought the Liberal Party into control in the 1973 elections for the shadow City Council set up in preparation for local government reorganisation. Big changes were occurring too in secondary education and, in a more technical field, the City Planning Department was pioneering methods for measuring the incidence of deprivation in its first social malaise study.[1]

Liverpool had long been fertile ground for experimental projects and social surveys. It attracted every one of the series of national projects: educational priority in Paddington; the neighbourhood project in Brunswick; community development in Vauxhall; and SNAP in Granby. As soon as the Secretary of State made his statement in the House of Commons, the Leader of the Council, the Chief Executive and the City Planning Officer were ready to respond.

Figure 2
Inner city projects

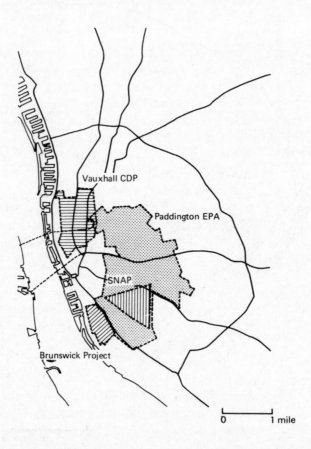

0   1 mile

(1) Amos F J C, *Social Malaise in Liverpool* (City Planning Department 1970).

Development of the study

The Liverpool Inner Area Study was a partnership between the Department of the Environment and the Liverpool City Council, later joined by Merseyside County Council after local government reorganisation. To that end, the responsible minister in the Department of the Environment invited the Leader of the City Council and other leading members to form a Steering Committee for the study under his chairmanship. This Committee met regularly during the study to approve the work programme drawn up by the consultants, and to receive progress reports and recommendations for action from them. It was advised by a group of chief officers under the chairmanship of the Chief Executive.

We were given six months to develop a basic approach, choose a study area and draw up a programme of work. The study was then expected to last 'several years'. Our initial discussions with officials during this pilot stage revealed the existence of a great deal of information. The City Planning Department already had a working definition of the inner area based on a city-wide system of planning districts and was proposing to revise the first social malaise survey. Detailed, unpublished data from the 1971 Census of Population were awaited. The various experimental projects were producing new insights. There was a surprising consensus about what was wrong in inner Liverpool, particularly among officials, but no such certainty about what should be done.

The total approach figured largely in these discussions. Peter Walker had referred to the need for a total approach in the context of the urban guidelines studies, and had asked the inner area studies to look at the needs of the selected study areas from the point of view of the people living there. The need for a total approach at the local level was confirmed by our initial discussions which covered a wide spectrum of issues. They ranged from the management of council housing to the problem of single parent families; from uncertainty about the future of individual streets to crime and prostitution; from the opportunities for adult education to street sweeping and litter. The list seemed endless.

We adopted as the underlying principle for the study Peter Walker's request to examine inner area problems from the point of view of those living there. Such an approach appeared to have many advantages. It focussed our attention on the services actually being delivered to inner city residents, the sharp end of the policies laid down grandly in Parliament and Town Hall. Yet it put no limitation on our field of concern, beyond our own capacity to undertake action and research.

The study area

A study area with a population of about sixty thousand was chosen to be the focus for the study. The main criterion for its selection was that it should exhibit broadly the range of inner area problems anticipated by the consultants. A number of possible areas were identified forming a series of overlapping wedges emanating from the city centre. The one containing the Vauxhall CDP was ruled out; that incorporating the South Docks was felt to have special problems which went

13

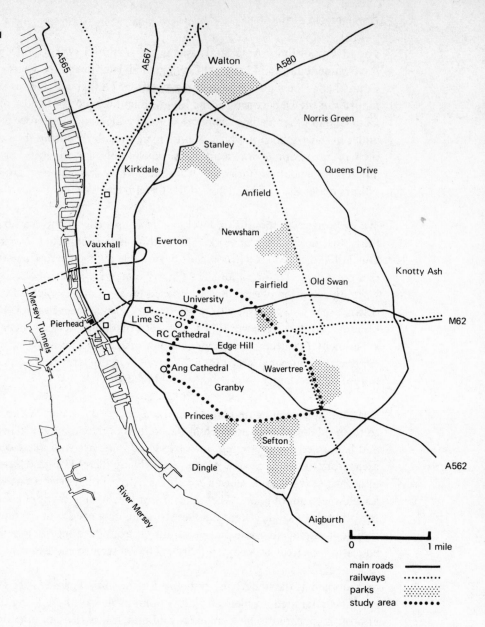

Figure 3
The study area and the inner city

A565

A567

Walton

A580

Norris Green

Stanley

Kirkdale

Queens Drive

Anfield

Newsham

Vauxhall

Everton

Knotty Ash

Fairfield

Old Swan

University

M62

Mersey Tunnels

Lime St

Pierhead

RC Cathedral

Edge Hill

Ang Cathedral

Wavertree

Granby

Princes

Sefton

Dingle

A562

River Mersey

Aigburth

0   1 mile

main roads ————
railways ··········
parks
study area ●●●●●●

beyond the scope of the study; that surrounding Everton was felt to be too much
in the throes and aftermath of clearance. The chosen area lay south-east of the
city centre. One special reason for its selection was that it contained most of the
city's multi-occupied housing, a phenomenon traditionally associated with the inner
city. Although it contained few of the poor, stable working class council estates,
found mainly near the docks, it did contain most of Liverpool's black and
immigrant areas which no study of inner city problems could ignore.

While the study area may not have been fully representative of inner Liverpool
the problems found were typical. It achieved its main purpose as a point of entry
for the study team into inner area life. We opened a small office in the study area

14

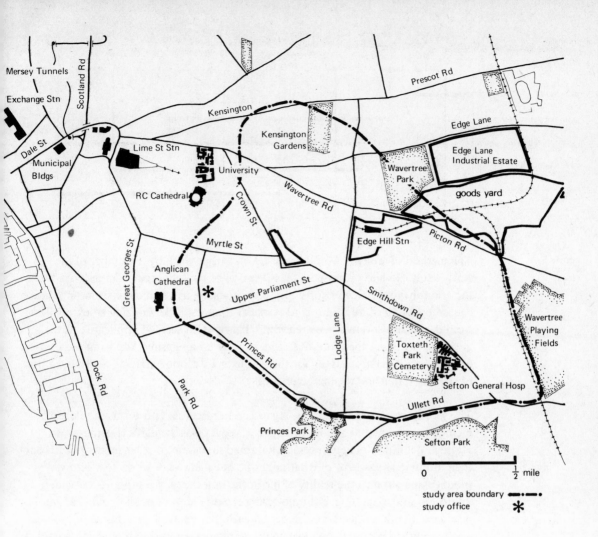

**Figure 4
The study area**

and a number of the team made their homes locally. But in the event our work took us far beyond the boundaries of the study area, to the rest of inner Liverpool and further afield.

The Project Report

The Project Report, written at the end of the pilot study,[1] proposed two main strands of work. On the one hand, we sought to bring together the many pieces of research already carried out and to use existing sources of data in arriving at a clear description of the inner area and its social characteristics. We adopted this tactic rather than undertake a new home interview survey because inner Liverpool had been surveyed remorselessly for so many years. A new survey would add little to our understanding and engender further alienation among already disillusioned residents. The greater need was to be able to describe the inner area systematically and place it in its city-wide context. If possible, too, we should be able to compare Liverpool with the inner areas of other cities.

(1) IAS Liverpool, *Project Report* (Department of the Environment 1974).

15

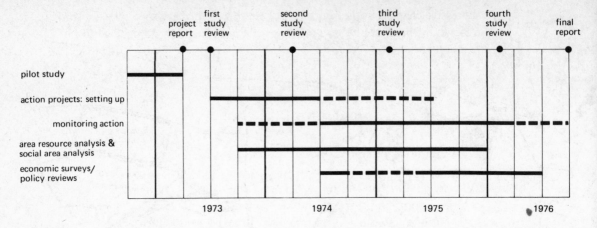

project report · first study review · second study review · third study review · fourth study review · final report

pilot study

action projects: setting up

monitoring action

area resource analysis & social area analysis

economic surveys/ policy reviews

1973   1974   1975   1976

**Figure 5
Structure of the
study**

The method of analysis would be based on earlier work by a member of the study team. He had proposed a classification of twilight areas in cities based on the relationship between people and their housing, between changes in population caused by aging or migration and physical changes in the housing stock resulting from decay, improvements or renewal.[1] This system seemed applicable to the study area. We proposed therefore to test its validity by analysing data from the Census and the social malaise survey for the whole of Liverpool, arriving at a description of the inner area and its characteristics.

The second main strand of work lay in action research. Our terms of reference included experimental action for which a budget was available. Furthermore, Halsey's definition of action research quoted in chapter one harmonised with our then intuitive assessment of what might be our method of work. It would give us practical insight into the reality of life in the inner area, yet support our wider interest in understanding and influencing the direction of public policy. Mounting a series of action projects would face us with the practical constraints of political acceptability, day-to-day management and financial control all of which would be of crucial concern in recommending any major changes in policy at the end of the study.

We emphasised that the study would be a learning process for all concerned; the study team, the local authority and the Department of the Environment. This implied that the study would evolve, building on experience and changing course when necessary. In fact, significant changes of course did occur, adding new dimensions to the study and complementing the action research and social analysis. For example, area management had been included in the original terms of reference for the study but it grew in significance as our understanding of the local authority procedures deepened. Eventually a major action project was set up, supported by its own body of research into the allocation of resources to the inner area. Another major change came with the realisation that we would have to widen the scope of our work beyond those issues capable of exploration through action research, particularly into questions of Liverpool's economy and housing market. The

(1) Watts C F, 'The Role of Twilight Areas,' in Gutch R E and Kettle P B, *Essays in Urban and Regional Planning* (Department of Town Planning, University College London, 1971).

16

successive changes in the course of the study were marked by a series of study reviews in which we reported our emerging understanding to the Steering Committee.

First Study Review: Action research

At the outset of the study we identified four areas of concern: bad housing conditions, public and private; the poor quality of the physical environment; the ineffectiveness of local authority services; and the effects of regional economic decline in poor job prospects and high unemployment. These were based on consultations with most of the voluntary organisations and community groups active in and around the study area, and an intensive series of discussions with local officials.

The voluntary groups were most concerned about housing and social issues. They could not understand the apparent inconsistencies in the life expectancy given to different housing areas and felt themselves unable to influence housing policies. They saw a drop in the standard of environmental services in areas threatened with clearance. They were concerned, too, about dwellings in multiple occupation, contrasting sympathy for the plight of those living in unsatisfactory conditions with fear of the spread of multi-let dwellings into their own neighbourhood. There was widespread indignation about the management and maintenance of council housing. Young people were seen to face special problems; homelessness, inadequate opportunities for training and further education, and a shortgage of recreation facilities. Much of this concern sprang from the street fighting amongst youths in the study area in the summer of 1972. Prostitution, kerb crawling and widespread vandalism were frequently mentioned.

The consultations revealed an overriding sense of alienation amongst local people from the activities of the local authority: a deeply-rooted distrust of many officials and members and a cynicism about the likely results of their activities. This alienation was expressed in the pages of community newspapers and in the activities of community groups, and in the lack of participation in the formal procedures of local government democracy.

The discussions with officials confirmed many of these fears from a different viewpoint. The McKinsey reforms had introduced a formal corporate, decision-making machinery for the city as a whole. But this had, if anything, reduced the sensitivity of the local authority to the special needs of particular parts of the city. There was no way in which the same corporate decision-making could operate at the local level. Furthermore there was little information about whether services varied between different parts of the city. The doubts of many officers of their corporate effectiveness formed a counterpoint to the alienation expressed by community groups.

The results of these consultations were reported to the Steering Committee in the

First Study Review.[1] They provided the framework for the provisional list of action projects drawn up at the same time. This was subsequently developed into the complete action research programme described in chapter three.

Second Study Review: The area perspective

By the time of our next study review, we had clarified as a central theme for the study the role of central and local government in the inner areas.[2] We would be looking at the scope for government intervention in the context of its existing policies. We would be testing its effectiveness in identifying needs or delivering services. We would be assessing the scale of government investment and its relationship to the declining levels of private investment in the inner area. We saw the attitudes of society to the inner areas as crucial. Conventional government programmes were acting as a form of charity, contributing to a view of inner area residents as relatively helpless and in need of support.

Much of our understanding derived from setting up the action projects. This had forced us into detailed consultations with officials and with residents of our study area, with councillors and voluntary organisations. It had led to detailed negotiations with officers and members to gain the approval of council committees for each project, further clarifying the workings of the local authority. Furthermore, we had explored in some depth the scope for area management and gained approval for an experimental project to start as soon as possible after April 1974. What was meant by area management as included in our terms of reference had been unclear. We saw it as taking a comprehensive view of local authority policies and services from the perspective of a single area, in contrast to the more orthodox perspective of service committees and departments.

Area resource analysis

Quite early in the study, we asked a simple question. 'How much did the local authority spend each year in our study area in relation to other parts of the city?' This question was designed to lead on to others. 'Is the area receiving its fair share of resources?', 'What should the expenditure be to meet the residents' real needs?' and 'How does that relate to the total available?' Not surprisingly, as there were no consistent boundaries to the administrative decentralisation practised by most departments, such information did not exist. Moreover nobody had thought to ask. We therefore undertook, in collaboration with an enthusiastic City Treasurer and the departmental accountants, an estimate of a single year's allocation of resources by the Corporation, item by item, to Planning District D, one of the eleven districts into which the city was divided by several departments, and nearly coincident with our own study area.

We soon found that, despite a highly developed budgeting system within the

(1) IAS Liverpool, *Study Review* (Department of the Environment 1974).
(2) IAS Liverpool, *Second Study Review* (Department of the Environment 1974).

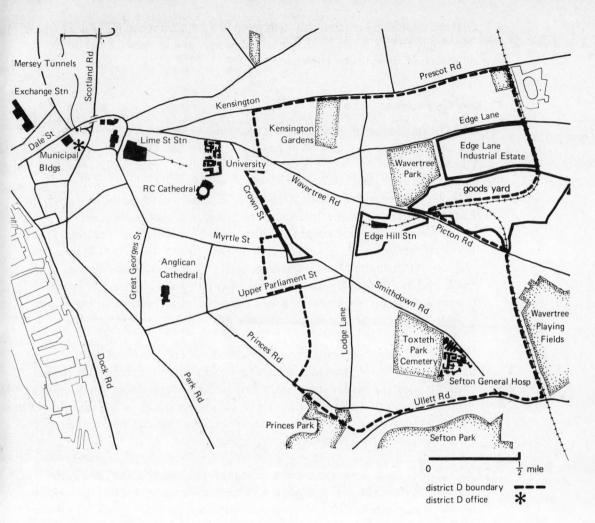

**Figure 6
Planning District D**

Corporation, information was not readily available in a suitable form to begin to answer our questions. Nor, apparently, had any other local authority worked out an appropriate system of area measurement. We found that the best estimate could be given by measuring the provision of services to the area (eg the school places taken up by children living in the district) and to multiply these by a standard unit cost for each service. While such a method does not take into account differences in unit cost or quality of service between districts, it does allow for direct comparison in 'output' terms between districts or between a single district and the whole city. This so called area resource analysis firmly refuted the hitherto prevalent impression that District D had become one of the more favoured parts of the city, getting more than its fair share of resources. It did this by looking at the total expenditure on a particular service rather than the marginal shifts brought about by special initiatives. It showed that in many services the District D was getting less than the average for the city. Clearly, area resource analysis would be much more useful if applied to other districts as well, and for other years. The City Treasurer is working towards this, through the development of more refined measures of output, and by recasting the city budget into this output format.[1] There

(1) IAS Liverpool, *Area Resource Analysis, Methodology* (Department of the Environment 1974); and *District D Tables, 1973–74* (Department of the Environment 1976).

is, too, a continuing requirement to develop more refined measures of need which can be related on the one hand to political objectives and, on the other, to the allocation of resources by output measures.

Area management

The Liverpool experiment in area management was approved by Council in December 1973 to start as soon as possible after the new District Council had taken office following local government reorganisation. Arguably, this was very bad timing. The arrangements for reorganisation were bound to dominate the thoughts of both members and officials, even more so in Liverpool where the new council had been won by the Liberal Party for the first time in very many years. Furthermore, a reaction had set in against many of the McKinsey reforms. Thus the newly established Programme Planning Department was to be disbanded and the new style corporate budget was to be replaced for several years by the traditional line budget. It meant that there was little strong backing from any of the political parties for introducing area management at this time: at best it was regarded as a probably shortlived experiment.

We nevertheless felt it essential to continue with the experiment. It had been set for us in our terms of reference and at least some chief officers, including the former chief executive and his successor in the new authority, were strongly in support of the idea. If we were to have sufficient time to observe its operation, it could not be long delayed. We persevered and, after intensive consultations, prepared a report which formed the framework for the experiment.[1]

We saw area management as a technique for bringing parts of the local authority administration closer to the people it was designed to serve, through the actions of elected members and officials. It would foster a corporate approach to the needs and problems of particular areas, especially in the allocation of resources. This was made clear in the aims we set for the project namely, to examine ways for devolving parts of the administration so as to better identify needs and provide services; to identify the role of councillors and community groups in area management; to consider the possible involvement of other government agencies; and to establish whether area management could or should be applied to other parts of the city.

The experiment had started by the end of 1974. The area chosen for the experiment coincided roughly with our study area. It comprised District D, one of the city's planning districts, with a population of about sixty thousand. An Area Executive was appointed, directly responsible to the Chief Executive. His office was in the city centre, close to the municipal offices and he had a small area management unit of two technical staff and administrative support. He reported to a district committee of councillors from wards in District D and the rest of the city, with its regular place in the committee cycle. He was advised initially by a group of middle management officers from all the service departments although this was soon replaced by ad hoc working parties on particular topics. Attempts were made to

(1) IAS Liverpool, *Proposals for Area Management* (Department of the Environment 1974).

20

set up a district forum where community groups from the area could express views but this failed to get properly established owing to conflicting views about its status and function.

For most of its life, area management has thus consisted of a district committee and area management unit. In practice, its role has differed significantly from that described in the IAS proposals.[1] It was argued that before any part of the corporate administration could be decentralised it would be necessary to make changes at the centre, introducing an area perspective to enable the needs of a single area to be seen more clearly than when fragmented by the traditional system of service committees and departments. District D thus became the case study from which illustrations could be drawn, showing ways in which focussing attention on an area could bring a fresh insight into the activities of the Corporation. Examples are given in chapter ten.

At the time of writing the area management experiment has been in operation for almost two years. It has been incorporated into the Department of the Environment's trials across the country and will continue for a further two years, its progress being monitored by the Institute of Local Government Studies (INLOGOV). But the Liverpool experiment has already shown the strength of deeply entrenched departmentalism and centralised control of policies in the main service committees which has caused them to get out of touch with the needs of small areas, and fail to achieve a corporate impact at the local level.

Third Study Review: Issues and policies

We wrote our Third Study Review: Issues and Policies, about halfway through the study.[2] At this point we felt sufficiently confident of the direction of our work to put forward what we thought were the most important issues facing the residents of inner Liverpool: the lack of economic opportunities, the low educational achievement, many aspects of housing and the provision and take up of government services. Cutting across all of these were the central questions of responsibility for the future of the inner area and the resources required for change. The review discussed a variety of ways in which government could tackle these issues.

We moved from our original statement of local issues which gave rise to the action projects, to one which raised wider issues of fundamental importance to peoples' opportunities for housing and a job. We were able to extend some of our action research to exploring aspects of these wider issues. But we found it necessary to supplement this work by surveys into subjects where action research was inapplicable, and by analysing the impact of major policies on the inner area.

The Third Study Review emphasised the paramount importance of economic

(1) IAS Liverpool, *Area Management Progress Report* (Department of the Environment 1975).
(2) IAS Liverpool, *Third Study Review: Issues and Policies* (Department of the Environment 1975).

issues, which dominated the remainder of the study. We had already undertaken two local investigations into economic matters during the summer of 1974. One was a series of structured discussions with a group of young people, many of them black or unemployed, about their opportunities for, and attitudes to, training and employment.

The discussions gave rise to a consultation paper entitled 'No One from Liverpool 8 Need Apply', a quotation from a job advertisement in a local newsagent. The paper was very widely distributed and discussed with officials and voluntary groups with an interest in problems of employment, training and placement. We followed it up with more formal surveys: a sample of young people who had left schools in the Edge Hill section of the study area three years earlier; and all those men on the unemployment register at the Leece Street Employment Exchange who lived in the study area. These surveys, and consultations with officials in the Careers Service, Manpower Services Commission, Employment and Training Services Agencies led to our preparing a major report on the training and placement of young people in Liverpool.[1]

The other 1974 survey was of vacant land in our study area, which led to recommendations of an administrative nature designed to limit the problem of vacant land.[2] But vacant land was only a symptom of the far wider economic malaise afflicting inner Liverpool. During 1975 we interviewed a number of employers in and around our study area. We analysed changes in employment and reviewed the impact of regional economic policies and land use planning on inner Liverpool. Others were also busy on economic problems. The Building Research Establishment was compiling a detailed, firm by firm, record of changes in employment in Merseyside; they made available to us the results of their pilot data processing for Liverpool 7. The Area Management Unit reviewed the availability of industrial land in the inner area. And the Merseyside County Planning Department was analysing economic issues as part of its structure planning. We used data from all these sources to prepare a substantial report and conclusions on economic issues, which, after discussions of a draft with central and local government officials, was completed in the summer of 1976.[3]

The other issues identified in the Third Study Review were examined through surveys and policy reviews, though not in the same degree of detail as the economic issues. We analysed the problems of urban renewal in the private sector using the example of the area where we were carrying out the action project in environmental care. The background research for the housing projects provided additional information on wider aspects of housing policy. We built up our understanding of the working of local democracy in a series of interviews with study area councillors about their work, and in a survey of community groups active in and around the study area, tracing the history of the community

(1) IAS Liverpool, *Getting a Job: the Training and Placement of Young People* (Department of the Environment 1977).
(2) IAS Liverpool, *Vacant Land* (Department of the Environment 1976).
(3) IAS Liverpool, *Economic Development of the Inner Area* (Department of the Environment 1977).

movement in Liverpool in the previous ten years. We reviewed the debate on education policies in the context of inner Liverpool and the work of the educational priority project. And we examined the evidence on crime and vandalism in inner Liverpool.

Fourth Study Review: Inner areas in a wider context

This was the last in our series of study reviews, written towards the end of our active involvement in the affairs of Liverpool.[1] The Fourth Study Review marked the completion of our formal research. The Second Study Review had nominated as our central theme the role of government in the inner areas. The third review identified the key issues where this intervention would be most crucial. But we still had not produced a formal description of inner areas and their characteristics, nor placed inner Liverpool in a wider regional or national context. This was the main contribution of the fourth review.

The new evidence came from the statistical analysis of data from the 1971 Census of Population and the revised survey of social malaise carried out by the City Planning Department in 1973–74. This work had been part of our programme from the beginning of the study in 1973. But difficulty in obtaining the Census data meant the work was not complete until the end of 1975. The social area analysis was carried out for us, and the City and County Planning Departments, by the Planning Research Applications Group of the Centre of Environmental Studies.[2]

The work took the form of a so-called cluster analysis of forty variables from the 1971 Census for each of 420 basic data areas (groups of adjacent and similar census enumeration districts) which made up the City of Liverpool. The forty variables included housing tenure, number of rooms and provision of basic housing amenities; socio-economic status, car ownership, travel to work and educational attainment; employment and unemployment; age, household structure and migration.

Basic data areas in different parts of Liverpool were grouped together into twenty-five clusters each of which was relatively homogeneous within itself and sharply differentiated from all others in terms of its socio-economic status, housing tenure and other variables. For instance one very small cluster, concentrated in a single part of the city, identified the main area of recent migration into Liverpool, where the black population, poor housing and high unemployment were found together. Another cluster picked out the most recent area of private house building occupied by middle class families with young children, many of whom had moved from outside the city. A third, widely scattered cluster, identified the tower blocks built by the local authority in the 1960s and inhabited mainly by older couples and

(1) IAS Liverpool, *Fourth Study Review* (Department of the Environment 1976).

(2) Planning Research Applications Group, *Liverpool Social Area Study 1971*, obtainable from Centre for Environmental Studies, 62–65 Chandos Place, London WC2N 4HH; and IAS Liverpool, *Social Area Analysis 1971* (Department of the Environment 1977).

single people. Further extension of the analysis combined the twenty-five clusters into five so-called social areas, where the housing was of similar age and tenure, and the status of the residents fairly uniform.

PRAG later extended the original analysis to the remainder of Merseyside, placing Liverpool's inner area in its metropolitan context. Also, a similar form of cluster analysis was carried out on a much larger, national scale. The 623 parliamentary constituencies in Great Britain were grouped to form clusters and social areas, showing that urban deprivation is common to the inner areas of the nation's larger cities.

The meaning of the study

Over the four years we experienced a major evolution in our conception of the inner areas which had its foundations in the work which we undertook and in our relationships with the Department of the Environment, the local authorities and the wide spectrum of unofficial opinion. We started with an approach through action research which, almost inevitably, meant a close involvement with particular projects whose impact would be sharply limited to those directly involved in them.

Once into the study we, like EPA and CDP before us, realised the limitations of this approach. Action research within small areas would not be a sufficient basis for understanding, let alone reform. Like EPA we realised the interrelated character of inner area problems. Like CDP, we recognised that many of the ills demonstrated in the inner areas have their roots in society and are to be found throughout the country. However, we came to the view that the extent and concentration of deprivation within the inner areas of our larger cities could be influenced through effective government action directed specifically at the inner areas. The remainder of the report describes how we came to this view and the action which we now conclude is necessary.

3 Action research

Setting up the projects

From the beginning we conceived the action research programme as a series of probes into the life and government of the inner area which would evolve as a learning process as far as accountability and budgeting permitted. The study team was to be responsible for identifying each project, defining its objectives and carrying it through to the point where it could start. Thereafter we would be responsible only for its monitoring and evaluation. Each project would actually be carried out by others, in some cases a department of the Corporation; in others, a voluntary organisation or community group. The choice of executive agent for each project thus became a key factor in its development. Our aims for study and innovation would have to be reconciled with those of the particular organisation, usually to obtain money and backing to meet a need.

A key decision by the Steering Committee was that each project should pass through the normal procedures of Council in obtaining detailed approval and in reporting on its operation. After receiving outline approval from the Steering Committee, each project would become the responsibility of the appropriate programme committee of Council (eg Housing, Social Services, Education). A detailed proposal would have to pass through the full committee cycle of Council and, at the same time, be approved by the Department of the Environment in consultation with other, appropriate departments of central government. The effect of this was to involve the study as a whole much more closely in the procedures of the local authority than might otherwise have been the case. It contributed to the relatively orthodox character of much of the programme and to the slowness in getting the programme as a whole into operation. But there were great compensations in the insight which it gave us into modes of operation and attitudes of mind within the Corporation.

By July 1973, the main aims of the action research programme and the limiting constraints were clear and our first list of projects received outline approval. We started our detailed work and by the spring of 1974 what eventually proved to be the entire programme had received detailed approval. The list was as follows:

environmental care in an area of two thousand houses

maintenance of several small blocks of council flats*

a day care and referral centre for single homeless people*

a team of social workers to provide support to single homeless people

a short stay hostel for mobile young people at risk

a social worker to work with single parent families

a group of four small play projects

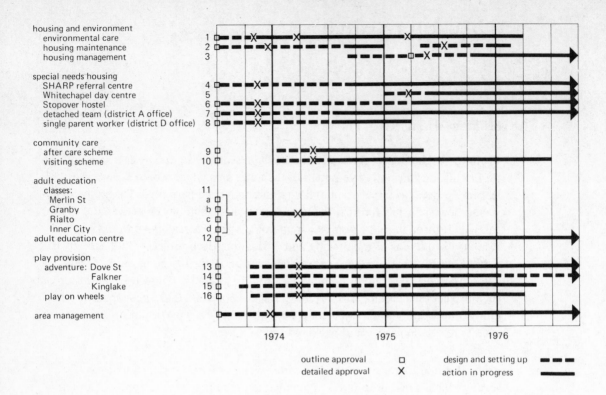

housing and environment
  environmental care 1
  housing maintenance 2
  housing management 3

special needs housing
  SHARP referral centre 4
  Whitechapel day centre 5
  Stopover hostel 6
  detached team (district A office) 7
  single parent worker (district D office) 8

community care
  after care scheme 9
  visiting scheme 10

adult education
  classes: 11
    Merlin St a
    Granby b
    Rialto c
    Inner City d
  adult education centre 12

play provision
  adventure: Dove St 13
           Falkner 14
           Kinglake 15
  play on wheels 16

area management

1974   1975   1976

outline approval   □   design and setting up ▬ ▬ ▬
detailed approval   X   action in progress   ▬▬▬

**Figure 7
Timetable for
action projects**

community based courses in adult education*

a visiting scheme for pensioners and a study of the needs of elderly people returning home from hospital.

Three of the projects (those marked by an asterisk) evolved into further projects or were considerably modified during the course of the study. The additional projects were:

management of two thousand council tenancies

day care centre for single homeless people

a community based adult education centre.

Some of the projects had started by the spring of 1974. Nevertheless, many took much longer to get into operation even after they had been given detailed approval from Council. There were delays in appointing staff; finding and leasing buildings or sites; obtaining planning permission; tendering; and construction work. It was not until the spring of 1975, two years after we had started preliminary consultations, that the greater part of our programme of action research was actually in operation.

Environmental care

The environmental care project was the first to be started, and was already in operation by November 1973, continuing thereafter for the rest of the study until April 1976, though with variations in emphasis being introduced for each financial

26

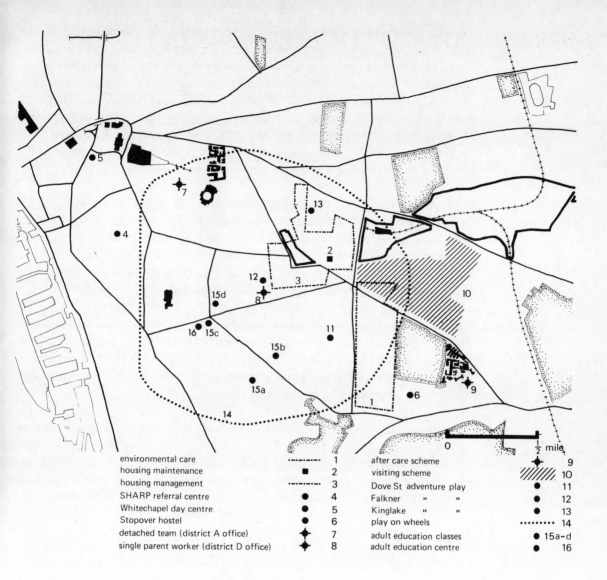

environmental care	1
housing maintenance	2
housing management	3
SHARP referral centre	4
Whitechapel day centre	5
Stopover hostel	6
detached team (district A office)	7
single parent worker (district D office)	8

after care scheme	9
visiting scheme	10
Dove St adventure play	11
Falkner " "	12
Kinglake " "	13
play on wheels	14
adult education classes	15a-d
adult education centre	16

**Figure 8
Location of action
projects**

year. It derived directly from environmental care trials previously carried out by the Director of Environmental Health and Protection.[1] The work was carried out chiefly by small local contractors and direct labour and did not require any lengthy preliminaries.

The project took place in Lodge Lane East, a run down Victorian residential area much of whose future was uncertain (see figure 38 on page 132). The smaller houses and some of the badly neglected larger ones were proposed for slum clearance. Others had been designated for limited improvement but only a short life. The Lodge Lane East Residents Association (LLERA) had been set up mainly to try to get their area declared a general improvement area. They were to play an active role in the project. Despite the variety of housing the surroundings were uniformly drab and depressing; decay had been accelerated by the area's uncertain future.

(1) Lees A M, *Environmental Care: The Raising of Environmental Standards* (City of Liverpool Health and Protection Department, 1971).

The aim of the project was to examine methods and costs of raising environmental standards in the area to an acceptable level and maintaining them. Priorities for action were worked out and progress reviewed at regular meetings between residents, local councillors, the district environmental officer and the study team. The first phase consisted of repairs to carriageways, footways, back lanes and drains; improvements in street cleansing and provision of litter bins; and treatment of vacant land and derelict property. In addition, noise, pollution, traffic and parking surveys were carried out, an experimental refuse container scheme organised and an exhibition of environmental care mounted.

In the second year about half the budget was used as a contingency sum, covering items which could not be planned in advance such as the disposal of dumped rubbish, securing derelict houses, treating vacant sites and gable ends, and repairing passageways. The remainder was used for new small improvements like repairing fences, an anti-litter campaign, and landscape treatment of stopped off streets. The experimental refuse container scheme was continued and another exhibition mounted.

The third year's work was far more limited and intended merely to consolidate the improvements and to allow a reasonable period over which to measure changes in the area. A further contingency budget was the main item together with extension to the refuse container scheme and extra street sweeping.

The results of the work were monitored in several ways. The regular meetings with representatives of LLERA provided some insight into the reactions of residents as did surveys made at the two exhibitions. Changes in the incidence of environmental defects, such as the amount of litter and of broken paving stones, were measured. The results were analysed and a report written at the conclusion of the project.[1] The chief conclusion was that basic repairs and improvements to the environment needed to be carried out parallel with the improvement of houses.

Grants are available for this type of work in general improvement and housing action areas. But our analysis showed the available sums to be inadequate; and no assistance is available for environmental improvements elsewhere. In addition a discretionary budget should be under the control of the district environmental officer. The current level of standard maintenance was adequate provided basic repairs were carried out and the discretionary budget wisely used.

Council housing maintenance and management

The maintenance and management of council housing in the study area emerged very early as a crucial local issue. As a prelude to a larger scale project on management, a small improvement scheme was carried out to the badly neglected communal areas of several blocks of 1950s three storey flats. The first phase was devoted to basic repairs and improvements. The programme of work was drawn up

(1) IAS Liverpool, *Environmental Care* (Department of the Environment 1977).

by the study team with the support of the district housing manager; it paid regard as far as possible to the wishes of the tenants who were contacted both at public meetings and, as only twenty four flats were involved, by personal visits. The scheme comprised private gardens or enclosed yards for ground floor tenants; tarmac areas relaid with both tarmac and paving slabs; provision of semi-mature trees, bushes and seats; doors for the front and back entrances on each block with entry phones in some instances; stairway windows glazed with toughened glass; individual stores on the ground floor repaired; and stairways and entrances redecorated in accordance with the tenants' own colour schemes. After completion of the first phase, and a further public meeting, a smaller final phase was carried out involving minor improvements such as clothes drying arrangements in private yards; repairs to the entry phones; some painting and removal of graffiti; and external painting of the blocks.

By the end of the project, the condition of the communal areas had been raised to a standard of design and repair more acceptable to the tenants. However the work carried out fell uneasily between two local authority programmes; normal maintenance which includes securing and redecorating vacated dwellings, and day to day repairs; and the council housing improvement programme which is at present concentrated on the inter-war tenements. It will be many years before the programme reaches the 1950s blocks which meanwhile fail to meet many tenants' needs because of basic faults in design. And the planned maintenance programme, which might have been expected to deal with some of the faults, consisted only of external repairs and repainting, carried out every six or seven years. The results of the project were presented in a report to the Steering Committee.[1]

Before the housing maintenance project was finished we started on a wider project on housing management, in close cooperation with officials from the Housing Department and from the Area Management Unit which by then was in being. At the request of the Housing Committee we had been asked to examine the scope for a project in tenant management. Consultation with tenants had been an integral part of the housing maintenance project and indeed its most successful elements developed from tenants' own ideas. Consultation and participation were features of many of our action projects. Nonetheless, our experience in the maintenance project and our more general talks with council tenants made us doubt the wisdom of a tenant management scheme in the study area.

District housing management offices each covered about ten thousand tenancies. The most detailed decisions on management policy were centralised and local housing personnel lacked status. The evidence of inadequate repairs and maintenance was overwhelming. Thus the first aim for a housing management project should be to explore ways of discharging existing responsibilities more effectively before seeking more direct tenant involvement. We were reinforced in this view by the weakness and scarcity of tenants' associations in the study area and were learning from other projects of the dangers of prematurely handing over responsibility to poorly based community groups. Finally many of the older council

(1) IAS Liverpool, *Housing Maintenance* (Department of the Environment 1976).

estates presented the worst possible basis for tenant involvement. They were unpopular, had a high turnover of tenants and a high proportion of poor, unskilled, large or single parent families.

The project was thus set up to improve current estate management as a basis for the later introduction of tenant participation in management. A small team of estate officers was located in a local office serving two thousand tenancies in a group of council estates of every type and age (see figure 40 on page 141). The team took on all responsibilities allocated to district offices except rent collection and each worker in the team had his or her own group of flats to look after. The office opened in the autumn of 1975 and by the early summer of 1976, when we wrote our report on the project, the team had removed a persistent backlog of repairs and were beginning to consider problems of general maintenance and rent arrears.[1] It was too early for firm conclusions to be drawn about the success of the project, or the validity of extending it into tenant management. The project meanwhile is continuing under the direction of the Area Management Unit and the Housing Department.

Special housing needs

A major early concern of the study was for those in greatest need of both housing and social support. They included young drifters who had recently left home; older people, mainly men, often recently discharged from prison or mental hospital and now moving around aimlessly; and single parent families. The one common feature of each disparate group was their ineligibility for council housing and their inability to afford adequate private housing. At best, they found insecure furnished rooms in multi-let houses. More likely, they moved from hostel to common lodging house, stayed with friends or relations or slept rough.

Our consultations with social services officials and voluntary organisations brought out the difficulties faced by these groups and the very limited local authority provision. Accordingly we devised a set of action projects with the aim of gaining a greater understanding of the circumstances of those with special housing needs through providing them with shelter and support. The four projects were:

  a day care and referral centre for single homeless people (subsequently split into two projects: SHARP, the referral centre, and the Whitechapel day centre)

  a short stay hostel for young people at risk (Stopover)

  a team of social workers for the single homeless

  a worker with single parent families.

A long tradition of voluntary activity, a lack of clarity about local authority responsibility, and a desire for innovation led us to the view that voluntary organisations would be more appropriate than the local authority to carry out the first two projects. Although not then active in Liverpool, the National Association

(1) IAS Liverpool, *Housing Management* (Department of the Environment 1977).

for the Care and Resettlement of Offenders (NACRO) was running similar schemes in Manchester and appeared to be the most willing and able voluntary organisation to undertake the projects. They were invited to cooperate.

The details of all four projects were quickly worked out and approved by November 1973 but there were lengthy delays in getting them started. The chief delays were in the first two projects for both of which premises had to be found, planning permission obtained, fire regulations met, improvements made and decorations completed. It was September 1974 before the referral centre could open and the following June for the hostel. Procedures for recruiting the social workers for the two latter projects were also protracted, having to pass through standard local authority procedures for advertising and appointment. In each case it was July 1974 before the staff were in post.

A condition set by NACRO for taking responsibility was that their projects should last at least three years, to justify the effort and expenditure involved. Accordingly the first three projects are still operating although we have drawn our conclusions and published our detailed report.[1]

The Single Homeless and Rehabilitation Project (SHARP) was set up in an old club in the centre of town. Initially it was intended to provide a twenty four hour referral service for single homeless people, a limited amount of emergency accommodation, and daytime sitting room and catering facilities, possibly with limited medical care. But very quickly the centre developed a much more limited operation which has changed little since. It has concentrated on providing an accommodation service, relying mainly on landladies, hostels and lodging houses. As the centre itself has no direct access to any accommodation, the service has been restricted to the daytime. Although about half the clients were middle aged or elderly men there were more young people and women than expected. Only a quarter of the total were in need of care and support.

The style of operation and the nature of the premises and the clientele made SHARP unsuitable for the intended day care service. Consequently a separate centre was set up in an old car showroom. There are perhaps a thousand middle aged and elderly men in Liverpool drifting from furnished rooms to lodgings to hostels or dossing in derelict houses or doorways. Although few men are now on the road looking for casual work, the group is constantly being added to by social casualties, an increasing number of whom are younger people.

The day centre was set up mainly for the older group. Prior to its opening there had been nowhere for men on the hostel circuit to go during the day, apart from the gruesome cafe in the basement of a notorious lodging house. All the major hostels closed during the day and many of the men were not accepted at ordinary cafes or old peoples' day centres because of their appearance or behaviour. The centre provided sitting space, television, papers, magazines and games, and tea and snacks during the daytime. A weekly surgery was introduced using volunteer doctors,

(1) IAS Liverpool, *Single and Homeless* (Department of the Environment 1977).

and some literacy work undertaken. The staff hope to use spare space for work shop schemes. On average, fifty or sixty used the centre every day, although only a few stayed all day. Some five hundred different men used the centre for varying periods during its first six months.

Stopover catered for young people who had left home or an institution, were drifting about the city looking for work and had come into conflict with authority. Shared flatlets were provided for up to eleven youngsters in a large, well converted house in a quiet residential street. Three full time staff, two of them residential, tried to provide an easy community atmosphere, whilst sustaining a maximum stay of eight weeks for individual residents. Their aim was to provide a breathing space for the youngsters and give them time to get a job, find more permanent accommodation or return home, and sort out some of their personal problems with the help of the hostel staff.

The team of four social workers provided care and support for single homeless people, referring clients to Whitechapel and Stopover and receiving referrals from SHARP and other organisations. The team was set up in part as a reaction against generic social work in providing specialist help for a particular client group found chiefly in larger cities.

Together these projects gave us a greater insight into the housing pressures faced by single people than could have been achieved by more traditional research methods. We also learnt a great deal about the relationships between the public, private and voluntary sectors in a field where they are particularly confused. We were able to put into perspective our early hopes for innovation in asking a voluntary body to carry out the work. The need to act quickly yet satisfy normal local authority procedures meant choosing a fairly large, acceptable voluntary body, and resulted in projects which were new rather than genuinely experimental.

Our original aims proved over optimistic. SHARP adopted a more limited role than intended; no new housing suitable for single people was set up, and little impact made on the city's housing policy. Stopover has been more successful because it was well planned, in the mainstream of NACRO's activities and had staff in a high ratio to residents. It showed the value of a refuge but alone cannot provide a solution to the lack of direction and opportunity experienced by young drifters. The Whitechapel centre provided only limited support but led to further projects; a drying out centre for alcoholics and a small research project into the primary medical needs of the homeless and rootless. The experience of the detached team has shown the value of a specialist approach by a small team for a group with special problems, most of whom are found in small parts of the city.

Above all, perhaps, these projects gave us a sense of the possible and helped us to appreciate the entrenched nature of just one, small set of urban social problems. The time taken to generate even the smallest change in one field brought home forcibly the extent of commitment and time that will be required to achieve any real change in the inner area, even for those who, superficially at least, excite considerable public sympathy.

32

The evolution of the single parent families project took it away from the special housing needs group as a whole.[1] The original intention had been to appoint someone to spend a year working with single parent families and then put forward proposals for a practical project. As responsibility for the homeless at the time lay with the Social Services Committee and as single parent families were classed as a vulnerable group, a social worker was appointed. In practice she was unable to reconcile the demands of casework in a district social services office with the task of preparing a future project and with the entirely different demands of research. She resigned after three months as did her replacement. The project itself proved abortive but did draw together some useful statistical material for Liverpool and confirmed the Finer Committee's conclusions that the most important issues facing single parent families were finance, housing and child care.[2]

Community care of the elderly

The community care projects stemmed from a desire to examine tasks which had once been performed by the extended family or special group, had increasingly been taken over by state organisations and professional agencies, but might still be performed more effectively within the community. Many elderly people were being referred to social workers who were able to do little once the immediate crisis had been resolved. A local community organisation, the Help and Neighbourhood Development Scheme (HANDS) had already been working with pensioners in the district for several years and were anxious to extend their work. Age Concern Liverpool had been researching into the problems of elderly people being discharged from hospital. Their report *Care is Rare* was very critical of the failure of the hospital service to ensure that conditions at home were suitable for convalescence and that adequate services were provided after discharge.[3]

A two part project was put forward and approved by Council in March 1974. Age Concern were to investigate the capacity of the voluntary sector to provide after-care services for the elderly discharged from hospital. HANDS were to operate a visiting scheme and informal social centre in the Smithdown Road area, itself adjacent to the large general hospital in which the Age Concern project was based. The basic objective in each case was to test the capacity of the voluntary sector to provide an effective service.[4]

Age Concern had previously devised and tested a form for the collection of information on elderly people entering hospital, interviewed staff and patients and experimented with co-ordinating after-care services at two Liverpool hospitals. Their report *Going Home?* recommended establishing the post of after-care

(1) IAS Liverpool, *Single Parent Families* (Department of the Environment 1977).

(2) *Report of the Committee on One Parent Families* (Cmnd 5629, HMSO 1974).

(3) Amos G M, *Care is Rare: a Report on Homecoming for the Elderly Patient* (Age Concern Liverpool 1973).

(4) IAS Liverpool, *Community Care of the Elderly* (Department of the Environment 1977).

co-ordinators in hospitals catering for the elderly.[1] We then sponsored them in establishing a small hospital-based team to explore how far the voluntary sector could respond effectively to the infinite variety of needs of elderly people returning from hospital.

Fifty six voluntary groups known to be interested or active, ranging from large national charities to small residents' groups, were interviewed. A sample of the groups was asked to visit patients shortly after their arrival home from hospital to assess whether their home circumstances were adequate for convalescence and whether any other services were needed. A follow up by the team assessed the agencies' performance in identifying needs, and provided a service. The experiment was tried in different forms showing better results when the agencies were briefed by a member of the survey team acting as a proxy after-care co-ordinator. The project demonstrated that community and residents' groups were virtually untapped yet could be most effective when their activities were sympathetically coordinated and supervised.

The HANDS project consisted of regular visiting amongst pensioners in an area of densely packed terraced housing with a population of about ten thousand. The project team assembled information during their visits about the needs of pensioners in the area and their material circumstances. The scheme itself was backed by a small social and information centre set up by HANDS in an old motor cycle showroom in a nearby shopping street. A number of socials were also run during the project using local schools and church halls. The project showed that visiting and carrying out routine tasks need a strong, very local base if they are to be responsive to needs. A locally controlled scheme, using local residents if possible, and built up from local needs, can be more effective than a city-wide scheme adjusted administratively to meet local circumstances.

Play in the inner areas

Our involvement in action projects on children's play came in a roundabout fashion. Early consideration of the temporary use of vacant sites led us to the view that playgrounds would be appropriate uses, as local play facilities were inadequate and play provision did not normally require heavy financial investment. Our original intention was to provide one fixed and one adventure playground and to compare their separate advantages. However, we found that both types of provision already existed in the study area but that the three voluntary adventure playgrounds were struggling to get established and very short of funds.

Approval was given in February 1974 for grants for the development of the Dove Street, Falkner and Kinglake adventure playgrounds and a 'mobile play resource unit', soon, happily, to be called Play on Wheels. The three playgrounds were at varying stages of development. All three had a form of local management committee

---

(1) *Going Home? The Care of Elderly Patients after Discharge from Hospital* (Age Concern Liverpool, 1975).

and grants for employing a play leader, either from the local authority or the Urban Programme. Our grants were to enable Dove Street to have a second play leader and to assist all three with buildings, fencing and equipment. The grant to Play on Wheels was for workers and equipment.

Dove Street was the most successful of the three playgrounds. Under strong management the Cuckoo play centre quickly became an important local base for several hundred children. A discotheque, painting, sewing and other activities were organised in the centre and many trips organised using a coach purchased from the grant.

Kinglake playground proved cramped and badly sited and did not sustain the degree of local support which was at first apparent. Nevertheless play activities continued spasmodically for over a year until both workers left and the building was heavily vandalised, and eventually demolished by the local authority.

The Falkner playground was built next to a new, tough, multi racial estate. It was more ambitious in its provision than the other two with a large concrete bunker play building in a two hundred foot long compound surrounded by a twelve foot concrete wall. But it proved too much for the few interested local residents to handle with the resources available and was taken over by the Education Department who, to date, have failed to organise any activities or appoint a play leader.

Play on Wheels grew out of experience of the Granby festival in the summer of 1972. It consisted of a truck equipped with discotheque, inflatable play structures, film projector and equipment for various play workshops – badge making, face painting, poster printing. An old warehouse provided an office and space for building inflatables, garaging the truck and storing equipment. Two workers and paid assistants took the truck to playgrounds, summer playschemes, schools, street parties and vacant sites. Heavy programmes were built up over the summers of the two years in which it operated. But when the financial support of the Department of the Environment was withdrawn at the end of the study, the local authority felt unable to take on responsibility for its full cost, and the project closed down. POW had nevertheless shown independence and flexibility of operation, responding to consumer demand yet combining this with the beginnings of an educational function.

The four projects led us into two further pieces of work which added greatly to our understanding of the complex relationship between the local authority and the voluntary sector. One was a survey of 1974 summer playschemes in which we jointly sponsored research with the Merseyside Play Action Council, the body set up to represent and coordinate the voluntary schemes.[1] The other was our participation in the work of a joint working party on play and leisure set up by the Community Development Section of the local authority in 1975. Our work in play convinced us of the useful role which voluntary groups could undertake in

(1) *Developing Play in Liverpool*, a Joint Report by IAS Liverpool and the Merseyside Play Action Council (1975).

complementing local authority services.[1] However a fruitful partnership between the two required not only a coordinating organisation such as the Merseyside Play Action Council, but also a more responsive attitude inside the authority.

Further education

Surprisingly little emphasis was placed on education in our initial consultations, either by officials or public. The lack of jobs and recreation facilities were given greater priority. The one exception was the concern that formal education was having little or no impact on many young people in the study area, particularly young blacks. In the first stage of our project seminars were conducted with local community groups, with a view to setting up courses based on the interests that came out of the discussions. There was a strong element of community development in the approach; encouraging people consciously to explore their own interests and be involved in providing for them. Four groups were selected and assisted to carry out their own further education projects: a woman's weekly social group at the Merlin Street community centre; Granby Resources, organised by local community workers in the nearby Princes Park Methodist Centre; a small sewing workshop for unemployed girls in the Rialto Community Centre; and the inner city study group, about fifteen young black people under the guidance of a tutor, discussing three aspects of inner city life: police, housing and education.

All four schemes were located within a quarter of a mile of each other yet had no common basis and in the end foundered. First, in order to speed the process of setting up courses, we relied on existing community groups. But the groups had set themselves up originally for different purposes; they lacked the skill, experience or motivation for developing ideas in adult education once the initial impetus was past. Secondly the project as a whole failed to acquire a clear field of interest or client group. However, the inner city study group focussed our attention more clearly on the special problems of young black people. Out of its experience, we extended the principle of learning through discussion by setting up groups to consider the employment problems experienced by young black people referred to in chapter two.

The project thus far had shown the necessity for having a much clearer set of aims if community education was to be pursued. The second stage of the project was directed towards one particular group, young unemployed blacks. An independent employment agency, South Liverpool Personnel, was working mainly with young blacks in the study area from an office in Upper Parliament Street. A management group was set up by the agency to develop this stage of the project. A young black woman from the locality who had teacher training experience was appointed to run an adult education centre opened in an empty shop in Upper Parliament Street in November 1974. The centre caters largely for the local black community. It provided information about existing adult and further education courses; helped people get accepted for courses provided by the local authority and Training

(1) IAS Liverpool, *Inner Area Play* (Department of the Environment 1977).

36

Services Agency; and set up its own courses to fill gaps in the existing provision. These included English and pre-O level classes, black studies and black music. The project is still in progress and has been guaranteed financial support as an experimental project for a further two years.[1]

The impact of action research

Action research is intended primarily to inform social policy by examining critically the consequences of minor, and successive, changes in programmes. It is a learning process for decision makers and administrators, the cumulative result of which could be quite significant shifts in policy. But it also has other purposes. It can in itself raise standards, or improve methods of providing a service. And it can lead to a deeper understanding of clients' needs and a wider knowledge of the administrative and decision making system within which it is operating.

Action research in the Liverpool Inner Area Study, excluding area management, involved a direct expenditure of about six hundred thousand pounds between March 1973 and March 1976, and several projects are to continue for some time yet. In addition, on a conservative estimate, preparing, monitoring and writing up the projects occupied about a third of the total resources of the study team. This excludes the contributions of staff time by the local authority. The effort was substantial yet, at its peak, the action expenditure represented a net addition of less than five percent to the annual level of expenditure by the local authority in roughly the same area of the city.[2] A full account of each project is given separately in the various reports but it is appropriate to consider here the combined effect of the action research programme.

The direct benefits to the different client groups are clear. Expenditure on each project has brought tangible results during its operation, whether hostel, playground or visiting scheme. But these short term gains could quickly lose their impact if the improvements are not maintained or if lessons learned are not applied by the local authority in their normal services. The whole exercise might have aroused expectations which may not be satisfied in the future. And indeed the same amount of money could have been spent in different ways which might have given greater benefit. Considerations such as these raise doubts about the ethics of experimental action, which can be allayed only to some extent by the knowledge that at least for a short period some people obtained a measure of benefit from the action expenditure.

Action research gave the study team a much greater insight into the nature and government of the inner area of Liverpool than would have been possible by more formal methods of research. The projects themselves, in probing into the life of the study area, gave us a picture of real conditions. Because they required us to work

(1) IAS Liverpool, *Adult Education* (Department of the Environment 1977).

(2) IAS Liverpool, *Area Resource Analysis, District D Tables 1973–74* (Department of the Environment 1976).

closely with the local authority in its standard modes of operation they gave us at least some understanding of how the departments and committees function. The selection of projects, and the agencies chosen to implement them, gave us insight into the variegated spectrum of community action and voluntary effort, its strengths and weaknesses and its relationship with the local authority.[1]

Nevertheless, even with the addition of area management, the action research was not sufficient on its own. It could not provide the rigorous framework for an objective understanding of the inner area in the wider context of the city as a whole. Nor could it take us far into the basic economic issues which emerged increasingly as the dominant ones facing any effective planning for the future of the inner area. These were tackled by other means in the development of the study.

But the real test for the action research programme must be how far it has informed policies and their implementation directly within Liverpool. In the end this must be a question for the local authority to answer. We have written reports which have gone from the Steering Committee to the desks of chief officers and, in some cases, the agendas of committees. But whereas we, the study team, have been involved in every project, involvement by the local authority has been much narrower; one or two officials in particular departments, often low in the official hierarchy, one or two councillors. But the local authority has not looked at the programme as a whole, asking the questions which we have had to ask. Arguably, it should be doing so. The Inner Area Study is not the first and will probably not be the last programme of experimental action projects carried on in Liverpool. Yet there is little evidence of clear evaluation by the local authority, or of continuity from one special programme to another.

The chief difficulty for the local authority in gaining any lasting benefit from the action research is that the scale of action was comparatively small and its impact marginal, in terms of the overall work of the local authority and the problems being tackled. Furthermore, the degree of commitment to the programme within the local authority was small. Both the initiative and the resources came largely from outside. The study team was appointed by, and accountable to, the Department of the Environment which also met three-quarters of the cost of the action. The benefits of outside intervention and independence of view point have to be weighed against the resulting lack of commitment within the authority which has the most immediate responsibility for action.

Examination of the projects shows two conflicting views. The more deeply embedded a project was within a department of the local authority, the more likely it was to be accepted and its results used constructively in the improvement of services. The environmental care project was little more than a continuation of current research by the local authority for which funds were no longer available. The housing management project might well lead to significant changes, particularly if additional resources can be made available.

(1) Davies H W E, 'Setting up Local Research Projects', in *The Use of Action Research in Developing Urban Planning Policy* (Department of the Environment 1975).

Executive responsibility for the more innovatory projects lay outside the local authority. The adult education centre, for instance, is run by an independent management group and Play on Wheels by a group of community workers. Each represented a real change in ways of meeting local needs but in neither instance was there any commitment to their future development within the local authority. When financial assistance from the Department of the Environment came to an end, so did Play on Wheels. It is an open question whether the same will happen to the adult education centre. It may even occur with the hostel, day care and referral centres being run by NACRO even though they are more orthodox in their style of operation and less likely to be in conflict with prevailing attitudes within the local authority.

The conflict between innovation and commitment is real but both are essential if action research is to lead to lasting and effective improvements in social policies. On the one hand, local authority departments are capable of generating the commitment to social policy but are slow to change their methods, particularly the means by which policies are implemented. At best, they seem to have been capable of no more than marginal improvements in operating efficiency. The more fundamental changes of style of action and the relationship between those providing a service and its recipients have been much more difficult to achieve from within individual departments. The reasons are many but must include a limited capacity for self analysis in the face of the day to day pressures for fulfilling their main functions.

Voluntary agencies on the other hand appear to have a greater, and more flexible, capacity for innovations through action research given the right circumstances and leadership. But they require substantial support and a degree of continuity in management which together pose the question of what is to happen when the support is withdrawn or the continuity broken. Ideally, if the need for the service still remains, it should be taken over by the local authority yet the characteristics which made it a success may be in conflict with established practices which the authority may be unwilling or unable to change.

Certainly, social policies and their means of implementation need to be kept continuously under review and action research affords a method of doing this. As the main provider of services and the prime source of funds, responsibility for innovation through action research should be with the local authority both in developing ideas internally and in being responsive to outside initiatives. If the existing departments are unable to discharge this role, then there would seem to be need for a non-departmental unit with corporate responsibility for policy review and action research. But in a wider sense, the questions raised by our action research go to the heart of the relationship between people and government in the inner area, questions which we take up more fully in chapter ten.

4 The Inner Areas

The city and the inner areas

The city of Liverpool is a densely built-up area of forty three square miles. Its population in 1975 was estimated to be five hundred and forty nine thousand. Since April 1974 it has been a district of the metropolitan county of Merseyside, a conurbation with one million five hundred and eighty eight thousand inhabitants. Liverpool is the core city, but the continuously built up area extends northwards through Bootle to Crosby, north eastwards to Kirkby, and eastwards through Huyton and Prescot to link up with St. Helens. Formby and Southport are separate seaside towns north of Liverpool and 'across the water' is the Wirral with Birkenhead as its core.

Liverpool had its origins near what is now the Pierhead, in the docks and small town hemmed in by the sandstone ridge of Everton Heights a mile inland. It grew rapidly during the eighteenth and nineteenth centuries as the port expanded and new industries came in its train. It grew also as many immigrants crossed from Ireland to Liverpool, three hundred thousand in the first five months of the potato famine years of 1846–47.[1] The first houses had been on the low lands between the river and ridge. About the turn of the eighteenth century, elegant terraces and squares were laid out for the wealthier classes on the high ground, but engulfed, as population pressure grew, in a sea of small terraced houses running in a great arc from the Dingle in the south to Walton in the north.

Working class housing followed the same basic form right up to the First World War. By 1914, the continuously built up city reached out just beyond the inner ring of Victorian parks. The population of this built up area continued to grow, reaching its zenith in 1921 when the city's population was seven hundred and twenty six thousand including the detached, but similar area within the city near the docks at Garston. Beyond lay open farmland, landed estates and small villages such as West Derby or Much Woolton.

The Liverpool of this period was a diverse city. The professional and middle classes still lived in the squares and terraces although change was already occurring. The author, Nicholas Monsarrat, was born in 1910 in the heart of this area, in Rodney Street, the son of a surgeon and university professor. He records the first incursion of trade into the street, a car salesroom, and by 1921 his father had bought a car and the family were living in Allerton, 'ten miles from Liverpool.'[2] Abercromby Square was already being colonised by a growing university and nearby Falkner Square had become 'a Liverpool Bloomsbury, a place of cheap studios and lodgings

(1) Woodham-Smith C, *The Great Hunger: Ireland 1845–9* (New English Library 1975).
(2) Monsarrat N, *Life is a Four Letter Word: Book 1, Breaking In* (Pan Books 1969).

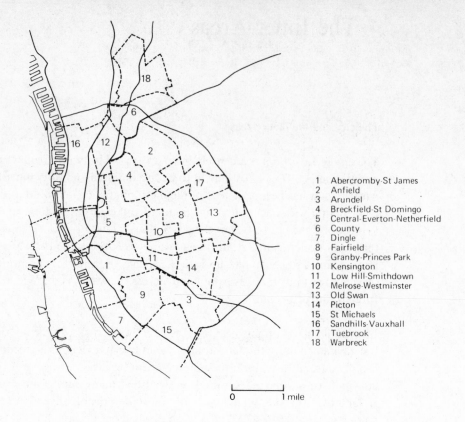

Figure 9
Inner city wards

1 Abercromby-St James
2 Anfield
3 Arundel
4 Breckfield-St Domingo
5 Central-Everton-Netherfield
6 County
7 Dingle
8 Fairfield
9 Granby-Princes Park
10 Kensington
11 Low Hill-Smithdown
12 Melrose-Westminster
13 Old Swan
14 Picton
15 St Michaels
16 Sandhills-Vauxhall
17 Tuebrook
18 Warbreck

0   1 mile

for actresses.'[1] Below, in the vicinity of Great George Square was where the 'foreign element lived, Orientals and Scandinavians, their condition depressed.' But most of the city was formed of endless terraces then hardly touched by the early municipal tenements which had replaced the worst cellar dwellings and court houses.

From 1921 onwards the population of the then built up area of the city declined at an accelerating rate. By 1971 it had fallen below three hundred and thirty thousand.[2] The character of this area changed greatly during the half century after 1921. The blitz caused many people to flee the city if they could. Others sought new homes and more attractive surroundings in the suburbs both before and after the war. The larger houses left behind by the families moving out were converted to rooming houses and cheap lodgings. Slums were cleared and replaced by new council housing. And the residential areas nearest the city centre were whittled away by the expanding university, colleges and hospital and the growth of city centre commercial activities.

Industry and commerce

By 1971 the industrial and commercial scene had changed radically compared with

(1) Reilly C H, *Some Liverpool Streets and Buildings in 1921* (Liverpool Daily Post and Mercury 1921).

(2) Population estimates for 1921 and 1971 based on Census data for the wards shown on figure 9 (1971 boundaries) and the detached St. Marys ward (Garston). These wards correspond closely with the three social areas described on pages 45 to 53.

fifty years earlier. The city centre was still thriving. Much of it had been rebuilt since the war. Lord Street, the main shopping centre, had been rebuilt after the blitz. A new covered shopping centre, the St. John's Precinct, had replaced earlier shops and the market. New offices were being built to the north, at Old Hall Street. A scattering of new hotels had opened. Only Dale Street and Castle Street with the municipal buildings and town hall remained substantially unchanged. And east of the city centre, even more new construction was to be found in the growing complex of university and hospitals.

In contrast, the docks, railways and industries were in decline, much of their employment lost. Now, for several miles north and south of the city centre, the docks lie idle. What is left of the trade has been rationalised into the Seaforth complex, north of Bootle. The collapse of the docks has hit nearby industry hard. The north end is crumbling and polluted but tobacco warehousing, sugar refining, brewing and food processing struggle on. But it is a precarious survival. Tate and Lyle, whose vast bulk overshadows all and in which several thousand workers are employed, has been threatening to pull out for years.

The industrial scene in the south end is, if anything, still more depressing. Acres of docks lie unused, save for a little storage and packaging. The impact of abandoned docks, empty warehouses, crumbling factories and mills and acres of derelict land add up to a form of environmental anarchy. The firms that survive and the new ones that spring up, often only for months, use the buildings and their surroundings virtually as they please. But for those who live in the nearby tenements, such dereliction can only remind them that their jobs have been taken away.

The most obvious impact of industrial decline in the study area itself is in the railways. Edge Hill station was the terminus for the first railway passenger line in the world. Opened in 1830, on the inauguration of the Liverpool to Manchester railway, all trains into Liverpool finished their journey here until the tunnel to Lime Street station was built. Young people now employed on job creation schemes clearing up derelict sites above ground, might like to remember the eccentric philanthropist who, in the 1830s, was disturbed by the large number of men queuing for work on the railway tunnels. For twenty years he employed men to dig his own system of tunnels, starting from the basement of his house in Edge Hill.[1]

Edge Hill station now stands, almost derelict itself, in a sea of abandoned railway sidings and half demolished engine sheds. The Edge Hill Goods Yard, once a major local employer, is now almost at a standstill. The redundant Crown Street Goods Yard is nearby, linked by a half-blocked tunnel and an abandoned railway cutting to Edge Hill station. The site is dominated on one side by a great, red-brick ventilation shaft. On the other can be seen the last remnants of once prosperous coal depots.

(1) Whittington-Egan R, 'The Mole of Mason Street', in *Liverpool Colonnade* (Philip Son & Nephew, Liverpool 1955).

There is little industrial dereliction elsewhere in the study area. Major local industry is confined to the Edge Lane Estate, comparatively prosperous and well-insulated from surrounding residential areas. Apart from the north and south dockside belts and industrial Aintree, it is the largest industrial area in inner Liverpool. Edge Lane is dominated by three firms, all Liverpool owned until recently. Their fortunes are therefore of great importance to the stability of the local economy. Fortunately the manufacture of biscuits and telecommunications equipment and the running of football pools and mail order have been relatively stable occupations, although each has rationalised or cut back in recent years. Nearby, south of the railway land, several small firms, and a gas works overlook the wasteland that once held the small railway terraces of Earle Road. Immediately north of the station is a building of some significance. A low, neat, partly prefabricated builder's depot, it is the first new industrial development in the area for many years, apart from a new workshop put up by a firm of armature winders within its own site.

A scattering of small industries in the rest of the study area reflect and reinforce a general air of decay and depression, rather than causing it directly. These are backyard industries, mainly panel-beating, paintspraying and vehicle-repairing and builders' yards.

The inner areas[1]

Inner Liverpool is a complex, mainly working class area exhibiting a wide diversity of life styles and social organisation. Most people live an ordinary family life typical of anywhere in the country. They live in small terraced houses with a growing number in council flats and houses. Many form stable communities, the tough, close knit Catholic communities near the docks; the remnants of the Orange Lodges now largely broken up by early slum clearance programmes; the complex 'foreign' communities of Liverpool 8, Arab, Pakistani, Chinese, African and black Liverpudlian; the terraces of Smithdown. They are communities brought together by shared interests, by family relationships built over several generations.

But inner Liverpool is the home too of other, more diverse groups. The students and nurses, the young professional people in their self contained flats near the parks, for these inner Liverpool is a waystage, a place which they pass through for a few years before moving on. Their numbers are small, as are those at the other extreme, the alcoholics and ex-mental patients living in rotting commercial lodging houses or dossing in derelict houses; the squalid bedsitters in crumbling mansions.

But for most of its residents, the inner area creates pressures. There are the personal pressures of poverty, of family breakdown, the strained racial tolerance. There is the loss of jobs, the destruction brought about by slum clearance, the stress from

(1) *Inner Liverpool/the inner areas* in this report refers to that part of Liverpool covered by the three social areas described in this section and illustrated in figures 10, 11 and 12. It corresponds closely with the group of wards shown on figure 9 but they also include small, scattered pieces of the two social areas found predominantly in outer Liverpool (see figures 13 and 14). See footnote on page 42.

living in cheap, inadequate housing and the vandalism of a decaying fabric. For some the inner city is a refuge, for others a trap. Some are just passing through. Others are happy to spend their lives there. Many who have left want to come back. There are compensations for the unemployment and urban decay of the inner areas in living in a close knit community near the city centre.

The Census analysis identified three types of social area in the inner city in 1971, each with its distinctive features, differing not only between themselves but also contrasting with the two social areas found predominantly in the rest of the city. The three inner city social areas with their 1971 populations are:

the older terraced areas	170,000
the rooming house areas	55,000
the inner council estates	55,000

The older terraced areas

About sixty percent of the population of inner Liverpool lives in the older terraced areas. The terraces form huge swathes in a great arc around the city, separated from the city centre or interspersed by the great dockside tenement areas, the new estates of Scotland Road, Everton and Edge Hill, and broken by the rooming house areas in Everton and Granby and around Newsham, Stanley and Princes Parks. The older terraced areas retain nearly two thirds of the city's stock of privately rented, unfurnished dwellings, though with an increasing proportion of owner occupation. Nearly two thirds of the houses still lacked an inside wc in 1971.

**Figure 10
Older terraced
areas 1971**

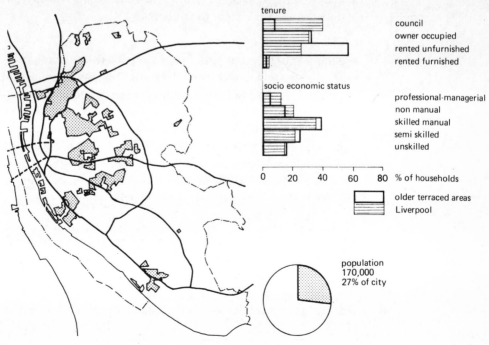

45

Despite a degree of poverty and generally poor living conditions, strong, stable communities have developed over the years, predominately skilled and semi skilled workers and their families. The older terraced areas had the fewest people moving within the city in the five years before the 1971 census. There is nevertheless a hierarchy of status, tenure and housing condition. Many of those furthest away from and north of the city centre have been bought from the old private landlords. The houses are in better condition and the occupants include a small proportion of professional and managerial workers, though in status the areas remain below average for the city. Conversely, the terraced areas closest to the city centre are in the worst condition, with the smallest houses, most lacking in basic amenities. Their social status is low and fewer houses are owner occupied.

However the gradations in income, house type and customs, even accent, are subtle ones. The overriding impression is of poor, proud and introverted communities, over-laying small groups of identical streets: for instance, the Welsh streets in Princes Park (Voelas Street, Rhiwlas Street, Powis Street); the Holyland in Dingle (Moses, Isaac and Jacob) and the Flower Streets area in Kirkdale (Snowdrop, Pansy and Harebell). Such communities have developed over a long period and an extended family network still thrives in many areas. In one small neighbourhood in Smithdown over ninety percent of pensioners had lived there all their lives. Judging by the age of the housing they would all have been children of the first families to move into the area when it was built at the end of the last century.

Outward appearances are staunchly maintained. Front steps, window sills, stretches of front pavement and even back lanes are regularly scrubbed. Neat lace curtains, washed every few weeks, are discreetly pulled back to reveal brass ornaments proudly displayed or football rosettes pinned up. Rooms are still wallpapered annually, partly against the damp, and house fronts regularly painted and rendered by those who have bought their houses.

A glimpse into the front parlours of a small terraced house reveals the pressures for space that modern family living demands. Three-piece suites and colour television sets vie with smart prams and chopper bikes, in rooms which open straight onto the street. Cars jostle for parking space on a fine summer evening with parents sitting in the doorways, younger children on the pavement with toys and books; older ones in the street with balls and bikes. Even the once sacrosanct front parlour now often bows to modern living as the wall is cut away to combine it with the back kitchen. Nearby relatives, neighbours, pubs, clubs, bingo, the 'bag-wash' and the corner shop form the basis of social and community life for many people.

The older terraced areas thus have an apparent degree of stability but they are nevertheless under pressure. Until recently the main threat has been slum clearance. For many, the threat was real, but necessary. The very oldest terraced houses and the even earlier court houses and cellar dwellings offered such bad living conditions that clearance was the only remedy. But the process was long drawn out and its effects are still being felt although the main clearance programmes are coming to an end. One of the last major clearance areas in the recently curtailed programme was in the study area around Earle Road. The scale of the exercise and delays in the programme had devasting effects. An air of uncertainty hung over the area for several years before final decisions were made as to the extent and boundaries of clearance areas. Thereafter a period of five years was to elapse before rehousing was complete. Elderly people were often the last to leave because of their long associations with the area, yet often the least equipped physically and emotionally to remain behind. Increasing vandalism and dereliction made going out a nightmare. Thefts were commonplace, often because it was not even clear whether a house was occupied or not. The complex network of relationships which allowed even housebound elderly people to remain fairly independent broke down. For many, isolation became complete. As the people left, so the shops on the nearby Earle Road steadily declined, despite the Corporation's policy to retain the shopping facade. A series of clumsily boarded-up shops, with their hopelessly optimistic 'To Let' signs were interspersed with derelict properties abandoned to the vandals, and the odd second hand shop or corner grocer waiting for the people to come back.

In 1975, eleven percent of land in the study area was lying vacant much of it the cleared sites of terraced houses. For those who have to live with the day to day reality of large, rubble-strewn sites the impact is immediate, unsavoury and depressing. Packs of half wild dogs scavenge among bags of abandoned household refuse. Pools of water collect where badly filled cellars have subsided. Children build fires with cardboard cartons and the abandoned timber from demolished houses and play among the piles of brick rubble and broken glass. Half bricks provide a ready and almost endless supply of ammunition for the frequent destruction of the windows of surrounding houses. Mattresses, furniture, gas cookers, prams and even cars that have outlived their usefulness are dumped. There is a pervading smell of old town gas from the partly buried gas pipes of demolished houses and the stopped off gas mains. It cannot be surprising that nearby residents, faced with five to ten years of dereliction, feel abandoned by an impersonal and uncaring bureaucracy.

Now the nature of the pressure on the older terraced areas is changing. The very worst of those shown on figure 10 have been cleared since 1971 but much of the housing has continued to deteriorate. Unimproved houses can still be bought for under a thousand pounds; soundly built but damp, quarry tiles on an earth floor, no bathroom, an outside toilet, sometimes only gas lighting and a single cold water tap. The problem is how to maintain and improve these houses and their environment. On the one hand, there is the cost of improvement and where the resources are to come from, for even grant aided expenditure would be beyond the means of many occupiers and many landlords would be unwilling to meet the cost. On the other hand, there is the problem of ensuring that the process of physical improvement does not lead to hardship or change unduly the social fabric by displacing the present occupants and attracting in new, more affluent residents. Already, too, signs of housing stress and multiple occupation are beginning to appear in some of the remaining areas of poor housing as adjacent rooming house areas are cleared or improved.

The rooming house areas

The rooming house areas are clustered in Abercromby, Granby and Princes Park, and in several smaller enclaves north and east of the city centre chiefly around the parks. They contained roughly a fifth of the total population of the inner area in 1971. Their chief characteristic is that they contain nearly two thirds of all private rented furnished accommodation in the city, chiefly large houses split into furnished flats and rooms. Nevertheless this form of tenure constitutes only a quarter of the total in the rooming house area. Most of it is either privately rented, unfurnished, or owner occupied.

The rooming house areas are the city's main reception area for young single people, newly married couples or poor families. Forty percent of residents had moved during the previous five years, the majority from outside Liverpool. They are people who do not qualify for a council tenancy, cannot afford to buy a house or want to spend a short period living in a flat before buying their own home.

Many of the larger old houses of the rooming house areas were built near the ring of Victorian parks that mark out the inner city. These were the parading grounds of the Victorian middle class; Princes, Newsham, Stanley, Sefton; each with its basic formula of grand approach, lake, grand drives and focal points of church spire or palm house. These were the ultimate, over formal, and stilted designs that were the baroque expression of a long tradition of English landscape gardening. Today they are luxuriant and decadent in their vegetation, and taken over by football pitches, playgrounds, gangs of small boys, dog walkers, a pirate galleon, a Peter Pan statue, and lonely old men sitting in the palm house on a cold winter Sunday.

**Figure 11
Rooming house
areas 1971**

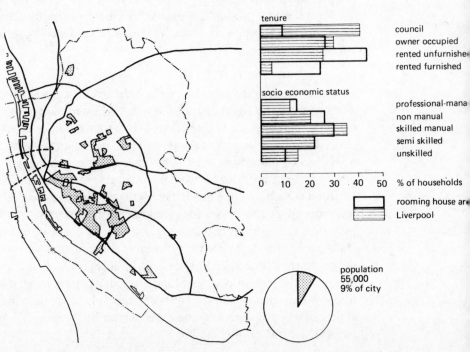

Throughout much of the inner city they provide the only relief from the old polluted industrial areas, the densely built housing and the vacant land.

It is chiefly around these parks that the higher status rooming house areas are to be found. Strictly, the term is a misnomer, for many of the more attractive large houses near the parks have been properly converted into modern self contained flats. Many have been offered for sale to young professional people and childless couples. Slightly smaller homes near the parks and hospitals, less suitable for conversion, are occupied by students or nurses.

Abercromby contains the remains of late Georgian and early Victorian Liverpool. The Anglican cathedral, started in 1904, dominates the whole area from its imposing sandstone ridge. It conjures up a vision of the banks of the Mersey one day restored to windswept grazing among its ivy-clad ruins . . . 'change and decay in all around I see, O Thou who changest not . . .'. And at the other end of Hope Street is the new Roman Catholic cathedral, built in the 1960s on foundations laid down massively in the 1920s.

The Crown Street Study suggested that the former well-to-do residents of Falkner Square had begun to leave as early as the nineteen twenties.[1] Many houses were abandoned during the Second World War. Others were split into flats and rooms and allowed to decay, cheek by jowl with those occupied by original residents, now aging or come down in the world. Small workshops were set up in mews, houses or back yard sheds. Now the wheel has turned full circle. What is left is being painstakingly put back together by housing associations; renovating, converting, rebuilding.

Ten years ago much of Granby and Princes Park was in a similar state, although much of the housing was later and less soundly constructed. Unemployment, overcrowding, prostitution, and above all, extreme poverty, provided much of the fuel for the notorious Liverpool 8 image which rebounded on the majority of ordinary, poor residents, black and white alike, and further tightened the noose of deprivation. These were the twilight areas of the city, areas of despair, the antithesis of community; a trap for the rejected, a refuge for those needing to escape. Landlords asked no questions and charged exhorbitant rents. Then, in the late 1960s and early 1970s, slum clearance reached the multi-lets of Granby. At the same time, a few years of generous improvement grants encouraged a dying spark of private flat conversions in the big old houses of Princes Avenue and around Princes Park and a rapid rise in the activities of housing associations. In addition the central part of Granby was declared a general improvement area. Granby started going up in the world; not the gentrification of Islington or Camden Town, but an influx of working-class families with steady jobs or a little capital.

Many of the families in the cleared multi-let houses moved out to new estates like Netherley or Cantril Farm. Indeed it was well known that a number of houses were

(1) Vereker C and Mays J B with Gittus E and Broady M, *Urban Redevelopment and Social Change: A Study of Social Conditions in Central Liverpool 1955–56* (Liverpool University Press 1961).

emptied several times over by sympathetic housing officials, as they were persistently relet to desperate families during the lengthy process of compulsory purchase, rehousing and clearance. However, many families were rehoused locally either into new council estates or older tenements. Already hard to let, an influx of poor, sick, large or unemployed families, rapidly made many flats lettable only to the toughest, most desperate or least caring households. Liverpool's twilight zone moved into the public sector.

However, not all the remaining multi-let housing has been improved. More houses have been split up, more scattered now as the supply of suitable, large Victorian villas dries up. Smithdown and Arundel wards further to the east now have their pockets of multi-occupied houses. A movement that has seen a steady and compact progression out from the city centre over the years is now being fragmented among the remaining large private houses of the inner city.

The rooming house areas have the special distinction in Liverpool of being the home of the immigrant communities. Ever since Chinese, West African and West Indian sailors settled near the south docks early this century, Liverpool 8 has been the home of the immigrant communities of Liverpool. Chinatown has settled onto the Great Georges area and through the extensive ownership of property and restaurants a self-contained and independent community has been established, although many Chinese families have quietly moved out into smaller terraced houses in other parts of Liverpool.

The focus of black Liverpool is further up the hill, in Upper Parliament Street and Granby. A history of inter-marriage with white Liverpool women and a tendency for different nationalities, African, Asian, West Indian, Arab, to cluster together has created far more complex and exposed communities than that of the Chinese. The impression is of a fragile truce maintained locally by an equality of poverty between black and white, and further afield by ignorance, indifference, or the presumed security of distance. Liverpool born blacks suffer most. Many have little knowledge of their original culture yet feel rejected from the one into which they were born. Granby Street, running through the centre of black Liverpool was, according to SNAP

> 'once one of the most prestigious local shopping areas in Liverpool with shopkeepers displaying prizes and awards. The character has changed and it now exhibits a new type of stimulating cosmopolitan brilliance . . . the occasional small supermarket, shops bursting with red and green peppers, yams, sweet potatoes, okra, aubergines, guaras and courgettes. All of them, including the Polish grocer, the Chinese 'chippies' and the ubiquitous betting shops, wear heavy protective grills at night which are rarely taken down during the day.'[1]

(1) Shelter Neighbourhood Action Project, *Another Chance for the Cities, SNAP 69/72* (Liverpool 1972).

The inner council estates

The inner council estates had roughly the same population in 1971 as the rooming house area and, in their own way, present as great a variety of conditions, not only in architecture but also in standards of maintenance, social character and popularity with tenants. Nearly ninety percent of the people live in council dwellings which include 1930s tenements, 1950s walk-up flats, 1960s high rise blocks and the most recent three storey flats, maisonettes and houses, each type reflecting the architectural fashion of its time. The estates are all built on the sites of cleared slums and the dwellings, nearly all flats or maisonettes, are smaller and have fewer rooms, than on council estates in other parts of the city. The great bulk of the older inner council estates are in the dockside areas of Vauxhall and Dingle. Others are found in Everton, Edge Hill and Old Swan. They are poor working class neighbourhoods, largely Catholic, strong communities into which comparatively few people have moved in recent years.

The 1930s tenements were hailed in their heyday as something of an architectural and social milestone in public housing. Even today, none can doubt the sturdiness of their construction. But thirty years of neglect, poverty and overcrowding have taken their toll. The gardens which gave many of them their names have long since been replaced by tarmac, now pitted and patched. Attempts to relieve some of the barrack-like squares with play equipment have mostly been short lived. Its charred or twisted remains lay neglected for years and add to the desolation. Long rows of drab, identical balconies, relieved by the occasional brightly painted flat, are piled five high. Attempts to install lifts in some blocks have been abandoned. They were out of action more often than they were working.

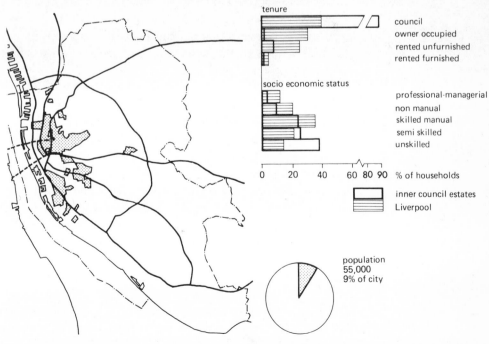

**Figure 12
Inner council
estates 1971**

tenure

council
owner occupied
rented unfurnished
rented furnished

socio economic status

professional-managerial
non manual
skilled manual
semi skilled
unskilled

0   20   40   60 80 90   % of households

inner council estates
Liverpool

population
55,000
9% of city

51

C

Two thirds of the workforce is unskilled in many of the tenement blocks. Up to a quarter of men are out of work. Most youngsters leave school with no qualifications and, if they can find work at all, drift into the same pattern of local, low paid, casual manual work their fathers had before them. Many flats are overcrowded. Children play on the balconies or in the glass and rubble strewn squares. Adolescents hang around the stairways, play football on patches of tarmac or waste ground or just drift around in groups. To an outsider the tenements, once inside the squares, seem tough and threatening. Hostility frowns down, it seems, from the watchful eyes of women, chatting on the balconies or hanging out washing.

Yet, despite everything, some of the tenements have remained popular. Certainly many people want to get out from overcrowded flats with old fashioned and inadequate fittings. But recently, some blocks have been fully improved. People value the comradeship and support that such an area can give, built up over many years, partly by a shared experience of poverty, partly by a similarity of attitude passed on from one generation to the next, and partly, perhaps, by the form and layout of the housing itself. Many young couples will try to get a flat in the block near to their parents rather than move away.

Scattered amongst the tenements are smaller blocks of three storey flats, built around communal courts to a common and spartan design in the early 1950s. Despite their smaller scale, many of these appear cold and inhuman, laid out in regimented blocks, neglected since the day they were built, lacking a single growing plant.

By contrast many of the new inner area estates of the 1960s and 1970s are popular and well cared for, especially those which are most like traditional private housing; two and three storey blocks in staggered terraces or built around open squares. Indeed fashion appears to have gone full circle. Much of it looks remarkably like the terraced housing it replaced with a bit more room, some gardens, a different layout, a few trees and some car parking spaces. Those which have employed industrial building methods or imposed extremes of architectural fashion are much less popular. But in certain locations and for single people or couples without children, even high-rise flats have become accepted and even popular. A secure, centrally-heated flat in a well maintained tower with a good caretaker and lifts which always work, combined with views across the park to the nearby city centre one way, and the Welsh hills the other, is for many, an attractive proposition.

A number of smaller estates and tower blocks have become notorious, with a high vacancy rate and, for council estates, a comparatively high rate of turnover of population. They include virtually every style and period, even the newest low rise, high density estates. They contain greater proportions of single parent families, new commonwealth immigrants, or problem families, chiefly as a result of rehousing families from nearby clearance areas or taking in those who had little choice of where to live.

Maisonettes with thin walls and large families, piled ten high to twenty storeys; with filthy lifts that seldom work and concrete stairs with broken lights and boarded windows, looking out over a sea of concrete and empty docks, make for trouble. Such have been conditions in one notorious tower block in Everton, the subject of a year's litigation between the tenants and the City Council about respective responsibilities for the communal parts of the block. A county court judge summed-up as follows:

> 'I was appalled by the general condition of the property and it astonished me that a city such as Liverpool could expect that tenants would live in and put up with conditions such as I saw ... I ought to draw attention to the fact that there was a considerable number of unoccupied properties in this block of buildings, which were apparently protected only by having corrugated sheets of iron put over the windows ... what a depressing appearance.'[1]

The outer areas

The outer areas of the city were the scene of steady population growth and new housebuilding from the green fields of 1921 to their present almost complete development. Although for much of the period, the physical form and density of private and council estates did not differ greatly, there has been a strong geographical separation into two social areas. They are, with their 1971 populations:

the high status areas   130,000

the outer council estates   200,000

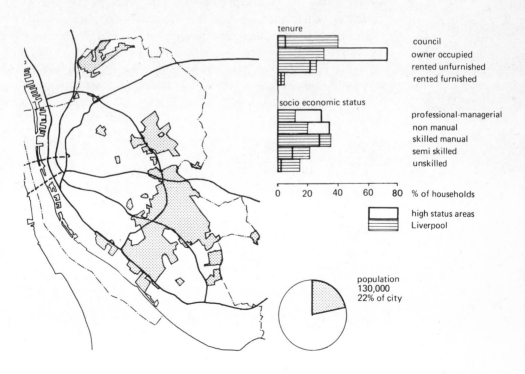

**Figure 13
High status areas
1971**

(1) Court of Appeal (Queen's Bench Division), Liverpool City Council v Irwin, quoted in an article by Murphy E in *Castle Street Circular* (Liverpool Council of Voluntary Service, May 1976).

The high status areas

Private housebuilding for sale was concentrated in the south east of the city around Calderstones Park and several golf courses, with smaller areas elsewhere. These high status areas contain nearly a quarter of the city's population and are very homogeneous, containing over seventy percent owner occupation, virtually no council housing and only a small proportion of private renting. The social area is so named because it is dominated by professional, managerial and non manual workers and their associated attributes of high educational attainment and car ownership.

In other respects, the high status areas do vary. Those of highest status are clustered around Calderstones Park itself with comparatively large houses. Elsewhere, there is a string of newly built estates of smaller houses on the city's eastern boundary north of Hunt's Cross where many couples with young children have come to live, moving to Liverpool from other parts of the country. But most of the high status areas are occupied by older people, many of whose children have grown up and moved away. These include the older, detached houses at say Grassendale, or the Wavertree Garden Suburb, developed chiefly in the 1920s and 1930s.

The outer council estates

The outer council estates are even larger and more homogeneous in character than the high status areas. The housing is overwhelmingly public sector and occupied chiefly by skilled and semi skilled manual workers; a social structure corresponding fairly closely to the average for the city. Their social characteristics correspond

Figure 14
Outer council
estates 1971

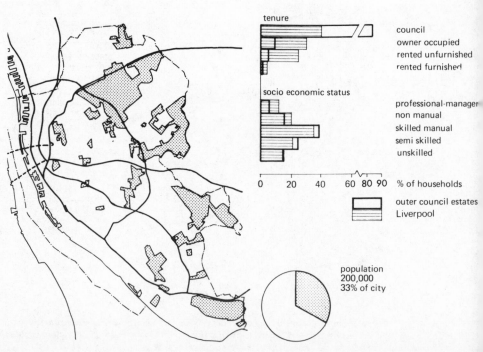

tenure

council
owner occupied
rented unfurnished
rented furnished

socio economic status

professional-manager
non manual
skilled manual
semi skilled
unskilled

0   20   40   60 80 90   % of households

outer council estates
Liverpool

population
200,000
33% of city

closely to successive waves of physical development. The oldest estates at Walton Clubmoor were built between the wars as garden suburbs, almost entirely semi-detached houses and short terraces. By 1971, the original population had aged and their children grown up and left home. They have become the most popular council estates in the city, many houses being bought by their tenants when offered for sale by the Council.

The next main stage of development was in the 1950s when a mixture of semi-detached terraces and houses with small numbers of walk-up blocks of flats were built, chiefly at Gillmoss and Speke. By 1971, the children of their first tenants were teenagers and young adults: youth unemployment was growing and overcrowding increasing. The most recent estates at Netherley and Cantril Farm have a much higher proportion of flats including slab and tower blocks. In 1971 there were many young families with small children and every prospect of increasing overcrowding.

Although the most recent outer estates contain a high proportion of flats the outer estates in general contain many more houses than those in the inner areas and all the dwellings have more rooms. And their social status is markedly higher than that of the inner estates. Tower blocks built in many parts of the city especially to rehouse childless couples, pensioners and single people from slum clearance areas form the only exception to this general rule. Although found in both inner and outer areas, they nevertheless correspond more closely to the latter in their social characteristics.

**Figure 15
The inner areas
1971**

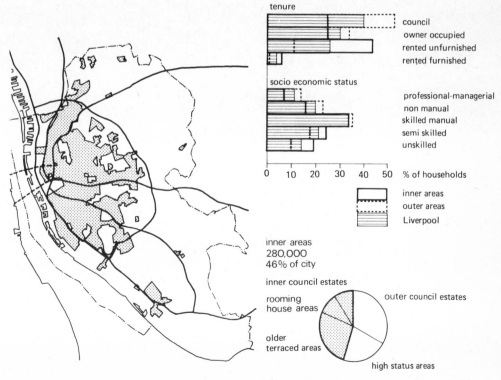

tenure

council
owner occupied
rented unfurnished
rented furnished

socio economic status

professional-managerial
non manual
skilled manual
semi skilled
unskilled

0   10   20   30   40   50   % of households

inner areas
outer areas
Liverpool

inner areas
280,000
46% of city

inner council estates

rooming
house areas

outer council estates

older
terraced areas

high status areas

55

Inner and outer area contrasts

The outer boundary of the three social areas making up Liverpool's inner area lies close to the line of Queen's Drive. Together, they contained a population of two hundred and eighty thousand in 1971 or about forty six percent of the total in the city. If, however, the small number of high status areas and tower blocks located in inner city wards are included, the population rises to about three hundred and thirty thousand.[1]

The greatest single contrast between inner and outer areas is their history. Since 1921, the population of the former has been declining at an accelerating rate whilst that of the outer areas has been rising, although at a diminishing rate in recent years. And for many years, the loss from the inner city has exceeded the gains in the outer areas so that the population of the city itself has been falling steadily.

Figure 16
Population change
1911–76

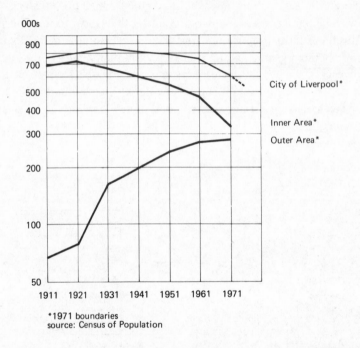

000s

City of Liverpool*

Inner Area*

Outer Area*

*1971 boundaries
source: Census of Population

The next significant contrast in the city is the greater proportion of private rented housing in the inner area and the generally lower status of its population. These contrasts in a sense replicate the difference between Liverpool and the country at large. The city is, to a considerable degree, a working class one. The social structure of the outer areas roughly corresponds to the national though even it has lower proportions of professional and managerial and non-manual households than in Britain. The inner area is thus much lower in status than the national average. The pattern of housing tenure shows a similar relation. Liverpool has less owner occupation and more council and private unfurnished renting than in Britain. But

(1) See footnotes on pages 42 and 44.

the outer area is closer to the national average than the inner area, with more owner occupation and less private renting.

In other respects, the differences are less significant. The age structure of the population is broadly similar across the city, its own population slightly younger than that of the country as a whole, with a higher proportion of children and young adults and a lower proportion of middle aged people. Both dwellings and households are slightly larger in Liverpool than the national average. Despite its history and reputation the proportion of people born in the Irish Republic is the same as in the whole of Britain, and only slightly greater in the inner area. Equally surprising, perhaps, is the exceptionally small proportion of the city's population born in Africa or the new commonwealth countries. At less than one percent in 1971, it was only about a third of the national average. However these figures omit the large numbers of Liverpudlians born of several generations of immigration and intermarriage.

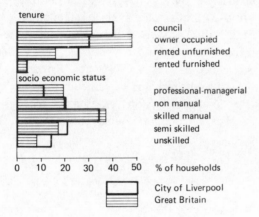

Figure 17
Tenure and status
1971

The most significant differences between Liverpool's inner and outer areas and between Liverpool and the rest of the country thus lie in population changes, housing tenure and social status. Liverpool as a whole, and its inner area in particular, have exceptionally high proportions of households either without an inside wc or sharing a dwelling. Unemployment is much greater and car ownership and educational attainment much lower in Liverpool than nationally, particularly in the inner areas.

Social polarisation and migration

Social polarisation is occurring in Liverpool not only between inner and outer areas but within different parts of the city. Thus the professional and managerial people moving into the high status areas in the five years prior to the 1971 census were raising the status of these areas still higher, whereas the increasing proportion of unskilled workers moving into the other council estates had an equivalent lowering effect. A similar divergence was occurring in the rooming house area, intensifying the social differences between its more and less affluent parts.

Only the rooming house areas and the new outer council estates gained new population in the five years prior to 1971. In the former over half of the resident households had moved to their present address in that period, over a quarter in the previous year alone, both from other parts of the city and from elsewhere in the country. Conversely, over three quarters of the residents of the most recently built outer council estates had moved in the previous five years, nearly all of them from slum clearance areas elsewhere in the city.

The population of the city itself fell by one hundred and thirty six thousand between 1961 and 1971 and has continued to fall thereafter at an average rate of about thirteen thousand five hundred people each year. This represents a gross loss of nearly forty thousand people a year, making due allowance for a small inward migration and natural increase. The greater part of this loss was from the inner areas, showing some disturbing trends. According to a recent study by the City Planning Department, the net loss of population from the city between 1966 and 1971 included a disproportionate number of young married couples with children whilst the numbers of elderly in the city were increasing.[1] But it also included above average proportions of professional, managerial and non manual workers and comparatively few unskilled workers. Although population loss was great, few people went very far. Nearly half of those leaving Liverpool between 1966 and 1971 went to the new Merseyside county districts of Sefton, Knowsley, St. Helens or Wirral. A further fifth went to the new and expanded towns of Skelmersdale, Runcorn, Ellesmere Port, Widnes, Winsford and Burnley. The rest were dispersed in the rest of the North West region, north Wales and the rest of Britain.

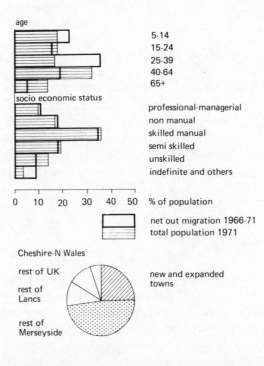

Figure 18
Net migration from
Liverpool 1966–71

(1) City Planning Department, *The Changing Social and Housing Structure of Liverpool* (1975).

A comparison of these trends suggests a number of important conclusions. The city has been losing population for a number of years, the loss from the inner areas being partially offset by new housebuilding in the outer areas. The loss from the inner areas is slowing down as the major slum clearance programmes of the 1960s come to an end, but the room for new development in the outer areas is now very limited. The population of the outer areas will continue to rise for some years through natural increase of the families recently moving in. But it is likely that the population of the city will continue to decline and its social class composition could become even more unbalanced, with an increasing proportion of unskilled workers. The social polarisation between the high status areas, including the more affluent rooming house areas, and the rest of the city may widen still further. The outer council estates are becoming an extension of Liverpool's inner area in terms of their social status.

The following six chapters describe in turn different features of inner Liverpool, relating them where relevant to the rest of the city and Merseyside. We then return in chapter eleven to the question of definitions when we have identified those characteristics of Liverpool's inner area which give greatest cause for concern.

An impression of inner Liverpool

The study area, looking west, September 1971.

Top left, the Anglican Cathedral and the Georgian terraces and squares of Abercromby. Top right, the Roman Catholic Cathedral of Christ the King and the University. Hope Street, between the two, marks the edge of the inner area. Beyond lie the city centre, Lime Street station, the docks and the river Mersey. Upper Parliament Street runs from top left to bottom right. To its left are the terraces of Granby (some since cleared) and 1950s council estates. To the right are 1930s tenement blocks and 1960s high rise flats at Edge Hill. Between are the cleared sites of slums, since redeveloped with two and three storey council estates.

Photograph by Aerofilm

The edge of the inner city; *top*, looking south along Hope Street towards the Anglican Cathedral; *bottom*, looking north towards the Roman Catholic Cathedral of Christ the King. Hope Street is now mainly offices, clubs, hotels and the Philharmonic Hall.

Liverpool formerly depended for its livelihood on the port and many people living in the inner city were employed in the docks. Today, much of the trade has left the port, or moved to new docks further down the river Mersey, and the south docks have been closed. *Top*, Wapping Dock, built in the mid-nineteenth century but now closed. Further north is Pierhead and the Royal Liver Building.

Bottom, food processing industries and other port related businesses were located near the docks but as trade declined, so many mills and factories closed, a further loss of jobs for inner city residents. The Tate and Lyle sugar mills at Vauxhall is one of the few remaining large dockside employers.

The inner city contained few big industries other than the docks. One of the largest employers was the railways but these too have run down since the Second World War. One group of industries (including food manufacturing, electronics and mail order/football pools) is located on an industrial estate at Edge Lane. The *top* picture shows the Edge Lane industrial estate in the background and one of the last of the big slum clearance areas in the city, the Earle Road site in the foreground. In between is the disused Edge Hill goods yard. The new building near the gas works is St. Thomas a Becket R C secondary school.

The inner city is the location, too, of a variety of small industries and service trades, many of them scattered in residential areas or, as in the *bottom* picture, around the edge of the former Crown Street railway goods yard at Edge Hill, now disused.

65

Much of inner Liverpool at any time in the past decade has been vacant. Slums were cleared but their sites could remain vacant for many years, particularly if they were reserved for some future use for which resources were not readily available, such as highways, extensions to schools or open spaces. The *top* view shows one such clearance area at Crown Street, Edge Hill, reserved for a proposed district distributor road. The original compulsory purchase orders were confirmed between 1966 and 1972, the sites finally cleared by about 1972. The part shown here was treated under the government's Special Environmental Assistance Scheme in 1972/73 and is still vacant. New University buildings are on the left of the picture.

A particular problem is unemployment amongst young people. The government's Job Creation Programme has provided a limited number of jobs, many of them on projects such as that shown in the *bottom* picture, an environmental improvement scheme in Everton.

66

The population of the inner city has fallen from 725,000 in 1921 to about 300,000 at the present time. Much of the loss of population has been due to people leaving of their own accord, for better housing, a more attractive environment or jobs. But much has been the result of slum clearance programmes, reaching their peak in the 1960s. These are now drawing to an end as the worst slums have been demolished, and future slum clearance will be on a smaller scale, in smaller sites.

The *top* photograph shows part of a clearance area in Abercromby, behind Upper Parliament Street, the tower of the Anglican Cathedral in the distance. The row of small houses on the left is Egerton Street, compulsorily acquired for clearance but, after local protests, the houses were reprieved and have now been improved by two housing associations. The large villa to the right has also been improved by a housing association and, beyond, a new block of flats is being built by another housing association. The *bottom* photograph shows Priest Street, part of a clearance area in Granby. Some of the houses are still occupied by people waiting to be rehoused; others have been vacated and boarded up to guard against vandalism.

The compulsory purchase orders for slum clearance usually apply only to the houses themselves. Groups of shops on the main road were not included but nevertheless fell into disuse following the loss of their local customers. The *top* picture shows a group of shops in the Earle Road clearance area at Smithdown.

The slum clearance schemes affected old people particularly badly. Often, they were less willing to be rehoused, less able to adapt to new conditions but increasingly were left isolated as their neighbours and relatives moved away to new council estates in other parts of the city. The *bottom* photograph is in part of the Earle Road clearance area at Smithdown. This was just about the last of the very large clearance areas of the stage 1 programme. Future clearance areas are to be much smaller and more selective.

A quarter of the population of the inner city is now living in council estates, ranging from walk up tenement blocks built in the 1930s to high rise blocks of flats in the late 1960s.

The *top* photograph shows the contrast. Windsor Gardens, Edge Hill, was built in the 1930s but in recent years its condition rapidly deteriorated, it became a 'hard to let' block of flats occupied by those least able to choose where to live. It stood empty for two years pending a decision whether it should be improved or demolished, and in 1976 was demolished. The block of flats in the background is Milner House, built in the 1960s, chiefly for pensioners and childless couples.

Bottom left, the entrance to a ground floor flat in Myrtle Gardens, Edge Hill, a tenement block similar in style to Windsor Gardens. *Bottom right*, Entwistle Heights, Edge Hill, part of the same group of 1960s flats as Milner House.

69 The Inner Council Estates contain many of the most deprived people in inner Liverpool, the families of unskilled workers exposed to risk of unemployment; and large families with many children living in small, unsuitable flats, often poorly maintained and vandalised. This is true particularly of the 1930s tenement blocks such as Myrtle Gardens, Edge Hill. The *top* photograph shows one of its courtyards with a children's play space in the middle; *bottom*, one of the small corner shops in Myrtle Gardens, still in use, its windows boarded up against vandalism.

The Inner Council Estates: a different style of building was introduced in the 1950s, three storey walk up flats such as at Beaumont Street, Granby (*top*). The flats themselves are to a more modern design which can provide good living accommodation provided the common staircases and entrances and the surrounding open spaces are well maintained. But conditions in some inner area blocks have been allowed to deteriorate and these too may become hard-to-let flats.

The most recent council housing is entirely two storey, wherever it is located, in the inner city or outer suburbs. The *bottom* picture shows part of the Chatsworth estate at Edge Hill, built just before the height restriction on council houses. Nevertheless, it is mainly two storey terraced houses, with a few three storey flats and maisonettes. It was used to rehouse people from slum clearance elsewhere in the inner city, and is a popular estate as yet showing little sign of vandalism.

The Inner Council Estates: *top left*, 1950s council flats off Smithdown Lane, Edge Hill, showing the state to which the communal areas and entrance ways can deteriorate. *Top right*, a small corner shop in the Falkner estate at Edge Hill, slightly older and at a higher density than Chatsworth, with a greater proportion of three storey flats and maisonettes. This is becoming a hard-to-let estate, with growing vandalism.

High rise blocks of flats and maisonettes were built in many parts of the city in the late 1960s, chiefly to rehouse older people and childless couples from slum clearance and the waiting list. Families with children, too, were accommodated in the maisonettes but they have usually since been transferred to more suitable council tenancies. The *bottom* picture shows a group in the inner city, on Everton Brow with the docks in the distance.

The Rooming House Area: a fifth of the population of inner Liverpool lives in the former middle class town houses of the city, around Abercromby and Granby, overlooking Sefton Park and near Princes Avenue. Some of the houses have been converted into self-contained flats for young professional people, students, nurses etc. The majority are in multiple occupation with sharing, overcrowding and other symptoms of housing stress. They are the homes of many in poverty and distress, unable to afford better private housing, unable to qualify for council housing. Many of their inhabitants have only recently moved to Liverpool.

The *top* photograph shows Canning Street, Abercromby, now part of a general improvement area. The *bottom* picture shows a new block of flats being built for a housing association on a small cleared site at Huskisson Street, Abercromby.

The Rooming House Area shades off quickly into parts of the older terraced areas which, especially in Granby, have become the home of many of Liverpool's black population, including people whose families have lived here for two or three generations. Many of the houses are in multiple occupation or overcrowded. Some, such as Jermyn Street, *top*, are now included in the Granby general improvement area.

People in the most extreme stress may be sharing overcrowded, privately rented furnished rooms or be actually homeless, living in lodging houses or hostels. They include single people of all ages, from young people who have left home to older people with a history of psychiatric or medical problems. Many have been in and out of institutions such as hospital or prison for much of their lives. The *bottom* photograph shows a Shaw Street lodging house in Everton.

The Older Terraced Areas of the inner city still house over a half of its total population. They are all terraced houses built between fifty and a hundred years ago and in a variety of condition depending chiefly on age. The older houses lack basic amenities, such as an inside wc, and are usually privately rented. The more recent have sometimes been bought by their occupants and improved.

Top: Viking Street, Princes Park, a section which has recently been proposed for a housing action area, one of twenty one in the city.

Bottom: off Park Road, Princes Park, one of the remaining proposed clearance areas not yet demolished.

The Older Terraced Areas: houses in and around the Lodge Lane area, Smithdown. *Top*, a back lane off Smithdown Road. *Bottom left*, a recently improved terrace house. *Bottom right*, a closed house being bricked up.

Many of the main roads radiating from the central area through the older terraced areas are lined by shops. Wavertree Road, Edge Hill, is one such. As slums were cleared, land was reserved for a proposed district shopping centre and council offices. The *top* view shows the shops remaining on the north side, the building formerly occupied by a department store since closed on the south, and part of the reserved site. *Bottom*, informal street trading on the cleared site reserved for the new district centre.

Top, Granby Street is lined by a wide variety of shops serving a local population of very mixed origins, English, Irish, Arab, Pakistani, African and West Indian. The primary school also fronts onto the street.

Bottom, Nelson Street, St. James, below the Anglican Cathedral, is Liverpool's Chinatown.

Children's play in the inner area. *Top:* playing football in the courtyard of Myrtle Gardens, Edge Hill. *Bottom:* the 'Welsh' streets, Princes Park.

Play on Wheels visits a street party in Princes Park during the summer of 1974. Activities include inflatables, a discotheque, film shows and painting.

The edge of the inner city: the outer boundary is marked by the Victorian and Edwardian town parks of Liverpool. The *top* view is into Sefton Park. *Bottom*, the Lake, Princes Park, overlooked by nineteenth century villas now converted into self contained flats with a high rise block of council flats just visible through the trees.

5 People at risk

The new poor

A recent OECD report presents an authoritative analysis of poverty in a number of western countries and the ways in which it is being tackled by governments.[1] It makes the crucial point that the nature of poverty is changing and nowadays it chiefly involves two groups of people. First, there are those who are unable to work: the elderly (especially those living alone); the sick and the disabled; and people whose other commitments make regular, paid work an impossibility (eg single parent families). Secondly, there are those whose opportunities for regular, well paid work are most at risk, including those left with skills no longer required or who lack any basic skills; new entrants to the workforce, especially school leavers without any qualifications; and those who for one reason or another may be unfairly discriminated against.

In considering those most at risk in inner Liverpool it is important to distinguish between the economic and social pressures faced throughout urban society by those who are most vulnerable and the peculiar circumstances of inner Liverpool and other inner city areas. In practice it is almost impossible to disentangle the different elements involved. Decline of the docks in Liverpool has been the most direct cause of the loss of large numbers of unskilled jobs. But there has been an overall decline in unskilled jobs resulting from changes in technology and industrial processes which themselves have occurred at different rates in different parts of the country. Increasing affluence, a desire for independence and changing social mores have contributed to a breakdown of the three generation family system, changes in living patterns, and greater mobility. These also have occurred differentially throughout the country, and affected some classes of people more than others. And the changing international status of Britain coupled with rapid immigration from the new commonwealth in the recent past has challenged traditional class and social relationships.

The bad effects of these changes and pressures can be seen in unemployment, family breakdown, homelessness, sickness and racial discrimination. Most of the symptoms can be found in more than their fair share in inner city areas although few, if any, are peculiar to such areas. Nevertheless, inner Liverpool contains exceptional concentrations of many of the groups of people at greatest risk of poverty in our society. Our study looks at the concentrations, rather than poverty itself. This chapter, therefore, considers briefly the circumstances of those most at risk in the inner areas; unskilled workers, school leavers, vulnerable families and racial minorities. It looks at the local results of wider economic and social forces. The forces themselves are examined in later chapters. And chapter eleven considers

(1) *Public Expenditures on Income Maintenance Programmes* (OECD 1976); see also article by Beckerman W, *New Statesman*, 10 September 1976.

the extent to which the co-existence in certain areas of different kinds of deprivation in itself constitutes a further disadvantage for those living in these areas.

Unskilled and unemployed

Nineteen percent of workers who lived in inner Liverpool in 1971 were unskilled, compared with ten percent in the rest of the city. Extreme concentrations were found in the inner council estates, rising to a third of the resident workforce. Comparisons throughout the city at the small area level suggested that there is a hierarchy of values within Liverpool, such that a worker's risk of being unemployed in the inner council estates is about four times as great as a worker of the same level of skill living in the high status areas of the city. The hierarchy applies at every level of skill, but is especially pronounced for unskilled workers.

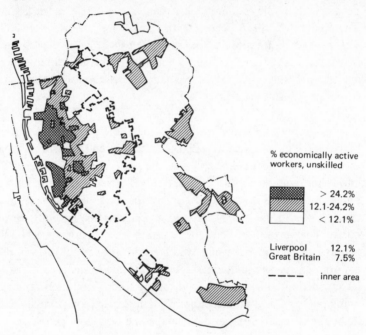

**Figure 19
Unskilled workers
1971**

% economically active workers, unskilled

> 24.2%
12.1-24.2%
< 12.1%

Liverpool 12.1%
Great Britain 7.5%

---- inner area

The most important single effect on the probability of a worker being unemployed is his level of skill. Men in our Leece Street unemployment survey whose last job had been unskilled were nearly twice as likely to be unemployed as their incidence in the population suggested. The level of educational achievement and formal training among the unemployed was also found to be very low. More than ninety percent of the sample had no educational qualifications. Even among the young, educational qualifications were the exception, eighty five percent of those under twenty having no qualifications at all. Furthermore, three-quarters of the men had received no formal training since leaving school, even when this definition was widely drawn to include instruction in the Armed Forces, and on-the-job training of more than three years.

Unskilled workers took longer to find work than skilled men and had held fewer jobs in the past five years. Many jobs were held only for a short period due partly

82

Figure 20
Unemployment by
skill and area 1971

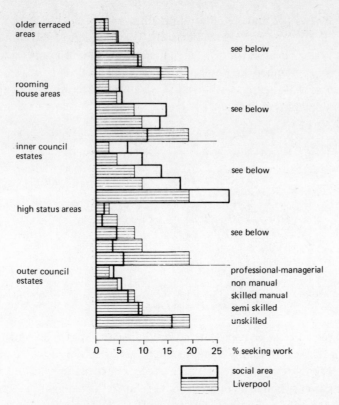

to the temporary nature of much unskilled work, for instance on building sites, and partly to the prevalence of taking seasonal work among inner Liverpool residents in holiday camps in summer time, or food factories at their autumn peak. Unskilled workers are forced to rely on this kind of work largely because of the decline of unskilled jobs in Liverpool. Few vacancies for unskilled work were notified to the Leece Street Exchange in comparison with the numbers registered for work. Unskilled workers who had permanent jobs tended to change employment less often than elsewhere in the country.

Among the unskilled there was evidence of a group that could be termed 'hard-core unemployed'. Half of the total unemployed had been out of work for more than half their time in the last five years, some almost permanently; and an overlapping group of over a third had been on the unemployment register for more than a year. This hard core included many of those who had never had any job other than an unskilled one.

Unqualified and untrained

The overriding problem facing school leavers in Liverpool is poor job prospects. Unemployment among people under eighteen in Liverpool is approximately twice the national rate. The position is worse for boys though it has recently been deteriorating for girls as well. Liverpool had more young people out of work than any other town or city in England, at most times more than Birmingham and London combined. For instance, in December 1973, the last year for which these figures were published, there were one thousand one hundred and sixty four unemployed boys under eighteen in the Liverpool travel to work area, compared with nine hundred in Greater London.[1] The situation has worsened significantly in recent years. The number of young unemployed doubled between 1970 and 1973, at a time when numbers leaving school were falling. The current recession and summer school leaving combined to give a total of more than six thousand young people unemployed in August 1976.

Figure 21
Youth unemployment, Liverpool 1966–76

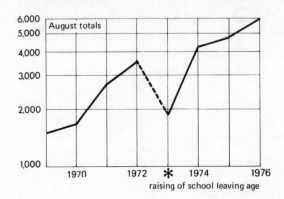

raising of school leaving age

Those most at risk of being unemployed are early school leavers and those without qualifications or training. A survey in 1973 showed that three-quarters of unemployed young people had been at secondary modern schools or in non examination streams in comprehensive schools.[2] Over eighty percent had left school at fifteen and only six percent had any 'O' levels or CSEs. Half of them had been out of work for more than two months.

Figure 22
First jobs entered, by training 1972

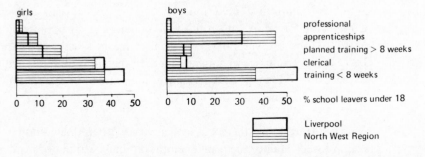

For early school leavers who do get jobs the prospects are little better. The proportion of boys and girls entering jobs requiring little or no training in Liverpool was greater than in the North West region. Two-thirds of boys leaving school at fifteen in Liverpool in 1972 entered unskilled work compared with well under half in Britain. For sixteen year olds the position is also worse than nationally, although among seventeen year old leavers a higher proportion enter both apprenticeships and clerical work, with the effect that the age group is slightly better placed in the city than nationally.

The prevalence of first jobs in the unskilled sector is due to the lack of apprenticeships and other training opportunities. Apprenticeships are of great

(1) *Department of Employment Gazette*, January 1974.
(2) Liverpool Careers Service analysis of its own records.

84

importance to boys. The failure to enter skilled training on leaving school effectively bars entry to skilled work, at least until adulthood, and normally for life. In both Great Britain and the North West, fifty five percent of boys take up work with training; in Liverpool, thirty eight percent. The proportion of boys entering apprenticeships in Liverpool has remained fairly constant over the last ten years. But there has been a rapid decline in the numbers available; one third fewer in 1974 than in 1966, compared with a slight increase nationally. And only sixteen percent of girls in Liverpool enter work with training compared with twenty eight percent in the North West. The shortage of training places is not balanced by opportunities in clerical employment, although a slightly higher proportion of young people enter this type of employment in Liverpool than nationally.

It is likely that young people entering unskilled work in the inner areas face the same difficulties as the rest of the local unskilled workforce. Certainly the Vauxhall survey[1] found that young people were faced with the same economic and social pressures as their parents had faced and were equally likely to go into dead-end casual or unskilled jobs. The social malaise study showed that job changing among inner city youngsters was higher than in the rest of the city. Both the Vauxhall survey and our own survey at Edge Hill suggested that this was a form of 'playing the field', and seeking out the least boring and best paid niche. Another study[2] found a very cavalier attitude among boys towards the very poor quality jobs that were available, though much less job changing when jobs were scarce than when the local economy was relatively buoyant.

However, although attitudes to work and the nature of the jobs available may differ across the city, young people face a high risk of unemployment right across Liverpool. The social malaise study showed that unemployment of over three months was at the same rate in the inner and outer areas. The Edge Hill survey showed a rate of nineteen percent among eighteen year olds compared with about seventeen percent in the city. More recent figures suggest that rates of twenty five or thirty percent are currently to be found in the outer districts as well as the inner areas.[3]

The family at risk

While the most widespread and damaging pressures on family life in inner Liverpool are poverty and bad housing, other factors directly connected with the family itself play an important part. Preliminary findings of the National Child Development Study,[4] at a time when the children were eleven, suggest that adverse family circumstances contribute to social disadvantage among children. Children in large, or single parent families were likely to have less help or attention from adults.

(1) Jones P, Smith G and Pulham K, *All Their Future: a Study of the Problems of School Leavers in a Disadvantaged Area of Liverpool* (Department of Social and Administrative Studies, Oxford University 1975).

(2) Parker H J, *View from the Boys: a Sociology of Downtown Adolescents* (David & Charles 1974).

(3) Liverpool Careers Service.

(4) Davie K, Butler N and Goldstein H, *From Birth to Seven* (National Children's Bureau and Longmans 1972).

The Study suggested that six percent of all children in the country satisfied their definition of social disadvantage. That is they came from either a large or single parent family, had a low income and were badly housed.

Large families are one of the types of family at risk identified in the National Child Development Study. They suffer more than most from low incomes for people are not paid according to their number of dependents, notwithstanding the addition of family allowances. But a further problem for large families in poverty is the availability of suitable housing. Most working class private housing in the inner area is in small, two or three bedroom terraced houses, unsuitable for large families by current standards and expensive and difficult to adapt. Few families can any longer afford the larger houses, most of which have been converted into flats. Yet very little council housing in the inner areas is suitable for large families. There are few houses as opposed to flats or maisonettes and many of the latter are small or unsuitable nowadays for any families with children, least of all large ones. Consequently overcrowding is high in areas where there are concentrations of large families.

Although overall numbers were small, the proportion of families with five or more children in Liverpool was about twice the national average, probably because of the high proportion of Catholic families, two percent of all households in Liverpool compared with a national figure of one percent. The great majority of large families in Liverpool now live in council housing, partly due to the high priority given to families in slum clearance areas but also probably to the persistence of Catholic communities in some older council estates. A number however were living in the newest housing in the outer council estates, where there was a high proportion of large dwellings. Many of them would have moved recently from inner city clearance areas and for them, overcrowding is not serious. Smaller concentrations

Figure 23
Large families 1971

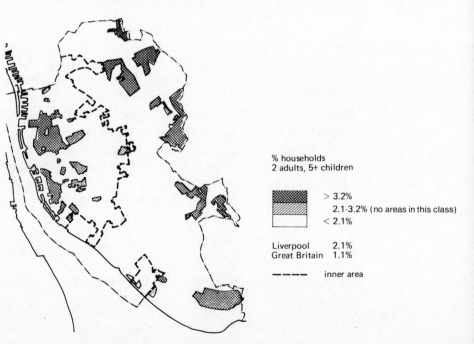

% households
2 adults, 5+ children

> 3.2%
2.1-3.2% (no areas in this class)
< 2.1%

Liverpool 2.1%
Great Britain 1.1%

- - - - inner area

86

live in some inner council estates and also in the rooming house areas in both of which overcrowding is serious.

Another type of disadvantaged family identified in the National Child Development Study was single parent families. The 1971 Census showed single parents with dependent children to form four percent of all households in Britain, five percent in Liverpool, but much higher proportions in certain parts of the city. The highest concentration was found in the inner council estates, up to fifteen percent of all households in some of the least popular areas. Parts of the rooming house area and the most recent of the outer council estates had nine to eleven percent.

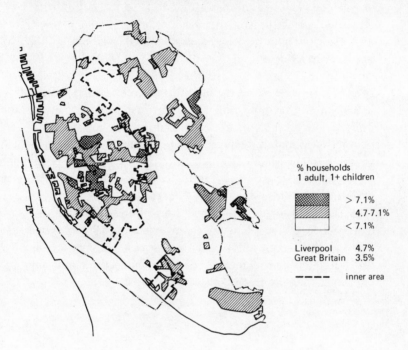

**Figure 24
Single parent
families 1971**

% households
1 adult, 1+ children

> 7.1%
4.7-7.1%
< 7.1%

Liverpool 4.7%
Great Britain 3.5%

– – – – inner area

The Finer Committee concluded that the most severe problems faced by single parent families were the complexities and inequalities of family law, income, housing and child care.[1] Although accurate small area figures were not available, the take-up of supplementary benefits in the study area appeared to be low. While the complexity of means tested benefits may not have actually deterred many people from claiming, it did mean that many did not get their full entitlement.

A further particular need is for child care. After school provision may be suitable for older children but properly financed, community based child minding would be more suitable for the younger ones. The real need for child care stems from a mother's desire or need to work. A dual standard prevails in which single parent families are expected to maintain economic independence on very low incomes yet retain full responsibility for their dependents. Many single parents do find a way of coping, particularly those who are able to get reasonable jobs and secure housing. But the long term situation faced by others is bleak. The most acute problems are faced during the period when a marriage breaks up. At a time of severe emotional

(1) *Report of the Committee on One Parent Families, Vol. 1* (Cmnd 5629, HMSO 1974).

stress, mothers (mainly) have to find their way through one or more court systems, the complexity of local authority housing rules, and a wide range of possible income support benefits.

The elderly

An increasing proportion of the elderly are living alone as greater economic independence and the breakdown of extended family networks allow the formation of independent and smaller households. But greater independence has often been accompanied by a drop in status. Many old people feel they are no longer as useful as they once were. They retire earlier and live longer but many no longer have an important social role, either within the family or community. Of course many maintain close family ties and have an active social life, but many others become isolated and lonely.

During the course of the visiting scheme to the elderly, HANDS found that several kinds of need were not being adequately met. Many pensioners were simply isolated and lonely and required little more than a regular social call. Others, poorer or less mobile, required a range of small everyday tasks carried out which would be done unthinkingly by a fitter person. But many were not always getting the specialised services they needed, and were entitled to, such as meals on wheels or disablement aids. Many of these tasks could best be carried out by a local organisation firmly rooted in the area, with the detailed knowledge and understanding of people's needs. Pensioners were found to be particularly vulnerable to the pressures of slum clearance as they were often reluctant to move, yet faced the disappearance of shops, declining community support and increasing crime and vandalism as rehousing progressed.

Figure 25
Pensioner
households 1971

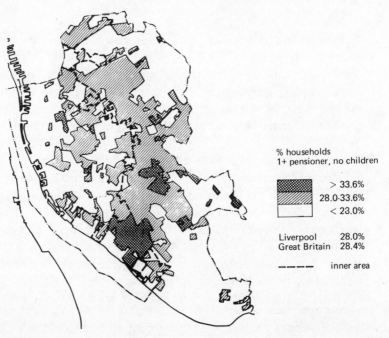

% households
1+ pensioner, no children

> 33.6%
28.0-33.6%
< 23.0%

Liverpool   28.0%
Great Britain   28.4%

– – – – inner area

88

The elderly now form about sixteen percent of the country's population and this is increasing steadily with improved health care and social provision. Between 1961 and 1971 on Merseyside there was a two percent increase in the proportion of elderly people, higher than any other region except Tyneside. The corresponding figure for Liverpool was over three percent. As young people move out from the conurbation, a greater proportion of the elderly are left behind, often in poor housing with few amenities. Adult households including pensioners (not the same as the elderly) were found to comprise over a quarter of all households in the city, although less than half of these were pensioners living alone. Households with pensioners were widely distributed across the city. But single pensioners living alone were more concentrated, particularly in the rooming house area and in scattered tower blocks built especially for small households.

People living alone

Nineteen percent of all households in Liverpool in 1971 consisted of one person living alone compared with eighteen percent in Britain. About two thirds of these were pensioners. Single non pensioner households in the city therefore formed some seven percent of all households. Although small, this group is very mixed, ranging from affluent young professional people living in self-contained flats to alcoholic single men living in common lodging houses. It includes nurses, service workers, students, divorcees, prostitutes and ex-convicts. They are drawn together in one or two small areas of the city where they can find cheap flats or anonymity near the city centre. Many are on their own by choice, quite able to look after themselves, living temporarily in the city, or at college or with a job. Others are seeking refuge because they cannot fit in anywhere else. A cheap room in a boarding house, a bed sitter or even a bed in a common lodging house is at least independence. The only alternative for those at the bottom is an institution however sympathetic.

Many single people in the inner city are on the edges of society, ex-psychiatric patients, alcoholics, ex-prisoners or drop-outs. Many are in and out of institutions all their lives; borstal, prison, mental hospital, reception centre, infirmary. Young people are particularly vulnerable. Boys drift into crime, girls into prostitution; well-established routes for young people who have left home after a row, come out of children's homes or borstal or merely come looking for a job but without money or skill. For a great majority the major problems are financial ones, particularly when there are so few jobs available. But some have more complex needs, ranging from almost complete emotional and social support to a sympathetic and caring environment.

Over eighty percent of those who came to the SHARP referral centre needed only adequate, secure housing to retain complete independence, but a small minority faced a wide range of personal and social difficulties and needed either temporary help to see them over a difficult period or longer term support. The detached team of social workers provided a degree of support. Over eighty percent of their clients were men, nearly all of them single, a few being widowed or divorced. They were of all ages, roughly two thirds having either psychiatric or alcoholic problems.

The majority were either living in hostels and common lodging houses or had recently been discharged from hospital. Nevertheless, despite the clear personal and social difficulties, forty percent of the team's clients would be able to manage adequately given secure accommodation of a reasonable standard.

Many of those using the Whitechapel day centre had already reached the bottom. There are at any time in Liverpool perhaps a thousand people, mainly middle aged and elderly men, who drift from furnished room to lodgings to hostel or doss in derelict houses or doorways. Some find their way permanently into institutions. Others are in and out of jail and mental hospitals. And the group is constantly being added to by mental breakdowns, excessive drinking and mental stress. It also appears to contain increasing numbers of young people and women. The proportion of men on the road for work is declining but the proportion of social casualties is growing and there are disturbing signs of a new breed of rootless young drifters forced to share what little accommodation is available with older men much more set in their drifting ways.

The demand from many single people for small, often furnished flats near the city centre and the supply of large, Georgian and Victorian town houses which are suitable for subdivision in Abercromby, Granby and Princes Park and parts of Everton has led to concentrations of single people in these areas. In most parts of the city between three and six percent of households were single non pensioners. But in the rooming house area they were much higher, reaching nineteen percent around Upper Parliament Street and near Sefton Park; twenty seven percent around Princes and Newsham Parks; and thirty six percent in Abercromby and around Princes Avenue. In total, over a quarter of the single non pensioner households in the city lived in the rooming house area. Two other kinds of council housing showed significant proportions; the widely scattered tower blocks, and

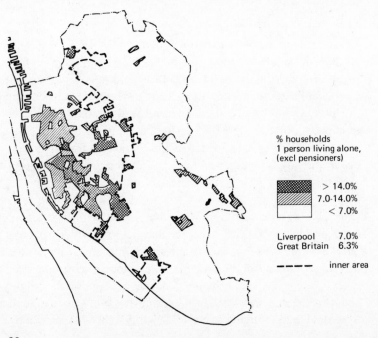

**Figure 26
Single person
households 1971**

% households
1 person living alone,
(excl pensioners)

> 14.0%
7.0-14.0%
< 7.0%

Liverpool   7.0%
Great Britain 6.3%

— — — —   inner area

90

some inner council estates adjacent to the rooming house area which had been used for local rehousing.

Racial discrimination

The proportion of new commonwealth immigrants in Liverpool is small by British standards. Less than one percent of the city's population was found by the 1971 Census to have been born in the West Indies, Africa, India or China, compared with over two percent nationally. But recent immigrants form an unknown proportion of the black population. Several generations of settlement and intermarriage have produced a unique situation in Liverpool. It was estimated in 1954[1] that there were then probably under a thousand Chinese men, women and children and a total of about six thousand Negroes and Liverpool born coloured people, with small groups of different Asian nationalities. The Race Relations Board has recently suggested that the non-white population of Liverpool is now nearly six percent of the city total, some thirty five thousand people.[2]

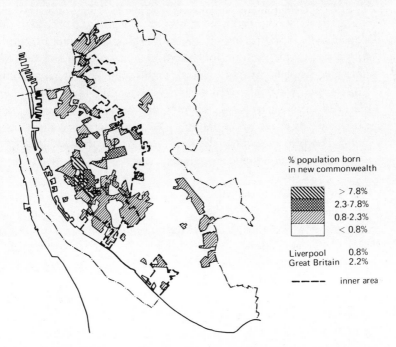

**Figure 27
New commonwealth immigrants 1971**

% population born in new commonwealth

> 7.8%
2.3-7.8%
0.8-2.3%
< 0.8%

Liverpool 0.8%
Great Britain 2.2%

– – – – inner area

Immigration from China, the West Indies and West Africa started on a significant scale at the beginning of this century when seamen began settling in the southern part of the city near the docks. A working party set up by the Liverpool Council of Voluntary Service in 1967[3] suggested that in the area lying within half a mile of Upper Parliament Street on the southern side, about forty percent of the population was coloured. In 1971 a seventh of all new commonwealth immigrants

(1) Richmond A, *The Colour Problem* (Penguin Books 1954).

(2) Reported in *Liverpool Daily Post* 2 June 1976.

(3) Liverpool Youth Organisations Committee Working Party, *Special but not Separate: a Report on the Situation of Young Coloured People in Liverpool* (Liverpool Council of Voluntary Service 1968).

lived in one small part of the rooming house area in Granby, few of them second generation. More dispersed parts of the rooming house area further from the city centre and nearby older council estates had a more equal balance of first and second generation immigrants.

The appearance of small numbers of immigrant families in many parts of the city suggests that a degree of dispersion has taken place recently. The early 1970s saw the first large scale clearance of housing in Granby, for long the main black and immigrant area of Liverpool. Small proportions of new commonwealth born are now to be found in the most recently built outer council estates, at Netherley. However, most of the resulting movement was very localised around Upper Parliament Street, into the remaining terraced housing, hard to let council flats and indeed some of the newest inner council estates.

The LCVS working party concluded its 1967 enquiry 'with a deep sense of unease', saying that there was a long-standing myth in Liverpool of non-discrimination which disguised a lamentable indifference and lack of understanding. Although they found some overt hostility within the areas where considerable numbers of coloured people were living, it was more evident in the exclusively white 'downtown' areas. Prejudice in the middle class areas took the form of indifference with assertions of non-discrimination being made only because young black people were not giving any trouble. A more recent report by the Community Relations Commission, which explored unemployment and homelessness among young blacks in various parts of the country, drew special attention to race relations in Liverpool.[1] Newness to the country was seen to have become a less important factor than race. They predicted constant friction because black youngsters would not accept rejection like their parents.

Our own work suggested that young Liverpool born blacks are developing an aggressive culture and life-style of their own that is in effect creating a new community where none existed before. The discussion groups on employment and education suggested that many young black people who were born in Liverpool feel a strong alienation from their parents or grandparents whom they never knew, whether African, West Indian, Arab or Asian. But they also feel excluded from the English culture into which they were born: 'The thing about being black in Liverpool is that you can't get away from it; . . . it's everything in your life'. The English Language classes, black studies group and black music workshop set up at the Adult Education Centre are not only helping to foster a common interest and culture but are also developing a greater awareness, albeit among a fairly small group, of why they have remained in a consistently depressed position and how self help and solidarity can help to get them out of it. The move must be seen as encouraging to those who want to see black groups assert their identity more strongly on English society rather than as individuals making their way up the social scale. But it must equally be seen as a threatening tendency for those who cling to ideas of a single, universal culture.

(1) Community Relations Commission, *Unemployment and Homelessness* (HMSO 1974).

On a more practical level, black workers experience higher levels of unemployment than whites. Figures from the Leece Street unemployment survey suggest that about a quarter of the new commonwealth immigrants were unemployed, nearly twice the rate for the population as a whole. The survey was able to identify immigrants among the unemployed, but not colour. Few immigrants in the sample were recent arrivals in this country, and their average age was higher than that of the British born. However, despite a similar level of training and education qualifications they fared worse in a number of respects. They were overrepresented in three low paid occupations; shops, clerical work and personal services. They also experienced greater difficulty in finding jobs, with a lower proportion of immigrants finding a job within six months than among the indigenous population.

Further evidence is given in our survey of employers in and around our study area. Only thirteen of the thirty four firms in the survey employed non-white workers, largely in unskilled jobs. The medium and large manufacturing firms were the most likely to employ coloured workers, but only one had more than two percent employed, and only three more than fifteen coloured workers. The only compensating factor was that, according to the Leece Street survey, immigrants hold jobs for long periods: forty eight percent had held their last job for more than a year, compared with twenty eight percent of the British born. No firm interviewed currently had a non-white apprentice, despite the fact that around two hundred boys in the sample of firms were undergoing this form of training.

The economic and social position of black people in Liverpool is currently declining further as the recession hits hardest those who are most at risk. But unemployment is endemic to this part of Liverpool. People have learnt how to cope with it, making enough money locally to get by in more or less legal ways. The Merseyside Community Relations Council felt that while help with jobs would be welcome, 'the community has a resilience and intelligence which enables it to survive in appalling conditions and to organise and manage its own affairs.'[1] They thought that Liverpool 8 should be given a break from the continual harping on 'gangs and ghettos, vice and violence', an understandable reaction when statements like 'today white people are not encouraged to go into Liverpool 8 unaccompanied' appear in the press.[2]

Whatever aspirations past immigrants into Liverpool may have had towards total integration, and whatever may be the wishes of those who still come to the city, that may no longer be the wish of many Liverpool born blacks. They are turning for identity and pride to black music, African history and in some cases the politics of black power, rather than the culture of English society from which they have felt rejected for so long. Although their position in society is closely paralleled by poor whites, they feel they have little in common with them. Whether their future position in society is to remain one of conflict and rejection or whether it can be accepted that peaceful separatism is a feasible alternative depends to a great extent

(1) Merseyside Community Relations Council, *Fifth Annual Report 1974.*
(2) *Daily Telegraph* 15 January 1976.

on how well our institutions can respond. The aspirations of many young black people can be summed up in the words of one young interviewee:

> 'I'd like to work with my own race and in my own area, helping to get homes for those who have none, more things to do for the unemployed – I never had the chance to do this sort of work; there are not many jobs in the way of what I would like to do.'

Social malaise[1]

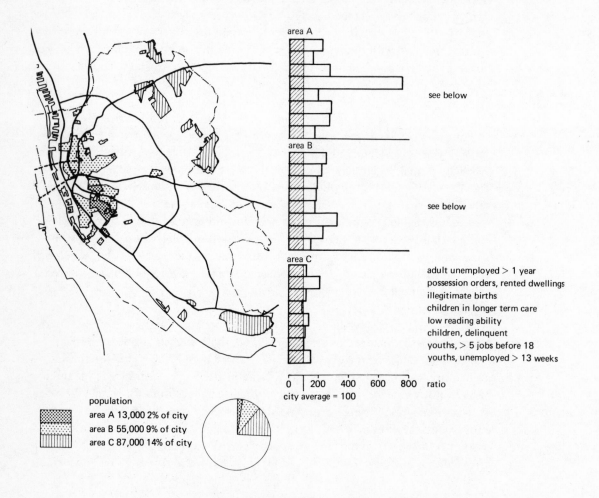

**Figure 28
Social malaise
1971–74**

The previous paragraphs have shown the concentrations in parts of the inner area of certain groups of people who are most vulnerable to economic forces, bad housing and social pressures. Geographically, many of the more extreme concentrations overlap in the inner council estates and the worst rooming house areas. But evidence from the social malaise survey shows the degree to which the concentrations of those at risk overlap with the incidence of social problems.

area A

area B

see below

area C

adult unemployed > 1 year
possession orders, rented dwellings
illegitimate births
children in longer term care
low reading ability
children, delinquent
youths, > 5 jobs before 18
youths, unemployed > 13 weeks

0   200   400   600   800   ratio
city average = 100

population
area A 13,000 2% of city
area B 55,000 9% of city
area C 87,000 14% of city

(1) The City Planning Department's first social malaise study was carried out in 1968. This section draws on the revised and improved survey made in 1974.

94

The evidence on social malaise covers a number of problems including indicators of poverty (eligibility for free school meals, possession orders, unemployment); of family instability (illegitimacy, children in care), of delinquency and other youth problems (unemployment, job instability), and of educational attainment. A small selection of the full list of variables is given in the map of Liverpool showing that the areas where social malaise is most concentrated fall into three categories.

The worst social malaise corresponds with the worst rooming house areas, in Abercromby, Granby and Princes Park. Nearly every indicator is present in an intense form, but particularly those relating to family instability, with relatively high proportions of children in care. The second area coincides with the council estates in the inner city. As with the first area, every social malaise indicator is present at a level roughly twice the average for the city as a whole, but the inner council estates lack the evidence of extreme family instability. Their social problems are more those attributable to a general level of poverty and malaise.

The third type of area is particularly significant for it is found not in the inner city but in certain of the outer council estates, especially those built in the 1950s, such as Speke, where by the time of survey families were growing up and many of the children of the original occupants were in the later teens. The pattern of social malaise almost exactly mirrored that of the inner council estates, but at a less intensive level, about one and a half times the average for the city. Placed in the context of population movements within the city, this suggests that social and economic problems having their origin in the inner city are being exported to the outer council estates. It suggests too that the problems reach their peak in the second decade of the life of an estate, when children reach school leaving age. If this is true, it could explain the low level of social malaise in the oldest outer council estates such as Walton Clubmoor, built in the 1930s, although other factors may apply. It also carries a warning of future social malaise in the most recently built outer council estates such as Netherley where, as yet, the children were still in the primary school age group at the time of survey.

Multiple deprivation

The concentrations of those most at risk of poverty in parts of the inner areas and outer council estates where the greatest incidence of social malaise is also to be found poses questions about the nature of multiple deprivation. The causes of the poverty and deprivation actually experienced by many people in these groups at greatest risk lie beyond the terms of this report, in personal and family characteristics and in the structure of society and its institutions. But the concentrations of those most at risk are different. We shall show in the following chapters that the build up of concentrations can be traced back to economic and social forces, and the location, availability and quality of the housing stock. And these forces themselves add a further twist to the poverty and deprivation which in chapter eleven we shall describe as the accumulated disadvantage from living in areas where concentrations of those at risk are to be found.

But in reviewing these concepts of multiple deprivation and accumulated disadvantage, three provisos need to be borne in mind. First, it is easy to assume, when considering areas where there are concentrations of deprivation, that a majority of those living there are in some way deprived; that many (or any) suffer more than one form of deprivation; or that the deprivation found in such areas forms the majority of deprivation in that city. Several studies have shown[1] that in fact in any deprived area only a minority is likely in any way to be deprived and that there are invariably more deprived people living outside deprived areas than within them. These conclusions are borne out by our own analyses. Whereas in the worst areas those most at risk, unskilled workers for example, sometimes formed a majority, those who actually suffered unemployment or serious overcrowding were in a minority. And while the inner city contained the greatest concentrations in small areas of people at risk, over half of the city's large families and single parent families lived in the outer areas.

A second argument is that there are personal failings leading to unemployment and social stress which can be handed on from one generation to the next. But in this, too, the evidence points to a different conclusion.[2] Certainly some determinants of economic and social failure may be inherited; for instance low intelligence or personality difficulties. But the more general case is that successive generations living in deprived areas are faced with similar economic and social circumstances which in turn restrict their opportunities for advancement.

The third proviso concerns the degree to which concentrations of those most at risk in themselves lead to a further, more widespread incidence of poverty within the deprived areas than would otherwise be the case through, as it were, a form of multiplier. But this ignores the extent to which many people living in such areas nevertheless maintain reasonable standards of behaviour, care for their homes and keep in employment. In fact the reality appears to be the opposite: that economic and social forces ensure that those at greatest risk of poverty are trapped in, or forced into, areas where the worst housing and most depressing surroundings already exist.

(1) Barnes J H and Lucas H, 'Positive Discrimination in Education: Individuals, Groups and Institutions' in Legatt T (editor), *Sociological Theory and Survey Research* (Sage Publications 1974); Halsey A H, 'The Juxtaposition of Social and Individual Approaches in Compensatory Education Projects', with addendum by Smith T and James T, paper at The Council of Europe Compensatory Education Workshop (Strasbourg 1975).

(2) Rutter M L and Madge N, *Cycles of Disadvantage* (Heinemann 1976).

6 Economic decline

Employment changes in Merseyside and Liverpool[1]

The need to provide special incentives for investment in Merseyside has been accepted by central government since 1949 when it was first scheduled as a development area under the Distribution of Industry Act. The major problems of the area, high unemployment and low skills, have their historical roots in the reliance on the docks and port related activity. The aim of regional policy has been to provide a new economic base centred on manufacturing industry, with a better trained workforce distributed more evenly across Merseyside so as to relieve pressure on the older areas such as Liverpool. Development policies have operated through three main methods for twenty five years. The Board of Trade and now the Department of Industry have provided incentives for firms to move to, or expand in, the Merseyside Special Development Area. The Department of Employment has organised industrial training and encouraged labour mobility. The Department of the Environment and local authorities have been concerned in the building of new towns and housing estates and renewal of the area's infrastructure. This chapter briefly reviews the decline of Liverpool's economy and its impact on the inner area, in particular the lack of investment in the inner area, unemployment and the skills and aptitudes of the remaining workers.

Regional policies have been broadly successful in their overall impact. Despite the port's continuing decline new manufacturing jobs have been attracted to Merseyside. In 1950 fourteen percent of all employment in Merseyside was in port-related activities (water, transport, sea transport, shipbuilding) and a further twenty one percent in associated industries. By 1973, the proportions had fallen to five and thirteen percent respectively.[2] Between 1945 and 1971, one hundred and seventy five firms moved to Merseyside, bringing with them ninety four thousand new manufacturing jobs. Three quarters of the firms moved into Merseyside from outside the North West Region, or were newly established, and their average workforce was twice that of those moving within the region. In contrast only a few firms moved out of the Merseyside Special Development Area, taking with them no more than three thousand jobs in total since 1945.

The change in the structure of employment in Merseyside has been matched by a shift in the location of jobs. New settlements on the periphery of the special development area have been the focus of employment growth. There was a net loss of manufacturing employment from the Liverpool Exchanges Area of six thousand three hundred jobs between 1961–1971 compared with a growth of twenty six thousand jobs in the outer areas, and the drop in services was even more

(1)   This is discussed more fully in IAS Liverpool, *Economic Development of the Inner Area* (Department of the Environment 1977).

(2)   *Merseyside Structure Plan, Draft Report of Survey: Economy* (Merseyside County Council 1975).

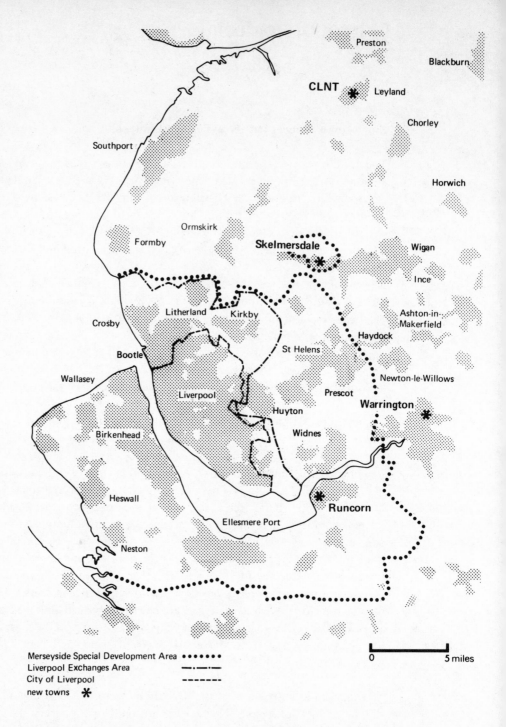

Figure 29
The Merseyside
region

Merseyside Special Development Area ● ● ● ● ● ●
Liverpool Exchanges Area ─ ∙ ─ ∙ ─ ∙
City of Liverpool ─ ─ ─ ─ ─
new towns ✳

0   5 miles

pronounced. In total, the Liverpool Exchanges lost more than fifty thousand jobs in the decade while the outer areas gained nearly nineteen thousand.

The Liverpool Exchanges Area extends beyond the city boundary to include Bootle and Crosby to the north, Kirkby to the north east and Halewood to the south. Although their loss of jobs between 1961 and 1971 was considerable, the loss from the city itself was proportionately greater still, particularly in service

98

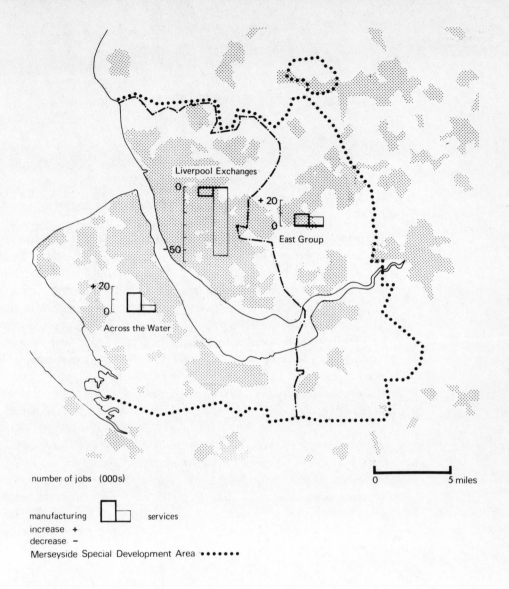

Figure 30
Changes in
employment,
Merseyside
1961–71

Liverpool Exchanges

+ 20

0

East Group

+ 20

0

Across the Water

number of jobs (000s)

manufacturing   services
increase +
decrease –
Merseyside Special Development Area ● ● ● ● ● ●

0   5 miles

employment for men. There was a net drop of twenty eight thousand in the number of workers in transport, construction and utilities in 1971 compared with ten years earlier. The majority of these jobs were lost from the docks and to a lesser extent the railways. The fall was nearly as great in wholesale and retail distribution, twenty one thousand jobs, mainly a consequence of the reduction in purchasing power and economic activitity following closures in the docks. To some extent the effect of these losses was balanced by growth in city centre services. Finance, professional and scientific services and public administration provided additional jobs. However most would not be open to those laid off from manual service employment; and their growth was less than that of similar commercial centres elsewhere in the country. In addition there was a net loss of thirty one thousand manufacturing jobs in the city during the decade; more than offsetting the increase beyond the city boundary achieved particularly by the coming of Ford to Halewood.

99

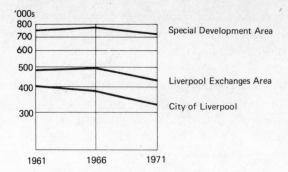

Figure 31
Employment
change 1961–71

'000s

Special Development Area

Liverpool Exchanges Area

City of Liverpool

1961　　　1966　　　1971

The total number of jobs for men in Liverpool fell by eighteen percent between 1966 and 1971. However the number of unskilled manual jobs dropped by twenty five percent, of semi-skilled by twenty four percent and of personal service jobs by forty one percent. The kinds of jobs disappearing were those for warehousemen and storekeepers, packers, caretakers, shop assistants, building labourers and unskilled workmen in the engineering and chemical industries, abbatoir workers and food processors, and, most important of all, unskilled dock workers. Low skilled jobs were declining in nearly all industrial sectors at a faster rate than the total level of employment in that sector, largely the result of mechanisation and productivity gains; the shake-out of the late 1960s. At the other end of the scale many of the more highly skilled jobs were actually increasing in number. More non-manual supervisory workers were employed in 1971 than in 1966, and the number of professional and managerial jobs remained fairly constant.

Opportunities for women have been less badly affected. A large decline in manual work is apparent. Much of this has been in semi-skilled and unskilled work but the limited number of skilled manual jobs was further reduced. However, some women at least were able to transfer to the generally better working conditions available in the expanding clerical sector. Where this was not available they could fall back on a variety of personal service work partly generated by the growth of offices.

There have thus been three main, cumulative causes of the relative decline of Liverpool in comparison with the rest of Merseyside. Most of the new jobs introduced to the region have been in the outer settlements; many offered good environmental conditions, modern housing, and new industrial estates with access to the national motorway network. Simultaneously some firms already established in Merseyside moved to new premises on the periphery. By contrast the traditional industries of Liverpool and Birkenhead declined rapidly, especially manual jobs including the docks and shipbuilding, and were not replaced by new jobs in the same locality.

The lack of industrial investment

Manufacturing industry in inner Liverpool is dominated by a small number of large firms whose fortunes have had the greatest impact on the general level of employment. There have been some significant closures. Other firms are under

100

threat. Some have reduced their labour forces through improvements in productivity. However there has been some growth, especially among small and medium sized firms serving markets outside Liverpool.

Local factors have had limited influence. Nevertheless falling demand in the Liverpool economy has particularly affected suppliers to the local consumer market and providers of industrial services for other local firms. Employment in small firms has suffered too from the clearance programmes associated with urban renewal and motorway proposals.

Firms have left Liverpool for a number of reasons: lack of room for expansion on existing sites, fewer problems of premises and land availability in the new areas, rationalisation, motorway access, and the uncertainty of operating in the inner areas. They have been encouraged in these removals by the emphasis given to industrial and residential development in the newer parts of Merseyside. In contrast, the spasmodic but significant exodus of jobs from the inner area has taken place virtually without hindrance. There has been virtually no industrial investment in inner Liverpool in the past fifteen years.

There are complex reasons for this lack of investment which are of critical importance in any consideration of future plans. The inner area can offer labour, including many unemployed skilled men, an abundance of unused land, and an industrial and commercial infrastructure which includes many empty buildings previously used for commercial purposes and shown to be capable of conversion. In theory, the area should benefit from the wide range of investment incentives made available under regional policy. They have had a major effect in other parts of Merseyside, but have generated virtually no new employment within the inner city.

Firms profiting from regional incentives have usually been relatively large and often capital intensive. Thus three motor manufacturers' works provided a quarter of the new jobs attracted to Merseyside since the war. The average new firm has employed four hundred and seventy workers. There have been few sites allocated for industrial use in the inner area, none suitable for new firms of this scale. Much of the development has therefore had little choice but to settle on the periphery. The basic principle of regional policy is encouragement and incentive, not direct control. Firms have been won to Merseyside in competition with other development areas. It has been necessary to provide the best possible conditions for incoming industrialists.

The policy of the English Industrial Estates Corporation, which has responsibility for developing industrial land, has therefore been until very recently to look for green field sites. There, land acquisition and industrial building are likely to be cheaper. Large estates offer advantages of common services and estate management, and the possibility of subsequent expansion. The major switch in the past fifteen years from rail to road transport with the development of the motorway network has further increased the relative attraction of peripheral development. As a result, the Corporation has developed 3·2 million square feet of industrial space in Merseyside since the war, but none of it has been in the older areas of Liverpool and Birkenhead. However, a new programme of advance factories for Merseyside was announced in November 1975 including a special provision for the inner area: fifteen thousand square feet at Sandon Dock, on the north side of Liverpool and seventy four thousand square feet at Rock Ferry, Birkenhead.

Liverpool District and Merseyside County Councils both have industrial development offices, and the city has a number of industrial estates. Until recently, the emphasis in both organisations has been on attracting footloose industry through advertising, promotion, and direct approaches to firms. The county office has recently redirected some of its attention to supporting the indigenous economy of the inner areas and stimulating local growth by encouraging firms to take up grants; developing linkages between firms in the local economy; and making better provision of sites for existing firms. However the extent to which either organisation can stimulate employment in the inner areas is limited by the availability of sites on offer. The city's main industrial area is at Knowsley where there is one hundred acres of unused land. A further ten acres is available at Kirkby. Designated inner area sites are fragmented and none is larger than three acres. The city has developed some small advance factories in the past and has recently started a new programme. No provision has been made for larger firms in the inner city. This has not only prevented the arrival of new firms, it has also encouraged existing concerns to establish new subsidiaries away from the city.

Many county and district officers agreed that small industrial units were urgently needed for the inner areas as the inaugural step in a rolling programme of advance factories and sites. Nevertheless industrial development recently proposed by local authorities and the Department of Industry will provide only about one hundred and eighty five thousand square feet in inner Liverpool and Birkenhead, less than half the area currently under development at Skelmersdale. It will provide space for perhaps six hundred jobs at a time when the number of unemployed men registered at the Leece Street Exchange alone is more than twelve thousand.

Despite the large areas of vacant land, there is an acute shortgage of land allocated for industry in the inner city, and that which is available is of poor quality. Recently the Department of Industry was able to find only one suitable site for a small advanced factory unit in the entire Liverpool Exchanges Area. A recent report by the city's Area Management Unit[1] pointed out that while sites have been allocated for industry a number of factors prevented their development as serviced and readily lettable land. Low priority was previously given to industrial development in the city's budget. An industrialist urgently requiring more than two acres of land would have no chance of finding a suitable site.

To give some examples: four vacant sites were, at the time of writing, allocated for industry within the study area. One, wanted for expansion by the Gas Board, was owned by the Council and had been vacant since 1974. Negotiations had not

(1) Area Management Unit, *Economic Development Programme Issue 1: Land and Buildings for Industrial Development in District D* (Liverpool 1975).

yet opened, although the client appeared willing to purchase. Another in council ownership had been reserved, initially for the Central Electricity Generating Board and later for the expansion of an adjoining sugar mill. Despite the fact that neither client had been interested in the site since 1974, no attempt had been made to dispose of it elsewhere. The third, a three acre British Rail site in very poor condition, had been vacant since 1968. It was first placed on the market in 1975 at a price of forty two thousand pounds per acre, far in excess of its market value. The fourth was another railway site, vacant since 1975 and awaiting purchase by the Council. It too was in poor condition and would need considerable treatment before being available for letting, according to the Area Management Unit's report.

Sites available for industrial use elsewhere in the inner city may be in better condition. In particular some cheap floorspace was available on a short lease in disused warehouses in the South Docks. But because of the low level of effective demand in the inner areas, investors and sellers may be easily deterred by impediments that would be readily overcome in more buoyant conditions.

Many industrial sites for new industry were chosen by the local authority only after the needs of housing had been met, are of inconvenient size and shape, and are expensive to develop and service. Rents are higher than those for green field sites. The current review of land use allocations by the City Planning Officer may improve conditions, increasing the supply of land allocated for industry. But industrial development falls under the locally determined sector for local government finance and will require higher priority than in the past.

Investment by the private sector is also affected by the actions of the local authority. Private economic activity virtually ceases on the confirmation of a compulsory purchase order. House owners have little incentive to maintain or improve their property. Shops and small businesses will be looking for new premises and vacant property has no market. Few small local firms survive. Loss of population, inadequate compensation and their already probably marginal profitability in old premises force them to close. Even if new premises could be found, such firms could not afford the rent. Not until redevelopment is largely complete is the private sector invited back to lease shops, offices or industrial sites. Private economic activity virtually ceases for a period of at least five years.

A further deterrent to new industrial investment in inner Liverpool is the pervasive atmosphere of dereliction and decay. For instance, eleven percent of our study area lay vacant in the summer of 1974 (see figure 43, page 175). Much of it was the sites of cleared slums, nearly all of it awaiting redevelopment, usually for public uses such as housing, schools, open spaces or highways. Only six percent of the total had been given landscape treatment, the remainder being strewn with rubble and refuse, at best only levelled. Three quarters of this vacant land was likely to remain so for at least five years more as no resources had been firmly committed for its redevelopment.

However there is much dereliction for which the public sector cannot be held solely responsible. Parts of the inner areas suffer from an industrial dereliction far more serious than the impact of an originally poor environment and the blighting and vacant land resultant on slum clearance. One major example among many is the South Docks, now closed to port traffic, and with little prospect of further maritime use. Some of the warehousing is let on the basis of one year tenancies but most of the remainder of the area is abandoned and derelict.

The deterrent effects of dereliction are exacerbated by a reputation for vandalism, only too apparent in graffiti, smashed windows and damaged property. Theft and acts of destruction were referred to by many employers visited in the course of our industrial survey particularly those whose premises were in residential areas. Burglaries were frequent occurrences in companies carrying large stocks. Vandalism was said to be directly responsible for increased insurance premiums and the need to install elaborate security systems. The only exception was that none of the firms on Edge Lane industrial estate had suffered serious damage; the protection afforded by industrial estates was usually adequate.

Working in the inner area

A most significant feature of the inner area is the proportion of people who work locally. Car ownership in the inner areas is only two-thirds of that in the city, dropping to less than a quarter of the average in the inner council estates. Here, low ownership results from the predominance of unskilled workers amongst whom the rate is only about a tenth of that for professional and managerial workers. But this is not the complete explanation as car ownership is low at all levels of skill in the inner area.

**Figure 32
Travel area 1971**

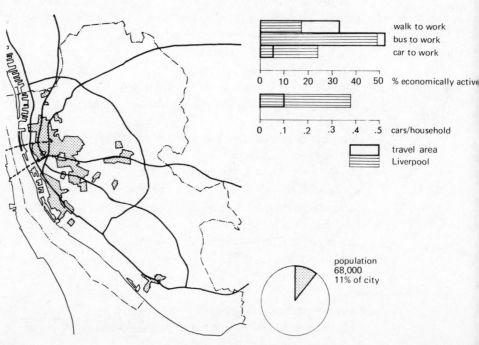

walk to work
bus to work
car to work

0   10   20   30   40   50   % economically active

0   .1   .2   .3   .4   .5   cars/household

travel area
Liverpool

population
68,000
11% of city

104

The majority of work trips for inner area residents in 1971 were by bus (fifty percent) or walking (twenty three percent). Only seventeen percent were by car. But in the inner council estates and some of the poorer parts of the older terraced housing nearby car ownership was only a quarter of the average for the city and a third of all work trips were made on foot. Much of the area is within walking distance of the North and South Docks, the docks at Garston and the Edge Lane industrial estate.

According to the 1966 Merseyside Area Land Use and Transportation Study (MALTS) virtually everyone living in the study area who travelled by public transport worked within the city boundary. Even of the small proportion travelling by car, three quarters worked within the city. The only significant place of work outside the city was the Ford factory at Halewood. But for the majority, work places were close at hand whichever means of travel was used. Forty five percent of bus trips and twenty seven percent of car trips were to the central area, the Edge Lane industrial estate or work places in the study area itself. More recently our survey of men from the study area who were unemployed in 1975 showed that ninety percent of them had held their last job in Liverpool, over sixty percent in south inner Liverpool.

Some examples of travel and costs in 1975 show the difficulty in getting from the inner area to new jobs outside Liverpool. The Falkner estate is a modern council estate near the centre of our study area. Many of its residents are poor, unskilled or black families from nearby slum clearance areas. Using the fastest available

Figure 33
Travel to work 1966

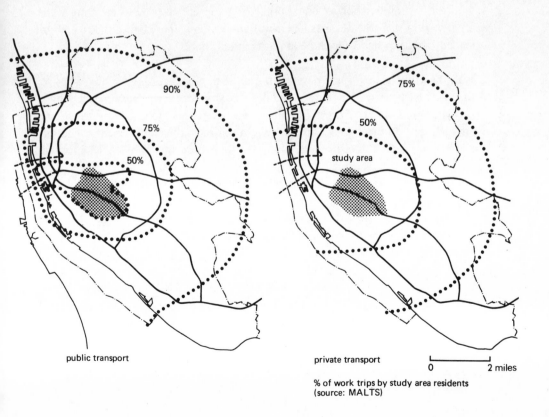

public transport

private transport

0 ⊢————⊣ 2 miles

% of work trips by study area residents
(source: MALTS)

105

public transport, the travel time to Ellesmere Port was fifty five minutes each way at a cost of £5·00 per (five day) week; to Runcorn, £4·40 per week and forty minutes each way; to Halewood, £2·80 and one hour. Furthermore each of these journeys would have presented special problems for shift work outside peak hours because of the lower frequency of services. Even so, the study area is near to Edge Lane and fairly well placed for public transport to the city boundary. Other areas do less well, especially the council estates near the docks. The boundaries of Liverpool can be taken as the effective travel to work limit for residents of inner Liverpool. To take up jobs further away means either having the use of a car, or being prepared to move home.

Our industrial survey showed the relationship between level of skill, area of residence and travel to work. Of the firms in and near the study area, including those on the Edge Lane estate, only a quarter employed a majority of workers from Liverpool 7 and 8. However a general distinction was made by employers between the types of area from which different classes of worker were drawn. Less skilled groups were mainly local; skilled workers were drawn from all over Liverpool; while managers generally lived outside the city. Only one respondent, the proprietor of a steel fabrication firm, lived in Liverpool 8 and expressed a strong personal loyalty to the area and its workers.

The type of firm interviewed partly explains these statistics. The majority were manufacturing concerns, many of whom had a high proportion of skilled workers. But other factors also emerged. Several companies had employed locally in the past. But a number of employers discussed the growing tendency of skilled workers, especially younger ones completing apprenticeships, to move from the area, buying their own homes in surburban estates. Others found that to recruit skilled men they had to look beyond the inner areas.

Half the firms however had never found difficulty in recruiting for any types of job and nearly all the remainder had only experienced problems in attracting specialist staff. All the firms found unskilled labour easy to get and were often embarrassed by the flood of responses to a notice at the employment exchange. Employers had a choice not available in more prosperous parts of the country.

Some firms operated the principle of first come, first served in recruitment, but others were particular in demanding a satisfactory appearance, a good work record and experience in the job. Employers in the survey discussed the reputation of the Liverpool labour force for being troublesome, strike prone and lazy, but the vast majority were generally satisfied with their workers. The largest firm in the sample said that industrial relations were the best of any of its plants in the country. One printing company with branches in Birmingham and Portsmouth found that the Liverpool workers had greater loyalty to the company, and a higher work rate than those employed at their other plants. These opinions however contrasted with comments made about the residential districts in which some of the firms were located. Many employers were aware of the problems of unemployment, social distress and violence in these areas, and a number had suffered the effects of vandalism.

The massive loss of unskilled work from Liverpool has meant that jobs are far more scarce than in other parts of the country. Department of Employment records show that at all times recently there have been more registered unemployed than notified vacancies, and the ratio of the two is consistently at least twice that prevailing nationally. This trend might have been more acceptable either if the number of men seeking this kind of work was also declining, or if the higher skills could be acquired that would allow better jobs to be taken on. However, the number of jobs available for male workers in Liverpool declined faster between 1966 and 1971 than the number of residents in every type of work except that of a professional or managerial nature. The difference between the rates of change was greatest for the worst jobs, those of a personal service and unskilled nature. Even in 1966 there were many more unskilled workers living in Liverpool than there were jobs available in the city, seventy seven jobs for every hundred workers. This deficiency was true of no other category in 1966 but within five years there were fewer jobs than workers for semi-skilled, as well as unskilled workers, and a virtual balance of numbers for personal service and skilled manual workers. The imbalance was growing for each category of skill and for only professional, managerial and non manual workers did Liverpool continue to have a surplus of jobs, attracting workers into the city from outside.

A chief consequence of this is the relatively high and persistent unemployment throughout Merseyside, and the even worse levels of unemployment in inner Liverpool. Unemployment rates in Merseyside have consistently been about twice the average for Great Britain, and slightly higher in Liverpool. The 1971 Census showed that eight percent of male workers in Liverpool were out of work, compared with eleven percent in the inner areas and over twenty percent in the inner council estates and worst rooming house areas. The numbers have risen rapidly in the last five years, for instance by over half in the Leece Street Exchange area which contains most of inner Liverpool. Unemployment rates in the most afflicted parts of the inner city could be as high as one in three at the present time. But concentrations of unemployment are not confined to the inner areas.

**Figure 34
Unemployment
change 1972–75**

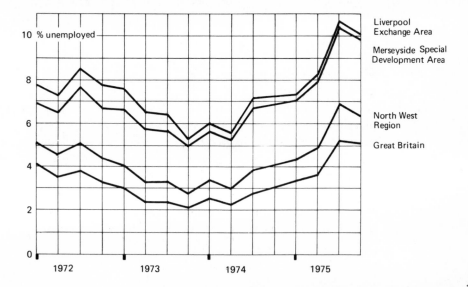

107

The 1971 Census showed that high rates of male unemployment were also to be found in many of the outer council estates such as Speke or, beyond the city boundary, in Kirkby.

Chapter five showed that unskilled workers, unqualified school leavers and black workers are particularly at risk of unemployment in the inner city. By far the largest group is the unskilled workers who not only form a larger proportion of the resident labour force in the inner city than elsewhere but also are more likely to be unemployed than other classes of worker or than unskilled workers living elsewhere in the city. Unemployment among young people in Liverpool doubled between 1970 and 1973; in 1971 it was about seventeen percent for those under eighteen. Figures for black workers are more difficult to obtain, but six out of ten black eighteen year olds in the Edge Hill school leavers' survey were out of work.

**Figure 35
Male unemploy-
ment 1971**

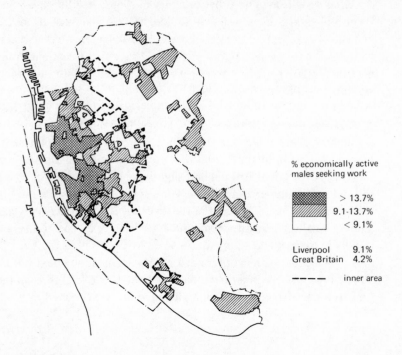

% economically active
males seeking work

> 13.7%
9.1-13.7%
< 9.1%

Liverpool   9.1%
Great Britain 4.2%

-------- inner area

Placement and training[1]

An active employment policy is of great importance in times of recession. The placement service is one of the main points of contact between an unemployed person and the labour market. It has an important role in disseminating information about jobs available locally and in encouraging movement elsewhere. It aims at increasing the attractiveness of an area to outside investors, and improving individuals' opportunities for work by maintaining and improving the levels of skill in the work force. But if the employment service is to respond flexibly

(1) See IAS Liverpool, *Economic Development of the Inner Area* (Department of the Environment 1977); and *Getting a Job: The Training and Placement of Young People* (Department of the Environment 1977).

to local opportunities, appreciate the special characteristics of the labour market in which it is operating, and develop special services for those who suffer most from economic decline, then it must be prepared to concentrate its efforts in areas of high unemployment and to exercise considerable autonomy at the local level.

Local officers of the Employment Services Agency saw their role as twofold. Firstly, they could reduce the mismatch between applicants and jobs; geographically through the Employment Transfer Scheme, encouraging the unemployed to move to other parts of the country; and in terms of skill through the range of training courses on offer. Secondly, they could speed up the placement process by ensuring that employers' requirements were met as quickly as possible. A number of changes have recently been made to improve the efficiency of the placement services. These include setting up job centres in which vacancies are displayed so that people can seek their own work rather than relying on employment officers to make submissions for them; placing higher grade staff in interviewing positions; and improving the rate of flow of job notifications.

Previously, placements were made by employment officers submitting the names to prospective employers. But under this method, more submissions were made for skilled men and for those who had completed an apprenticeship or attended a government training centre, than for unskilled workers and those with no training. The unskilled section of the live register of unemployed workers was so large in Liverpool that it proved virtually impossible to give individual attention to any but the most persistent applicants for work. Staff were encouraged to put forward those with the best prospects for placement in a job. The employment officer had to meet a certain placement target each week; he also had to generate a certain number of vacancies. No system of priorities existed, either for finding jobs for specified groups or for offering special advice or support.

This system has now changed but still Leece Street, the inner Liverpool employment exchange, has many more clients than it can cater for on an individual basis. Over sixty percent are classified as unskilled labourer, the category of worker for whom the ratio of unemployed to vacancies is highest. Jobs are filled before employment officers have made submissions for them. It is difficult not to become demoralised looking for an unskilled job. In effect, the employment service is providing only for those prepared to come to the exchange promptly each morning to have first chance of the current vacancies. The system is not unlike the old casual labour schemes operated at the docks.

The prospects of placement for unskilled men are further reduced by the practice of recording men as unskilled who nevertheless have some training or experience of better work. Around thirty percent of the sample of unemployed men in our survey had last held a job that would be classified as unskilled by the Register General's Classification of Occupations, but the actual figure recorded by the Department of Employment was sixty three percent. The difference arises because employment officers consider a man has a better chance of placement if he is in a category from which he may be considered for many different types of job. This practice discriminates against the least skilled for they are put in direct competition with men more attractive to employers. A second undesirable consequence is that a higher proportion of the unemployed of Liverpool are thought to be unskilled than is the case. There are many on the register who have held skilled and responsible jobs in the past, who would be attractive to employers seeking to locate a new plant in the city, but who are classed as unskilled.

The Employment Service Agency has recently launched an experiment in the Wavertree area, the Socially and Occupationally Disadvantaged Scheme. This is developing a casework approach to the hard core among the out-of-work to see if any improvement can be made in the rate of placements. The scheme has not been running long but it points to one way in which the needs of the worst placed among the unemployed may be met. However, a fundamental change of attitude would have to come in the employment service if it were to offer real assistance to many among the unemployed in Liverpool. This would require an awareness of the personal problems arising from unemployment; a willingness to advocate on behalf of individuals to employers rather than operate a referral agency service; and an abandonment of the strongly prejudicial attitudes held by many employment officers against many of their clients.

The Training Services Agency is involved in the training of both adults and young people. The training of young people is so closely related to their education that it is best discussed in chapter nine. For adults, the number of places available on Merseyside has recently increased to five thousand five hundred annually in skillcentres (formerly government training centres) located at Aintree, Runcorn, St. Helens, and Kirkby. The Aintree centre is one of the largest in the country with thirty three courses. The majority of courses provide basic skills; they are complemented by a range of other courses, including short industrial courses of a semi-skilled standard at colleges of further education and in employers' establishments.

It is clear that the low proportion of the unemployed to have benefitted from government training results primarily from the shortage of available places. A comparison between the numbers unemployed in Merseyside and the provision for training at any time shows that only seven percent of the currently unemployed could be accommodated on a course in any one year. In fact the proportion is lower than this, for courses are also attended by those in work; and more people move onto and off the unemployment register during the year than are out of work at any one time. More than twelve thousand unemployed men were registered at the Leece Street Employment Exchange at the time of our unemployment survey yet only six hundred and fifty places were available at the nearest skillcentre at Aintree which requires a journey of up to one hour from, say, south inner Liverpool.

Long waiting lists exist for most courses. It is not possible at present to be considered for any course for some months after applying, and for more popular skills (eg welding) the waiting period can stretch over two years or more. It is thus extremely difficult for a man who becomes unemployed to get onto a course. An added difficulty is the required standard of entry qualification. In a number of

110

cases these are very demanding and it has been estimated that fifty percent of applicants fail to gain admission to courses for lack of suitable qualifications or experience. Even where admission standards are not prohibitive there is a tendency to prefer the best qualified, in order to maintain placement rate among those completing courses. This again may lessen the prospects of low skilled workers with indifferent work records. Yet, when a sample of longterm unemployed men in Merseyside were encouraged to sit training tests in 1975, a high proportion succeeded in passing. But there is also a shortage of places for below skills training, a relevant introduction to training for men made redundant from unskilled jobs.

However, the Training Services Agency has not in the past been prepared to offer training unless prospects of placement are good. The Aintree centre has at most times been able to place seventy five percent of men within a short time of their having completed a course, but claims that it is difficult to sustain morale on courses if this figure is not reached. Thus the basic problem is that the number of training places on offer is a function chiefly of the current level and structure of employment in the region. Yet, as the Liverpool economy declines more rapidly than the resident population, unemployment increases and so does the need for opportunities for retraining or for learning basic skills.

The economic issues for inner Liverpool

A number of factors have worked together in producing high unemployment and low economic activity in inner Liverpool. There has been a rapid decline in the number of jobs available. There are many impediments to introducing new, or even sustaining existing, investment in the inner area. A significant minority of the workforce is trapped by lack of skill and opportunities for training and faces increasing risk of unemployment. Training programmes and placement services are geared to employers, skilled workers and those with jobs and not to the unskilled and unemployed.

Difficulties in travelling to work and concentrations of unemployment have focussed attention on particular areas of the city, for whose resident workforce the economic prospects are poorest. The economically most deprived part of the city contains only eleven percent of the city's population but has an overwhelmingly unskilled workforce and very high unemployment. It forms a tight ring immediately around the city centre and corresponds closely to the older council estates and worst areas of multi-let housing. It is the only part of the city to show unemployment rates and proportions of semi-skilled and unskilled workers significantly above the average for the city. Its residents have poor educational qualifications, change their jobs infrequently, have few cars and rely heavily on public transport or, in many cases, walk to work. Workers who live in this area rely to a greater extent than other parts of the city on jobs in the docks and railways and construction work and much less on manufacturing industry. The whole of this area showed exceptionally high levels of male unemployment in 1971, nowhere less than sixteen

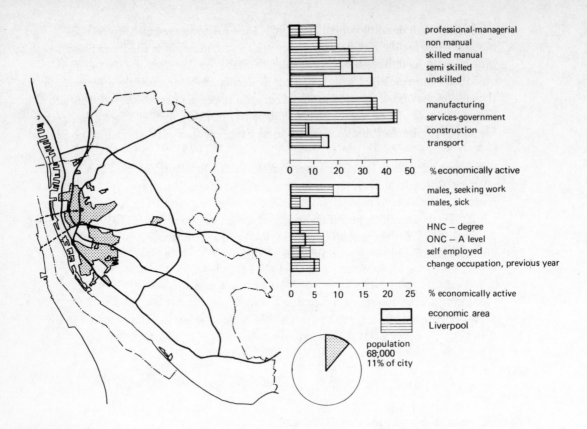

professional-managerial
non manual
skilled manual
semi skilled
unskilled

manufacturing
services-government
construction
transport

0 10 20 30 40 50   % economically active

males, seeking work
males, sick

HNC — degree
ONC — A level
self employed
change occupation, previous year

0   5   10   15   20   25   % economically active

economic area
Liverpool

population
68,000
11% of city

**Figure 36
Economic
deprivation 1971**

percent, and up to nearly fifty percent among unskilled workers in parts of
Abercromby and Granby.

Exceptionally high unemployment occurred in the inner council estates chiefly
because of the dependence of these areas on unskilled work. Their unskilled
workers were more likely to be unemployed than similar workers in, say, the outer
council estates because of their greater reliance on jobs in services, transport and
construction industries all of which are declining rapidly.

The rooming house area also had high levels of unemployment. But, unlike other
areas, the highest rates there were found amongst skilled manual and semi-skilled
workers rather than the unskilled. Part of the answer to this apparent paradox
lies in the presence of disadvantaged and transient groups drawn in by cheap
housing. There are high levels of family instability, such as illegitimacy, infectious
diseases, and children in care, many single people and much serious overcrowding.
There is also a high proportion of new commonwealth born immigrants, ten times
the city average, and also of Liverpool born blacks. Whilst these areas contain a
high proportion of unskilled workers, their dominant characteristic is a
preponderance of those whose personal or family circumstances make them unable
to work whatever their level of skill or past experience.

The economic future of inner Liverpool cannot be divorced from the general state
of the Merseyside economy. But within the county, the location of new industries
on the periphery of the conurbation to replace jobs lost from the inner city has

112

left behind high unemployment. There has been no new investment to provide manual work for the largely unskilled work force remaining in the inner areas. Nor have opportunities for training been available on sufficient a scale to enable unskilled or unemployed workers to compete effectively for new jobs either within the city or elsewhere, a factor which affects young people particularly as chapter nine will show. Indeed, there are growing concentrations of people in the inner area for whom personal or family circumstances make regular work difficult to obtain.

Any economic policy for inner Liverpool thus has two requirements. There is the need for a greatly increased training programme designed to improve the ability of inner city residents to compete for work. And there is a parallel need to create the conditions under which new industrial investment can be attracted to the inner city, to provide jobs for those who live there. We shall return to these in chapter eleven, after considering other aspects of inner city life.

7 Access to housing

Liverpool's housing stock

The huge influx of population into Liverpool in the middle of the nineteenth century contributed perhaps more than anything else to the Corporation's first attempts at influencing housing conditions in the city. Before becoming the city's first Medical Officer of Health in 1846, William Duncan conducted a campaign against bad housing by comparing the mortality rates of different areas. Court housing and cellar dwellings had been built by businessmen, merchants and slave traders well before the end of the eighteenth century. By 1840 it was estimated that about thirty two thousand people were living in cellars and over fifty five thousand in court houses.[1] Local Sanitary Acts of 1825 and 1842 and 1864 imposed standards on private building layouts and allowed the Corporation to clear cellar dwellings. Between 1844 and 1851, over five thousand cellars were cleared and over twenty thousand people evicted. No alternative provision was made and the private building boom of the 1840s which provided only for those in regular work soon collapsed. The casual labouring and unemployed poor were forced into the shrinking and decaying supply of pre-legislation court housing. In the 1850s, a generation after the first Act, it was estimated that a quarter of the city's population of over one hundred thousand were housed in this way.

It was not until 1869 that St. Martin's Cottages, the first council housing in Liverpool and the country, was built in Vauxhall just north of the city centre.[2] But this and the sporadic initiatives which followed were really intended to encourage the private sector. Only about five hundred council dwellings were built between 1875 and 1900 in Liverpool compared with about thirty thousand by the private sector. In the same period about twelve thousand were demolished.[3]

The tradition of tenement building appears to stem from the 1880s when it was found that land scarcity and local byelaws would allow only about a quarter of the existing unfit dwellings in the city to be replaced on the same area if self-contained cottages were built. Thus the only way to make an adequate return on investment, for this was still the overriding concern of all housing, was to build five storey tenement blocks. When the Insanitary Properties Committee became the Housing Committee in 1900, and it became politically acceptable to provide subsidised housing for the poor, the tradition was firmly established. Between 1900 and 1914 nearly two and a half thousand dwellings, mainly in tenement blocks, were built by the Corporation.

(1) Taylor I C, 'The Insanitary Housing Question and Tenement Dwellings in Nineteenth Century Liverpool', in Sutcliffe A, *Multi Storey Living: The British Working Class Experience* (1974).

(2) Gauldie E, *Cruel Habitations: A History of British Working Class Housing 1780–1919* (George Allen and Unwin 1974).

(3) Parry Lewis J, *Building Cycles and Britain's Growth* (1965).

Between the wars the Corporation continued to build tenement blocks in the inner areas, where they were the sole providers of new housing. They also laid out extensive, cottage-style suburban estates, not unlike the large quantities of semi-detached housing then being provided by private builders. After the Second World War the same pattern of development continued, although much of the total effort went into repairing and replacing war-damaged housing, much of it in the form of small, low-rise blocks of flats. Between 1956 and 1965, some twenty three thousand six hundred dwellings were built by the Council. By 1966 they were in control of eighty six thousand properties, of which sixty seven thousand were within the city boundary, the rest mainly at Kirkby.[1]

The historical pattern of development largely accounts for the marked difference in tenure between the inner and outer areas and for the polarisation of social status discussed in chapter four. Despite the drastic clearance programmes, three quarters of the inner area housing stock was still privately owned in 1971, nearly all of it built before 1914. And nearly sixty percent of the private housing in the inner areas was rented unfurnished, compared with under a quarter in the outer areas.

The housing market in the inner areas

Owner occupation

Owner occupation has grown steadily in Liverpool in recent years, although not as fast as in the rest of the country. By 1971 a third of Liverpool households owned their own homes, compared with half nationally. However the figure is a distortion of reality as much of the private house building has been in the outer districts of Merseyside. Most owner occupied houses in the city have been built for sale since the First World War, but many older houses, mainly in the inner areas, have been bought from private landlords over the years. Although the financial benefits are greatest for those with a large, secure income or capital, the flexibility, and financial security of owner occupation has resulted in a steady growth of this tenure in the more stable parts of the inner areas.

The price of small terraced houses in the inner areas has remained low; in theory well within the reach of those on low incomes. But most building societies regard older housing as a marginal investment and impose rules as to the level, security and nature of income and the proportion of the value of the house which they are prepared to lend, which effectively exclude those who are badly paid, unemployed, doing casual work, have no access to capital or are in difficult family circumstances. That a market has existed at all in the older parts of the inner areas has been due to cash sales, the provision of often very risky rental mortgages by some estate agents and finance houses; and, more recently, municipal loans. But the lending capacity of local authorities has recently been restricted. Between October 1975 and March 1976, 446 applications for Corporation mortgages were redirected to

(1) Muchnick D M, *Urban Renewal in Liverpool: a Study of the Politics of Redevelopment* (Ball and Sons, 1970).

116

the building societies. Of these 304 were rejected because of the location of the houses concerned, although the condition was also a factor in some cases. Liverpool's lending resources have been cut back to one and three quarter million pounds for 1976–77. Yet in 1974–75 the city advanced nearly four million pounds and between April and June 1975, when the cut back was announced, application had been made for a further three million pounds. The Corporation now intends to concentrate its lending in priority areas.

However it is only unimproved housing which is still cheap in the inner areas. The recent reduction in improvement grants from seventy five to fifty percent, combined with escalating improvement costs, now means that the market value of an improved house may not cover the cost of initial purchase plus the owner's contribution to improvement. Thus much of the older inner area housing becomes, in a sense, detached from the main housing market. Those who already own their homes may improve them to better their standard of living. But they will do so in the knowledge that they will be unable to recoup their investments and, if prices elsewhere continue to rise, may be unable to move without finding further capital.

Lowering the income threshold of owner occupation could bring important social gains in the inner areas. A proposal by the Council to provide low cost housing for sale is now underway with a first scheme for 170 houses. The building societies are likely to accept them as part of their more usual field of activity and, being new and physically separate from old housing nearby, they may well be successful. However, this type of development could lead to lower standards and the diversion of local authority resources from areas of acute need. The price of any new housing for sale will be out of the reach of many people coming from the slum clearance areas.

A recent survey carried out in one clearance area and a nearby proposed housing action area by the Area Management Unit showed that only about ten percent of households would have been interested in buying a new house nearby.[1] This low demand must be qualified by possible fears that expressing such an interest might have prejudiced residents' chances of a new corporation flat. While such an approach might have value in widening the choice of housing offered by the Corporation, there are more urgent priorities. Extending owner occupation in the inner areas could be achieved far more effectively by reintroducing municipal loans.

Private, unfurnished renting

Despite the steady decline of private renting since the First World War, one third of the city's housing stock, some fifty eight thousand dwellings, was still privately rented in 1971, mostly in the inner areas. Nearly all of this was unfurnished. In inner Liverpool forty four percent of all households were in this category compared with twenty six percent in the city and sixteen percent in the country as a whole. The houses were generally in poor physical condition, few private landlords having

(1) *Housing Preferences of Families in the Handel Street CPO and Adjacent Housing Action Areas*, Report by the Area Executive to the District D Committee, 27 September 1976.

taken up improvement grants or kept the properties in good repair. In the older terraced areas where this tenure predominated, over sixty percent of households had no inside wc. The worst areas have now been removed by slum clearance and the recent change of policy to improvement and rehabilitation will involve further decline of this tenure as it has no commercial viability and does not attract new, private investment. So far, the shift has been towards owner occupation, although most strongly in the areas furthest away from the city centre. A parallel shift into social ownership through housing associations, mainly in the older housing areas, has accelerated recently with preferential funding arrangements through the Housing Corporation and the acquisition of large portfolios from property companies.

In the past the children of long stay residents who wanted to get married could be 'spoken for' with the landlord and given priority when a nearby tenancy became vacant. More recently young couples have rented houses for short periods before either moving into a council flat or buying their own house. At present neither of these opportunities is provided by the local authority or housing associations, both of which have long waiting lists and in the case of the local authority at least, inadequate transfer policies. Without this flexibility, considerable stress could result as many young families are forced to remain with in-laws, being ineligible for council housing and unable to afford to buy even the cheapest house because of restrictive lending practices or insufficient income.

Rehousing from slum clearance areas has redistributed resources to some of the poorest families in the city. Improvement policies will not operate in quite the same way. Although less disruptive than slum clearance, improvement requires an individual contribution which will discriminate against the poorest households, because they cannot afford to pay their share or because they cannot cope with the upheaval involved. Municipal action in housing action areas should be able to overcome these drawbacks, but, as discussed in detail later in the next chapter, such areas will cover only a small proportion of the older privately rented housing in need of improvement.

Private, furnished renting

Only four percent of households in Liverpool rent furnished accommodation from private landlords, most of it in small units for small households. During the decade prior to 1975 the number of such dwellings grew because it was the least secure tenure and gave the best return to the landlord. The 1975 Rent Act extended security of tenure to furnished tenants but there is no evidence of any significant decline as yet in Liverpool. However, in the cheaper areas there is considerable pressure from students and other single households, as well as some poorer families.

Furnished renting is found almost entirely in the inner areas, chiefly in the rooming house area. In the more attractive areas, large houses have been converted into self-contained flats and provide for more affluent, generally small, households who want a flat near the city centre. Houses in less attractive areas are let as bed-sits and small flats. Many of the residents are young professional or non-manual

118

workers or students and only stay for short periods. This multiple occupation forms a practical and acceptable use of large dwellings, recently given a boost by improvement policy. However it is unlikely to expand significantly and will probably remain restricted to small areas near the city's parks and major hospitals. Living conditions are, on the whole, good and the areas are stable in combining a rapid turnover of population and steady demand.

Abercromby, Granby, Princes Park and parts of Everton gave a less favourable picture. In some areas over forty percent of all dwellings were rented furnished, the average social status was lower, there was much unemployment and sickness. A rapid growth in the numbers of small, particularly single person households has been accompanied by a decline in the supply of furnished rooms, cheap flats and lodgings where students, nurses, unskilled workers or newcomers traditionally found somewhere to live. At the lowest level, the twilight areas contained a high proportion of poor families with children, living in expensive and overcrowded furnished rooms. Many of these, including the largest in Abercromby and Granby, have been systematically removed by public health regulations and slum clearance. Many of the families moved into nearby, cheap and unpopular council estates. But others found their way into smaller and more scattered areas of multi-let housing just beyond the current clearance areas.

Social ownership

Housing associations in Liverpool had their origins in early twentieth century philanthropic endeavour. Until recently they have been few and small. But, as in other cities, there was rapid growth in Liverpool from the late 1960s onwards, stimulated by the 1969 Housing Act and Shelter assistance. Since the Housing Act 1974 they have begun to concentrate on the inner city areas, being most active in general improvement and in converting bigger, older houses into smaller, self-contained flats. Housing associations provided nearly three thousand dwellings in Liverpool between April 1970 and May 1975. This represented approximately twenty percent of all improvement grants taken up in the city. Their activity has accelerated since the 1974 Act, particularly in the acquisition and improvement of older inner area stock, compensating for the collapse of private improvement following the reduction of grants.

The associations have also built housing for special need groups, especially sheltered housing for the elderly. Already completed or planned in Liverpool are bedsits for ex-prisoners, a sheltered home for single people, furnished flatlets, and houses for ex-mental patients. This development has great potential, particularly for involving voluntary groups, and in setting standards of provision. Generous grants from the Housing Corporation allow a more personal service and greater welfare involvement than is provided by the local authority. However there is a danger that rapid growth in the size of the individual organisations may cause restrictive bureaucracies to develop which will undermine their major value as sensitive, flexible, locally-based organisations.

There has also been some new building for general needs. It is vital that full nomination rights are taken up by the local authority as one way of ensuring that the tenancies go to those in housing need. But the fair rents are generally higher than those in similar council housing. Without careful management and strong social objectives on the part of the housing association an incipient grading can take place, whereby the poorer and less able are unable to obtain housing association tenancies, and gravitate towards unpopular council estates.

A number of tenants' co-operatives and a servicing organisation, Neighbourhood Housing Services, developed from SNAP in the late 1960s. In theory co-operatives can use tenants' interest in the details of improvement to involve them in the control and management of small groups of dwellings. But none of the Liverpool co-operatives offer any sharing of equity, one of the major advantages of joint investment. And the desire for democratic involvement in management may not be as widespread as is sometimes suggested. Our housing management project showed that it was the tenants in greatest housing need who were least able to take an active part in management. Nevertheless it will be important to retain the advantages of a small-scale, flexible and personal approach if they are to be a long term success.

Council housing

Just over one third of all households in Liverpool are local authority tenants. In the inner areas, the figure is a quarter. Many of the great differences between the inner and outer council estates can be traced back to the nature of inter-war developments; large suburban estates of mainly three bedroomed houses contrasted with inner city walk-up tenements of mainly two bedroom flats. Although a greater variety of housing has been built since the Second World War most of the houses have still been in the outer areas. There has also been a tendency to rely heavily on one type of development at a time. During the 1950s and early 60s flats and maisonettes were more usual in new development than houses, reflecting the preoccupation of that period with pressure on land and an increasing birth rate. There has now been a return to low rise, medium density dwellings with front doors and back yards. The change was marked by the recent decision of the Council to build no housing of more than two storeys in height.

**Figure 37
Council housing
stock, Liverpool
1975**

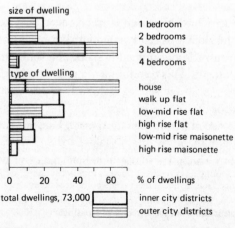

120

The difference between the inner and outer estates has thus been consistently reinforced. In 1975, thirty six thousand out of fifty three thousand outer area council dwellings were three and four bedroomed houses. This was in marked contrast to the inner areas where there were fewer than two thousand houses of that size, forming only nine percent of the total council stock. Half of all inner area council dwellings had only one or two bedrooms. With smaller dwellings, overcrowding was worse. In some areas with high proportions of tenement blocks and 1950s flats, one in ten of all households were seriously overcrowded. Nevertheless much of the older council housing remains popular, mainly because rents are low and young couples want to settle near their families.

Liverpool's recent policy for allocating council tenancies was designed to cope with rehousing from a slum clearance programme of thirty three thousand houses.[1] Consequently top priority, for a decade, was given to slum clearance families. Further ad hoc priority groups have been introduced during that period for modernising tenement blocks or older private houses or the special needs of the sick, and the elderly, or families with children in multi-storey blocks. But the over-riding priority given to slum clearance and special medical needs, has meant that the bulk of new housing and the most desirable relets have been offered to these two groups. Even special programmes have suffered. It was intended to rehouse three hundred families per year from multi-storey flats. In the first two years of this policy only about fifty families have been so rehoused, but the number has increased to two hundred in the most recent year and only two hundred and fifty one families are now left in multi storey blocks.[2]

The other major categories of housing need are the general waiting list and requests for transfer; currently about sixteen thousand and thirteen thousand respectively. The points system operating in Liverpool was split into two groups: high and low priority. It was so weighted that only those waiting list or transfer applicants living in particularly bad or overcrowded conditions gained enough points for group 1, from which an offer of a tenancy was guaranteed. Nevertheless, in the past year five hundred and fifty one tenancies have been allocated to group 1 applications and one thousand nine hundred and forty three to group 2 applications, both categories including a number of transfers.

Certain council tenancies have become unpopular, for reasons of obsolescence, bad design or layout; vacancies have occurred even on some fairly new properties. It is mainly these flats and maisonettes, more commonly known as hard-to-lets, which have been offered to group 2 applicants and others who were prepared to take

(1) A new allocations policy has been approved by the Council since we completed our main work on this subject, reported in IAS Liverpool, *Single and Homeless*, and *Housing Management* (Department of Environment, 1977). It reflects the shift in emphasis from slum clearance and rehousing to the improvement of private housing. It rationalises the previous system of categories, which had become very complex; gives greater priority to transfers; and enables the division of allocations between different categories to vary, reflecting local demand in housing districts. A more recent change has placed single parent families on the same footing as two parent families for allocations. The effectiveness of the new policy has yet to be experienced but it should meet some of the comments in this report.

(2) *Report on Allocations to the Housing Building and Planning Committee*, Liverpool City Council May 1976; more recent information from the Director of Housing.

them. However, applicants knew that once housed they were unlikely to be able to move. Those with bargaining power were thus encouraged to hold out for the more popular areas. In addition the grading of tenants persisted. Although of less importance than in the past, account was still taken of ability to pay and previous living conditions in making an allocation. The consequence in effect was to introduce a competitive market in public housing which has paralleled that in the private sector. Some estates, particularly the inter war houses at Walton Clubmoor, became very popular. Others, particularly certain tenements and walk-up blocks of flats in the inner city, have become a dumping ground for poor, homeless or difficult families.

Housing and social need

Trends throughout the city have led to a reduction in the supply of housing for those on low incomes. Clearance and closures have removed many poor quality, but readily available, furnished flats. Housing improvement policies have raised the standard of much privately rented housing but raised rents in the process. New council housing is more expensive than old. The decade of priority given to slum clearance families and special medical cases, either excluded non-priority applicants from council housing or forced them into unpopular and unsuitable flats. In addition the lack of an effective transfer policy restricted some families from moving to more suitable housing as their circumstances changed. Those suffering most from these pressures have been homeless and single parent families; single people; sub tenants and overcrowded familes in council flats; and insecure private tenants.

Homeless and single parent families[1]

When families living in council housing divorce or separate, the partner with dependents used to be offered a suitable alternative. And the other partner used to be offered a one bedroom flat. Those not legally separated have been able, since 1973, to register on the waiting list, subject to a social worker's report that the marriage has irretrievably broken down.[2] But for poorer families living in private housing whose marriage breaks up the amount of temporary accommodation is very small. About twenty places were provided in local authority accommodation for the homeless at Langtry House. Otherwise there were fewer than fifty places available for women and children in voluntary hostels.

Few single parent families gained enough points on the waiting list to be offered a house or flat in a popular area. If an offer was made, it would have been a hard to let flat. Homeless families, too, are offered only hard to let flats and in principle (although not always enforced) only a single offer is made. Single parent and homeless families have thus been concentrated in some unpopular estates, often in

(1) See footnote, page 121.
(2) *Allocations and Related Matters: Policies and Procedures*, Housing Department, Liverpool City Council, December 1973.

unsuitable conditions and surroundings and quite against any possible interpretation of housing need. For example, of 274 single parent families living in council housing in the study area, fifty eight percent had hard to let flats. Until recently an Express Service was operated by the Social Services and Housing departments which offered hard to let properties to applicants whom social workers considered to be in social need. This service included single people as well as families but it has now fallen into disuse following the reorganisation of the Homeless Service.

Following publication of the Homelessness Circular in February 1974,[1] a new Homeless Service was set up in the Housing Department in 1975, to find permanent housing for the homeless. It is based at the Housing Aid Centre in Granby. It shares responsibility for the reception of homeless families with the Homeless Families Unit of the Social Services Department which provides social work support.

Just over one thousand homeless families were referred in 1975 to the Homeless Families Unit, over half of them on matrimonial or domestic grounds. Of those found accommodation, nearly a third went to Langtry House, just under a quarter to hostels and nearly half were provided with bed and breakfast in cheap hotels because Langtry House was full. There are normally about twenty families in hotels at any time.

The single and homeless[2]

Accommodation for single homeless men in Liverpool ranges from night shelters and the DHSS Reception Centre through commercial lodging houses where a bed can be had for as little as 50p per night, to the Salvation Army Hostel where full board and a private cubicle costs about £12 per week. The Reception Centre, a converted RAF camp, is in the suburbs and open day and night. Residents are allowed to come and go as they please, but they must conform to the rehabilitative routine of the centre. The larger of two free night shelters run by voluntary groups is in the Crypt of the Catholic Cathedral and is full on most nights.

Commercial lodging houses are situated in the Shaw Street area of Everton. Their supply has been declining since they first had to be registered in the 1920s. In 1930, 120 premises provided nearly six thousand beds. In 1975 there were about three hundred beds in only four premises.[3] Standards are now desperately low: the largest commercial lodging house in the city caters for approximately two hundred men sleeping six to a room and has but one inside wc. However, the two remaining large hostels for working men have single bedded cubicles or rooms, adequate bathroom facilities and common rooms.

Just over one thousand single homeless men came to the SHARP referral centre in its first nine months; a third of them under twenty five. Two-thirds had

(1) *Homelessness*, Joint Circular by Department of the Environment (18/74) and Department of Health and Social Security (4/74), February 1974.

(2) This subject is discussed more fully in IAS Liverpool, *Single and Homeless* (Department of the Environment 1977).

(3) Stewart J, *Of No Fixed Abode* (Manchester University Press 1975).

previously lived in a hostel or lodging house or had no fixed abode. The main source of accommodation developed by SHARP was about eighty commercial landladies scattered over the whole of Merseyside, but concentrated in the older parts of Liverpool, Bootle and Birkenhead. Many of the landladies ran what amounted to common lodging houses. Otherwise SHARP was forced to rely on the dwindling supply of hostels and lodging houses. Very little success was achieved in getting clients into more permanent accommodation. In particular, very few people were found council flats.

Although most provision for women was of a better standard than the men's common lodging houses, it was restricted to about 150 beds, over half of them in a Salvation Army hostel; the remainder in a small number of voluntary hostels or houses, some of which also took couples or women with children. A refuge for battered wives was opened in 1974. Nearly 450 women came to SHARP in the first nine months of operation. Less than half were found any accommodation at all as many landladies were not prepared to take women. The shortage particularly of decent temporary accommodation was more marked for women than men.

Pressure of numbers and scarcity of accommodation focussed the attention of the referral centre on those in most urgent need. About half of those coming to the centre said they had nowhere to sleep that night. Accommodation was found for about half of these on their first visit and about two thirds of all those who came to SHARP were eventually found a place. The remaining third either could not be placed, or did not persist in seeking help. The shortage of adequate short-stay accommodation meant that SHARP was forced to use some accommodation that was either of a very low standard, or sharply discriminatory (usually against black people or women), or turn away people in urgent need. Faced with a classic dilemma of knowing that immediate help for the client often entrenches their circumstances, SHARP staff felt obliged to exclude only the very worst accommodation, but to ensure that all clients were fully aware of what to expect. Nevertheless, many clients accepted a bed in unsuitable circumstances.

Single people unable to afford private accommodation thus face severe difficulty. Anyone who has lived in Liverpool for twenty four hours may apply for a council tenancy. But the opportunity for a single person to stay in lodgings or other temporary accommodation is severely limited. And, legally, single people living with their council tenant parents may not even apply for a separate dwelling until they are twenty eight. During 1973 over seven thousand people were on the waiting list for one bedroom flats but only 336 single bedroom flats were let to non-priority waiting list applicants although more accommodation will be available as the last families are rehoused from multi storey blocks of flats. Whilst the service to the single homeless as individuals reflects the Council's lack of statutory obligation to secure accommodation for this group, positive action has been taken when hostels have been closed. Two major charitable hostels in Liverpool were closed during 1975 and in both instances Housing and Social Services Departments mounted a joint exercise to rehouse the residents. The Housing Committee is now gradually beginning to accept greater responsibility for the single homeless; partly by providing some furnished tenancies, partly by providing sheltered housing, partly by taking over and continuing our projects.

Sheltered housing

About a quarter of all those who came to SHARP were considered to be in need of care and support and referred to social workers; they included many people with alcoholic or psychiatric problems. This was confirmed by a night survey undertaken in January 1975 by the Merseyside Campaign for the Homeless and Rootless (CHAR). They estimated that approximately one third of the residents of the large hostels and lodging houses in the city were suffering from drink or drug abuse or were mentally disordered, that is were in need of care and support.

The Social Services Department's services to the elderly provided domiciliary services, sheltered dwellings, day care and old people's hostels. Homeless old people who applied for admission to a hostel were given a high priority. But the Department's residential provision for the mentally ill is still minimal sixteen years after the passing of the Mental Health Act. Currently three small hostels provide residential care for twenty four people. By the end of 1976 eight more hostels will have opened making available a total of one hundred and thirty six places. The Department plans to start an experimental lodgings scheme to enable mentally ill people to be looked after in private homes.

Voluntary hostels provide approximately one hundred places for homeless people in need of care and support. Two voluntary hostels, run by church organisations, provide for adolescents coming out of care, while three probation hostels and one bail hostel (opened in 1975) provided a total of approximately sixty places in Liverpool.

One particular type of shelter was afforded by Stopover, to provide a breathing space for young people who had come into conflict with authority, and give them time to find a permanent place to live and sort out some of their personal problems with the help of the hostel staff. Most of the seventy five young people who stayed at Stopover in its first six months had been referred there by a probation officer, social worker, voluntary agency or SHARP. Over a third were completely homeless, and two thirds were out of work. Over a third were girls, and the majority of both boys and girls came from elsewhere in Merseyside. A quarter of the young people stayed for the full eight weeks although the average stay was about three weeks. The great majority, particularly of those staying for the longer periods, did sort out their problems to the extent of either returning home or finding somewhere reasonably secure to stay.

Increasingly, institutional provision is aiming as closely as possible at a normal family situation in an average community. Ordinary houses are quietly converted into supportive housing for ex-psychiatric patients or young offenders. This takes time. Public resistance is often strong. At present the provision, often by local housing associations, is not keeping pace with the demand, particularly from those being discharged from mental hospitals. But there may be hope in the number of experiments in communal living which have sprung up in large old houses in parts of inner Liverpool (and elsewhere). At present they tend to be interest-based; a particular project, a religious community, a political group. But they also have potential for young people who would normally remain isolated; particularly if they can achieve a wide age range, a mixture of strong and weak, perhaps reproducing some of the advantages of a traditional extended family system among a group who might be unrelated except by the need for companionship and mutual support.

Council transfers[1]

Different housing types have dominated council building in different periods. And the policy of the Housing Department has been to match the size of the family and the dwelling closely at the time of letting. Consequently many tenants are now in unsuitable, unpopular or overcrowded accommodation. The rapid decline of job opportunities, for unskilled workers in particular who form an above average proportion of tenants in most inner city estates, has combined with strong community ties and an inability to move to produce complete economic and social stagnation in some estates.

Transfer policy has been in operation since 1969, in which at least a quarter of new and relet tenancies were to be made available for rehousing from within the same housing management district. In most years nearly a third of all lettings have been transfers. But most of these were priority cases in their own right, that is special medical cases, families with children in multi-storey flats or those being moved out of flats to be modernised. Transfers made on the basis of any kind of social need amounted to only about ten percent of the total. Since the loss of Kirkby and Cantril Farm at the reorganisation of local government, opportunities for transfer and letting for general need have been further reduced. For example in 1973 transfers in Liverpool accounted for thirty two percent of all lettings; by 1975 this had fallen to twenty two percent.

Applications for transfers could be either high or low priority and, for the city as a whole were divided roughly equally between the two. High priority groups were given first choice of where to live and low priority groups had to take what was left. By this means, housing districts in the city could be placed in a rough rank order of popularity with Walton Clubmoor at the top and Childwall (which includes Netherley) at the bottom of the list. The two inner city districts are low in popularity.

The pattern of relets in the housing management project area conforms to the general rule. With the exception of the most recent new housing (the Chatsworth estate) relets were distributed evenly through the area and the proportion going to high priority groups was low, suggesting that the area was rejected by applicants having some choice over where to live. This impression was strengthened by the small number of transfers coming to the area and the impression of the project

(1) See footnote, page 121.

team that the majority of these, exceptionally, were in low priority groups. Nearly three quarters of the lettings in the tenement blocks were to families with children, over a quarter to single parent families. Sixteen of the eighty families had three or more children; six had five or more. The flats were clearly let up to their full potential. One consequence of this policy was that overcrowding in the city was concentrated chiefly in council tenancies, mainly in the inner council estates.

Only one hundred and thirty three transfer requests had been registered in the project area for various reasons. Of these twenty five were seriously overcrowded and there were at least one hundred and twenty subtenants living with relations and waiting for their own home. Comparatively few people requested a transfer as there was so little opportunity to move, except into even more unpopular housing. Many of those living in walk up flats wanted to move to a house and were not interested in going into another flat for a little extra space. Where local transfers were requested it was usually for personal reasons, for instance to a nearby estate where relatives might be living. No transfer was allowed unless there were no arrears and the flat was in good decorative order. This requirement proved particularly difficult for those in financial difficulties through unemployment or for more permanent reasons.

Housing aid

The Granby Housing Aid Centre opened in 1972. Its manager is responsible through the Housing Services and Homelessness Officer to the Director of Housing. Its function is to help those who are homeless, in poor housing or have been placed in temporary accommodation. It does this by offering advice, by helping people secure accommodation in the private sector or with a housing association, or by working directly with district housing managers to assist a move into a council tenancy. Records kept between its opening in July 1972 and December 1973 showed that over half the seven hundred and seventy cases involved rehousing. The main problems were homelessness, overcrowding, eviction and repairs and improvements. These reflected the location of the centre in the centre of the city's main area of multi let housing. Half the cases were estimated to come from within a half mile radius of the centre, where at the time there was little council housing. The centre has adopted a casework approach, following through each enquiry until a real improvement is achieved in the client's housing.

A somewhat similar housing service is provided by the Vauxhall law centre located in an area of almost exclusively council housing. The first annual report of the centre's solicitor showed that of six hundred cases handled by the centre, a quarter concerned relations between council tenants and the local authority.[1] Indeed the complex case of responsibility for the communal areas of the high rise block of flats referred to on page 53, which is so far-reaching in its implications, has been handled throughout by the centre.

A particular need for housing aid is experienced by elderly people in slum clearance

(1) Linden J L, *Vauxhall Community Law Centre, Annual Report 1973–74.*

areas. Many of those visited by HANDS had strong ties with the neighbourhood, were not very mobile and needed small, ground floor accommodation nearby. They may therefore have had to wait longer than other groups to be rehoused. Five years elapsed between declaration of the compulsory purchase order and completion of rehousing for the two clearance areas involved in the project. As clearance and rehousing progressed the familiar surroundings became alien. Friends and neighbours left; landlords stopped doing repairs altogether; houses and then whole streets were boarded up and finally demolished; the corner grocers went out of business; dirt and rubble accumulated; vandalism was rife and many people dared not leave their homes unattended. The net result was the slow death of all established networks and values of the area. HANDS found that they had, in effect, to replace the community network for a time for some pensioners before they were rehoused.

A resettlement experiment carried out in 1973 by the Social Services Department on a new estate not far away showed the variety of problems faced by new tenants, but most keenly by pensioners.[1] Most of these involved full payments or social security benefits or related to the actual procedures of moving house. All the problems which arose were felt most keenly by pensioners.

Clearly, as the local authority intervenes in housing matters to an increasing extent, its relationship with those in need or simply seeking advice becomes more crucial. For the public sector, the organisation and heavy work load, the very appearance of district housing offices makes it difficult to achieve a satisfactory relationship between staff and public. One solution has been the appointment of housing area liaison officers (HALOs) but they deal with too many tenants to develop the face to face contact which was supposed to be a part of their job. Workers in the housing management project, with more time, found that most tenants had little idea of their responsibilities or rights. For instance, although many of the Angela Street and Carlisle Street tenants were highly dissatisfied with their housing conditions, none knew that grants were available from the Housing Department for installing fitments. The provision of a more localised and intensive management service allowed better relationships to develop with the public, clarified responsibilities between tenant and landlord, and kept tenants better informed about policies and programmes.

The means of identifying those in severe housing need are still inadequate. The Granby Housing Aid Centre has acted successfully on behalf of those facing particularly bad conditions in multi-let houses. But it is the only one of its kind, and its effective area of operation is very small. The aid and advice available to local authority tenants is negligible except in circumstances of dire need. The major slum clearance programmes are drawing to an end, but even so some clearance will continue and in any case major improvement programmes, in both public and private housing, cause considerable personal and financial stress for those involved, particularly the elderly. The decision to operate the Housing Department's new

(1) *The Toxteth New Housing Site Project, Interim Report*, District E Social Services Department, Liverpool City Council March 1974.

Homeless Service from the Housing Aid Centre and to open a further centre in the north end of the city was a welcome one. It provides an opportunity to develop a comprehensive approach to provision for those who are in greatest housing need in both public and private markets. But the gap between setting up the means of properly identifying housing need and having the supply of suitable housing and the right allocation policies to meet it, is still a very wide one in Liverpool.

8 Living in the inner city

The older private housing

Lodge Lane East: A study in private decay

Lodge Lane East is a run-down residential area of some two thousand, privately owned, mostly Victorian houses adjacent to a popular but declining shopping street. The housing varies from densely packed terraces of tiny two-up, two-down houses, larger terraced houses and small, semi-detached houses to more substantial, but often badly decayed villas in tree-lined streets. A few groups of council houses, including some old people's flats, have been built on infill sites. Most of the housing is rented from private landlords but a sizeable minority of people own their own homes. In terms of the description in chapter four, it is a mixture of older terraced and rooming house areas.

Despite a great variety of conditions and character, the environment is drab and depressing except for the few streets where the decay is hidden by overgrown vegetation. Streets are dirty, pavements cracked and dangerous, back lanes crumbling, badly lit and squalid. Empty or derelict houses are scattered throughout the area, many of them left open or poorly secured. Other houses have been demolished leaving ugly gaping holes, with exposed gable ends and rubble-strewn sites which invite dumping. The impression is of an area gone to seed; at the point where it needs either a determined effort to lift the standard of the environment, and then keep it there for as long as the housing is to remain, or to abandon the attempt altogether and merely ensure that the resulting accelerated decay does not actually become dangerous.

Lodge Lane East was the scene of our project in environmental care.[1] The future of much of the area was uncertain under the then housing policy of the Corporation. The smaller houses to the north and some of the badly neglected larger houses were due for clearance. The centre of the area had been designated for short life improvement: improvement grants were available for installing basic amenities but not for major improvements as such areas were to be cleared before the end of the fifteen year period, which had started several years previously. Residents of this section had set up the Lodge Lane East Residents' Association (LLERA) to try to get the area declared a general improvement area. The remainder of the area had been designated as a possible general improvement area.

Regular meetings with LLERA representatives and other residents during the environmental care project made it clear not only that their main preoccupation

---

(1) The project is fully described in IAS Liverpool, *Environmental Care* (Department of the Environment 1977).

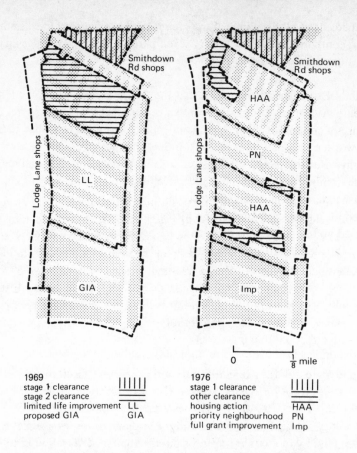

Figure 38
Housing policies,
Lodge Lane East

Smithdown
Rd shops

Lodge Lane shops

LL

GIA

Smithdown
Rd shops

Lodge Lane shops

HAA

PN

HAA

Imp

0   ⅛ mile

1969	
stage 1 clearance	‖‖‖‖‖
stage 2 clearance	═══
limited life improvement	LL
proposed GIA	GIA

1976	
stage 1 clearance	‖‖‖‖‖
other clearance	═══
housing action	HAA
priority neighbourhood	PN
full grant improvement	Imp

was with the state of their housing but that existing housing policies were both ineffective in themselves and had been wrongly applied in that area. We carried out a survey of housing and social conditions in the area through discussions with residents and local workers, examination of population and housing characteristics from the 1971 census, assessment of the impact of various powers used recently by the local authority, and the carrying out of a superficial survey of physical condition.

The surveys showed a wide variety of household and dwelling type and structure in the area as well as some housing stress. Overcrowding was average for the city but parts of the area showed higher levels. The proportion of under-occupied dwellings was slightly below the city average but varied between ten percent and forty six percent in different parts of the area.

The incidence of households which might have been particularly vulnerable to poverty or bad housing conditions also varied considerably. The proportion of one or two person households in census enumeration districts ranged between forty two and eighty five percent; of pensioner households between eleven and fifty seven percent; of single parent families between one and four percent; and of very large households between one and fourteen percent. Half the dwellings in the area were rented privately unfurnished, compared with just over a quarter in the city as a whole. Private furnished renting was nearly four times the city average, while a quarter of houses were owner occupied compared with a third in the city. However,

132

fifty percent of all dwellings in the area lacked hot water, a fixed bath and an inside toilet, compared with only twenty seven percent in the city. Once again local variations were very great.

All the LLERA members agreed that the area had been in decline for a number of years. At the same time, they valued many aspects of living there, in particular a sense of community and the convenience of shopping in Lodge Lane. Residents and workers alike felt that the continuing presence of older residents gave the area stability. But the recent subdivision of some houses into flats had meant an increase in the number of short term residents. With increased security of tenure for furnished lettings, many landlords would let only to students, who usually only stayed for a short period. Others, with smaller houses, were selling out. This had allowed young families to move into the area, buying their first house. Once there, they tended to stay several years. However, increasing mortgage rates had reduced the number of couples who could afford to buy and some houses remained empty and rapidly became derelict. Chinese, Pakistani and West Indian families were said to have moved into the area from nearby Granby, many of them shopkeepers who were able to pay cash for their houses.

Many families in the area were poor, judging by the high take up of free school meals and the number of children who could not afford to go on outings; but they were stable and parents cared about their children. Both health visitors and social workers were concerned about the physical and mental condition of old people. Many old people were said to have arthritic and chest complaints caused by dampness. The majority of houses were built without a damp course and some were said to have been built over streams. Also, many isolated old people whose families had moved away had become lonely and depressed. The social workers felt that it was the people moving into the area who were bringing the social problems, especially overcrowding. A young couple might buy or rent a small terraced house and improve it, then split up and one partner remain in the house with the children. A new partner would move in, more children arrive, and the house become overcrowded. In addition, single parent families moved into the area as converted flats became available.

The results of recent council activity in the area were not seen to be very impressive. Clearance, the most dramatic of the council's powers, had not yet reached the area, but it had thrown a shadow before it. Though central and local government policies now encouraged improvement, many residents thought that this would merely postpone clearance for a time. Owner occupiers who sought grants often found the procedures too lengthy and complicated to see through; many did not feel improvement worthwhile in short life areas. Landlords were reluctant to improve their houses and they would often not do repairs. Between 1970 and 1975, three hundred and thirty nine applications were made for improvement grants of which a third were approved. The highest proportion of enquiries was from the limited life improvement areas, and involved a third of all the houses, although only eight percent had grants approved.

Powers were used to close or demolish a small number of individual unfit houses in the area between 1963 and 1974. But landlords were not forced to carry out repairs because legislation made no provision for prosecution for failure to comply with the order. Instead, powers for urgent repair under the public health acts were used, although only where it could be shown that a statutory nuisance existed. In 1973 for instance, three hundred and fifty one complaints were received by public health inspectors. Nearly two thirds concerned either roofs or drains; the remainder covered rising damp, plaster work, windows and brickwork. In the majority of cases where notices were served and complied with, it took more than three months for the repairs to be carried out. Powers to carry out work in default were rarely used as there was little chance of recovering costs from the owners.

The Council's policies at that time were designed to cover a variety of conditions and allow owners and residents to take part in improvements. Yet in no part of the area had a decisive policy been expressed. Formal procedures had not yet started for the stage 2 clearance areas, the potential general improvement areas had not been declared and the limited life area was, by its nature, uncertain. Those owners who had wished to improve their houses had been confused and deterred by the improvement grant process. While the possibility of a general improvement area had given some stimulus to the conversion of houses, the likely future clearance of other areas had discouraged landlords from repair or improvement. Tenants had suffered as a result. Some landlords trying to improve conditions for tenants said they could not get an adequate return on investing in improvements. Most did not try. Because of increasing building costs, grants had become commercially viable only for small dwellings of which there was a shortage. And investment had been sluggish until necessary repairs were enforced.

Advance discussion of the stage 2 clearance programme, however welcome as an element of public consultation, probably put a final stop to repairs in these areas. The uncertainty reinforced a trend in which the most affluent and enterprising were leaving to find better conditions elsewhere, the remainder being left in houses needing repairs which would not be done. Newcomers to the area were often those least able to improve the houses into which they moved.

Housing proposals for Lodge Lane East changed radically in 1976, as part of the new policy for housing renewal adopted by the council following the 1974 Housing Act. The future of the area thus will be affected chiefly by the efficacy of this new policy, described below.

Conditions in the older private housing

That the Lodge Lane East area was typical of many areas of older, private housing in inner Liverpool which were rapidly changing socially and decaying physically was confirmed by the social area analysis. It comprised elements of both the worst rented housing in the older terraced areas and the low status parts of the rooming house areas.

Despite the beginnings of an improvement programme and demolition of sixteen and a half thousand dwellings in inner Liverpool between 1966 and 1970, the main concentrations of bad housing conditions in Liverpool in 1971 were still in the inner areas. Over thirty thousand houses, over one third of those remaining in the inner city, were still considered by the Council at that time to be in sufficiently bad condition to require demolition.

The most widespread indication of poor private housing in the inner areas, the lack of basic amenities, could be illustrated by lack of an inside wc. Of nearly a quarter of the city's households which lacked an inside toilet, eighty two percent lived in inner Liverpool, seventy five percent in the older terraced areas. The lack of amenities was mainly attributable to the age and tenure of the dwelling. Half of all households renting unfurnished had no inside wc. In addition a seventh of owner occupiers, most of them in similar small terraced houses, lacked this amenity. Although often in itself no great hardship, the absence of an inside wc is usually a good indication of more serious problems. Overcrowding as such was not serious in the older terraced housing except in the oldest, smallest houses, where space was tight for family living. To provide an inside wc (and a fixed bath) entailed either losing a room or building an expensive rear extension which takes up most of the backyard. And the widespread lack of an inside toilet in areas of private renting indicated a general unwillingness among landlords to provide modern amenities. The lack of amenities suggested a degree of poverty which may not be revealed by levels of unemployment.

A second indication of housing deprivation is given by the proportion of households sharing a dwelling. By any definition of sharing, the inner areas fared particularly badly. The census definition is a particularly narrow one, including only three percent of the city's households. However, nearly three quarters of these lived in the inner areas, chiefly in the poorer parts of the rooming house area, where up to a fifth of households were found to share dwellings. The incidence of sharing in these areas indicates adverse conditions for families, but the population included an above average proportion of students and other small households, for whom sharing may be perfectly acceptable. This is particularly a feature of private rented furnished households, among whom for instance fifty seven per cent share a bath. It is a feature also of the principal form of tenure in the inner areas, namely private rented unfurnished households. For these, five per cent shared a bath in 1971.

Although not as severe as in the inner council estates, overcrowding in the poorest parts of the rooming house area was also high. In the worst part, one in ten households lived at a density of more than 1·5 persons per room, and a quarter of furnished tenants at more than one person per room. Most of the overcrowding in the rooming house area occurred in multi occupied dwellings, although what proportion of the large households involved consisted of single families is not clear; some large households in the rooming house area may in fact have been groups of single people living together according to the census definition. In other parts of the rooming house area, proper conversions of large houses had been carried out. Sharing and overcrowding, consequently, were much less.

The Council spent the first post war decade replacing or repairing war damaged housing. But in the mid 1950s, the Medical Officer of Health resumed his statutory duty of representing unfit houses for slum clearance. It was clear that large numbers of dwellings had to be cleared and the only question was how quickly it could be done and new housing built to replace them. The pressure came not only from the Medical Officer of Health but from many of the occupants of the worst houses. Conditions were so bad that there was little to choose between different areas and the first to be cleared were those which would provide the best sites for redevelopment. Nevertheless, at this time many of those to be rehoused had to be found accommodation in the new outer council estates for there was not enough space to rehouse them locally even if they wanted.

By 1966 the rate of slum clearance was not keeping pace with the deterioration of the older private housing stock. The whole clearance and rehousing programme was reviewed and a new, accelerated policy of slum clearance was introduced. The National Building Agency prepared a three stage programme by which seventy eight thousand dwellings would be cleared by 1991. The first stage, to be completed by 1972, comprised thirty three thousand dwellings, a third of the total in the inner city. Allocations policy was changed to give priority to rehousing people from slums and the whole programme of clearance and redevelopment controlled by computer.

The slum clearance programme brought fifteen years of increasing upheaval for inner city communities in Liverpool. The Council's intentions were benevolent but firm. Undeniably, the living conditions of thousands of people were improved dramatically by rehousing in new council tenancies. But by 1971 there was a growing reaction against slum clearance for a number of different reasons, concerned more with the methods used than the policy itself. The programme had, of necessity, been on a large scale, involving wide areas of up to a thousand dwellings. The legal procedures for making and confirming compulsory purchase orders, the time taken to rehouse all the residents of a clearance area after allowing them a choice of council tenancies and shortages of staff combined to create slippages in the computer programme so that for each clearance area the process from making the first decision to completing redevelopment was protracted over periods of years. There was a growing public rejection of high rise living in the blocks of flats which replaced the slums. Yet at the same time, up to a half of the residents of clearance areas wanted to be rehoused close to their former homes. Towards the end of stage 1, too, the very worst slums had been cleared and people were less eager to be rehoused than had previously been the case.

This disillusionment came to a head as the time drew near to embark on the second stage of the original clearance programme. At the same time the 1969 Housing Act introduced the concept of general improvement areas and grants for the improvement of older private dwellings. The City Council accordingly reassessed its housing programme in 1971. The changes include a much smaller clearance programme; areas where standard grants only would be paid for improvement in the expectation that the dwellings had only ten to fifteen years' effective life; and a full improvement programme based on the declaration of general improvement areas and the payment of larger grants for houses with at least thirty years' life. This was the policy illustrated for Lodge Lane East in figure 38 on page 132.

To some extent the 1971 policy acted as a self fulfilling policy. It achieved results: some fifteen thousand houses were improved between 1970 and 1975; general improvement areas were declared. But the residents and landlords of properties in the limited life areas did not feel encouraged to invest in their homes. Physical conditions in the remaining clearance areas deteriorated very rapidly even though firm dates had not been fixed for their demolition. By 1974, the housing policy once more was to be reviewed, part of the stimulus once more being new legislation, the 1974 Housing Act.

The period of massive slum clearance is over and many of its lessons have been learned. But its consequences are still a reality in inner Liverpool. The cleared sites of slums still awaiting redevelopment is one; the legacy of distrust and alienation, expressed in the growth of community action is another. We shall return to these in chapter ten. But a third consequence has wider implications for it can affect the new policy of improvement described below, and could well have lessons for the future should clearance once more become a necessary policy. This is the conflict engendered by large scale, yet intricate programmes of the kind attempted in the 1960s, bringing together a complex jigsaw of clearance and redevelopment, resources and time. The conflict lies between the strong, central control thought necessary for the implementation of such programmes and the interest and concern of the individual people and families affected by the programmes. At its peak, precedence was given to achieving the programme and the local authority acted in effect with benevolent despotism. Whether it could have succeeded in carrying through the clearance and redevelopment programme in a manner which respected the wishes and needs of all the individuals affected is open to question. It had started with a genuine wish on the part of many to be rehoused for their living conditions were intolerable. But in fact, it proved so difficult to carry out the programme efficiently that, for the people living in the clearance areas, the problems of remoteness and centralised control were made far worse by delay and uncertainty.

Improving the older private housing

The 1974 Housing Act reinforced the change in direction of housing policy nationally away from slum clearance towards the improvement of the remaining older private stock of houses. It added two new concepts, housing action areas and priority neighbourhoods, to the general improvement areas introduced five years earlier. So, in 1974–75, a fresh survey was made of the remaining stock of pre-1919 houses in Liverpool and a new housing policy was approved by the City Council following public consultation on a draft policy.[1] The new policy

(1) *Housing Renewal Policies: Revised Proposals for Improvement and Clearance of Older Private Housing in Liverpool*, Report of the Chief Executive to the Housing Building and Planning Committee February 1976.

contained five categories of action affecting the total stock of eighty two thousand dwellings.

55	new, small clearance areas (and the remaining stage one clearance programme)	6,150 dwellings
22	housing action areas	4,800 dwellings
3	priority neighbourhoods	1,320 dwellings
13	new general improvement areas (and the already declared general improvement areas)	5,230 dwellings
	the remainder, where full improvement grants would be made available	64,500 dwellings

**Figure 39
Housing renewal
policy 1976**

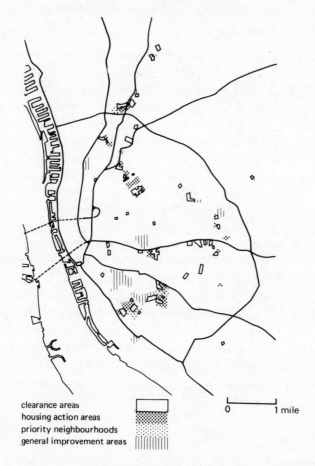

clearance areas
housing action areas
priority neighbourhoods
general improvement areas

0   1 mile

A section of these proposals for Lodge Lane East is illustrated in figure 38 on page 132. Under this policy, the local authority proposed taking direct action by the declaration of clearance or improvement areas covering a fifth of the older housing stock. Initially, in the remaining four fifths, the initiative for improving their houses would come from owner occupiers, landlords and housing associations making applications for grant. However, in principle, this is only the first stage of what is intended eventually to become a rolling programme for action.

The local authority's powers to clear and rebuild unfit housing are contained in the 1957 Housing Act. The real impetus for improvement, including the declaration of general improvement areas, is in the 1969 Housing Act. The 1974 Act was designed to deal with houses in the uncertain class between those for which clearance is the best course of action and those which, possibly with the help of the powers for declaring general improvement areas, can be effectively improved. Housing action areas were intended to be small areas of housing stress where intensive short term action could make conditions acceptable for some years; while the priority neighbourhoods were to be adjacent stress areas where no immediate intensive action was possible but certain powers were available to stop the spread of housing stress. The Act also strengthened the powers of housing associations, to help them to replace the private rented sector as an alternative to owner occupation or council renting.

Housing action areas were set up in areas where physical and social factors combined and interacted to create housing stress. A Department of Environment circular[1] suggested broad criteria which included areas of large dwellings and small households, with multiple occupation and shared facilities; low income and high unemployment leading to disrepair in some dwellings; areas where clearance would result in rehousing some people away from the area for lack of local decanting accommodation; areas where the prevalence of privately rented accommodation meant that improvement would be to the disadvantage of residents; and areas of low demand and unattractive surroundings where houses were being abandoned. Housing action areas were expected to contain between two and three hundred houses. Priority neighbourhoods were to be declared for adjoining areas, either concurrently with declaring a housing action area or shortly afterwards.

By these criteria a high proportion of the older housing stock in Liverpool could be said to suffer from housing stress and required action of the kind envisaged in the 1974 Act. Physical obsolescence was widespread, a high proportion of the housing being in poor repair, lacking amenities and rented unfurnished from private landlords. In many areas too, unemployment was high by London standards. The most severe housing stress was found only in small pockets in the rooming house areas characterised by multi-occupation, sharing of facilities, very high levels of unemployment and family and social problems.

In Liverpool the local authority has had to make a realistic appraisal of likely staff and financial resources, and concentrate only on those areas of housing which would require clearance if no action is taken immediately. The Chief Executive's report stated

> 'it cannot be over-emphasised that the current package is, of necessity, limited, dealing only with the very worst housing. If an impact is not made . . . within the next few years there will be no alternative left but total demolition.'[2]

He emphasised that even the proposed programme could not be achieved with the

(1) *Housing Action Areas, Priority Neighbourhoods and General Improvement Areas*, Department of the Environment Circular 14/75.

(2) See footnote reference, page 137.

existing levels of staff. But in choosing areas the Corporation would follow the Government's wish that, whatever the level of constraint on resources, priority should be given to the most difficult areas, even at the expense of other areas and services.[1] Staff appointments at the time of writing were being made for five area teams to cover the programme.

A further government circular attached great importance to the use of local housing associations to augment the resources available for tackling problem areas.[2] But the Chief Executive's report feared that national priorities would nevertheless lead to a major reduction in housing association activity. Nor would housing cooperatives be able to make a significant contribution. They have an important role in improving housing conditions in inner city areas but their limitations, described in the previous chapter, are such that they could not meet the scale of action required.

A further serious drawback is the low level of provision for environmental improvements. Grant-aided expenditure by a local authority on this can be no more than two hundred pounds per dwelling in general improvement areas, and fifty pounds in housing action areas, the Department of the Environment meeting half the cost in each. Yet our environmental care project showed substantially higher levels of expenditure would be needed on basic renewal of the environment, repair of back passageways, resurfacing of pavements, traffic management and environmental treatment and the like. The project itself gave figures of about two hundred pounds per dwelling in the proposed housing action area, and up to three hundred and fifty pounds per dwelling in the general improvement area. The difference in costs in the two types of area is a consequence of actual differences in their physical structure. But the low level of grants will not be sufficient to arrest decay.

In summary, therefore, there is a real danger that attention will be drawn away from the most important issue; the scale and nature of the effort required to create and maintain adequate modern living conditions in Liverpool's stock of older private housing. Housing associations and cooperatives can make a make a minor but important contribution to the effort required. But most of the burden will in the long run fall on local authorities, in carrying out improvements, administering grants, and in maintaining standards. In Liverpool, at least, staff resources appear to have been pushed to the limit in the proposals outline above. Although it is intended that these are the first stage in a rolling programme much will depend on how fast that programme can be implemented. The problems become particularly difficult as much of the action of necessity will be very local in scale, depending on the achievement of a partnership between the local authority, working through its area teams, and the local residents.

In the meantime, the future of the sixty four thousand pre-1919 houses not included in any of the priority categories must give cause for concern. Improvement grants

(1) *Housing Act 1974: Renewal Strategies*, Department of the Environment Circular 13/75.

(2) *Housing Cooperatives*, Department of the Environment Circular 8/76.

in these areas have been reduced from seventy five to fifty percent in the new legislation. This, in itself, will still further reduce the take-up of grants and accentuate the decay of housing which is at least sixty years old. Furthermore, the scale of expenditure required on environmental care, which should continue in parallel with housing improvement work, is very substantial. Without extra resources, the 1974 Housing Act will have little impact on much of the older private housing stock in Liverpool.

The management of council housing

Edge Hill Estates: A study in public neglect[1]

Some public housing in the inner area now provides living conditions worse than almost any in the private sector since the clearance of the worst slums. The blocks of three storey flats included in the housing maintenance project were built in the early 1950s to a design common to that period and repeated extensively on small sites throughout the inner areas. The basic layout is of blocks of six flats with access onto a common stair, and grouped around communal courtyards. Although structurally fairly sound and still providing reasonable living conditions, maintenance had been badly neglected; stairway windows were broken; paintwork was shabby and peeling; drains were blocked and kerbs damaged. There were also basic design faults, chiefly the lack of a clear demarcation between private, communal, and public areas, or definition of their function. There was no landscaping of any kind.

These few blocks were part of the densely packed area of council housing estates in the Edge Hill area chosen for the housing management project. Between them they contained about two thousand of the three thousand council tenancies in the study area; about one sixth of all those in the south city district. They contain examples of most ages and types of dwellings. Although the different types of housing are often close together, or separated only by a road or railway, they have no common identity. To some extent the distinctions are purely visual, the striking contrasts in architectural style, no linking landscape. But allocation policies

**Figure 40
Housing management project,
Edge Hill**

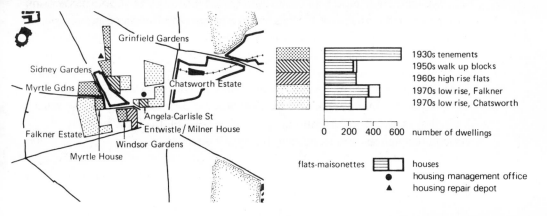

(1) This is described more fully in IAS Liverpool, *Housing Management* (Department of the Environment 1977); and *Housing Maintenance* (Department of the Environment 1976).

based on relative popularity reinforce architectural differences by contrasts in social structure.

Small households were a feature only of the high-rise blocks of Entwistle and Milner Heights, where they formed nearly three-quarters of the total. In contrast, large households were found everywhere except in these blocks. About a quarter of households in the tenement blocks and 1950s estates contained five or more people compared with an average for the city of less than one fifth. But most flats in these blocks are of two or three bedrooms. Consequently, serious overcrowding in the tenement blocks was found to be nearly three times the Liverpool average, and in the 1950s blocks, five times. Most of the overcrowding was among families with children. Over thirty percent of the population in the tenements and 1950s blocks consisted of children aged under fourteen, compared with eight percent in Liverpool as a whole. The low status of most of the area was confirmed by the very high proportion of unskilled workers, seventy percent in one block; and the degree of unemployment.

The oldest housing (six hundred and thirty eight dwellings excluding an empty block) consisted of four blocks of five-storey walk-up flats, the tenement blocks. There are now approximately six thousand of these flats left in Liverpool. They were built in the 1930s for slum clearance families to a grand and optimistic design. They were planned to have communal gardens. Some are elaborately terraced, others have great arched entrances to their courtyards. Each flat has its own balcony, often with built-in flower boxes. In some blocks, entrance to the flats is by gallery access, in others by separate stairways. They were the last stage of the development of model tenement dwellings which began in the first council house building in the late nineteenth century.

The tenements are usually now the lowest rung of the council housing ladder, difficult to let and so tend to be allocated to those on the waiting list with low priority, and to homeless families. Over the past two years, thirteen flats in one block have been let to homeless families. The rooms in each flat are small, although over half the flats are family sized. In the larger block, which has over three hundred flats and balcony access, thefts have been frequent and many of the tenants were convinced that their flat would be broken into whenever they went out. Some elderly tenants living alone preferred to have all their windows boarded up, rather than risk break-ins.

Consultation prior to the housing management project showed widespread dissatisfaction with the repairs service. The tenants complained that work was not done; the district office seemed unable to control or influence the repairs process; the maintenance depot was faced with a backlog of work; and the coding system on orders was too crude to distinguish any reasonable ordering of priorities. When the project started, many tenants were found to have been waiting weeks or months for repairs. The Dingle depot served the entire south city district of twelve thousand dwellings. Consequently, communication between tenants, management and depot was complex and tedious. Requests for repairs to the district office were put into a priority category which would mean, in theory, the

142

carrying out of the work within a guaranteed period. But this was done largely on the tenant's own assessment of urgency and without any reference to the complexity of the task or the work load of the depot. Nearly half of the orders were reminders or repeat orders.

Even the most casual observer on the estates could not have failed to notice the poor standard of general maintenance. Broken downspouts, missing roof tiles, rotted or broken bin store doors and gutters were commonplace. This state of dilapidation was too readily blamed on vandalism. Several factors in the organisation of maintenance militate against repairs being carried out. Undoubtedly shortage of resources was a major factor. But the less urgent repairs were given low priority and months could elapse before the work was done by the maintenance division. Many necessary repairs were never even ordered. Technical officers at the district office each covered an area with approximately five thousand dwellings; their first priority was to deal with vacant dwellings, and they were unable to cope with detailed faults on the estates. The other local officials, the housing area liaison officers, had other duties and usually were not able to initiate and chase up orders for repairs. In turn, tenants became demoralised and did not bother to report faults which would mean either writing or going to the district office and queueing at the repairs counter to get an order taken. The system of planned maintenance covered only those repairs identified at the time of external painting, every six or seven years.

The project area, like most inner city housing areas, had special problems which put additional pressure on the maintenance system. Crime and vandalism gave rise to a large number of urgent orders to secure dwellings after break-ins and to reglaze broken windows. Also the amount of work and the necessity to secure and sheet up vacant property quickly was greater than on quieter estates. The poverty and family circumstances of many tenants reduced their ability to do urgent jobs which other tenants might have done themselves (blocked sinks, plastering, door locks, reglazing). Dirty houses, although few in total, caused conflict. Some men would not work in them; yet management often wanted the work done to encourage the tenants to improve their standards.

One of the first priorities of the project, therefore, was to examine the repairs system and try to get some improvement. An opportunity arose of establishing a local sub-depot to serve the project area as part of a more general programme of reorganisation in the maintenance division. Only plumbers and joiners were employed there but other workers were available from the main depot. Although the size of the workforce in the sub-depot was no greater proportionately than elsewhere in the city, considerable benefits were felt almost immediately. The management team could contact the general foreman easily. Orders were made out in the knowledge of the state of the queue of orders at the sub-depot, thus avoiding giving unreasonable expectations to the tenants, in contrast with the priority system in operation at the district office.

The small geographical area cut down travelling time for the workmen and the frustration generated by tenants being out when the workmen called was reduced.

The small size of the group working at the sub-depot appeared to lead to increased morale and job satisfaction for the workmen. The project team members, who at the beginning of the project were in danger of being swamped by the amount of work caused by repairs, were soon able to give more time to other things, whilst still retaining control over the repairs.

The presence of a local office might have increased the demand on the repairs service and tenants who could not be bothered or could not get to the district office might have been more likely to report repairs to the local office. In practice, this does not appear to have been the case. It was estimated that one hundred and twenty to one hundred and thirty orders were issued weekly for the project area before the start of the project. The number issued from the project office, after an initial rise in the early weeks of opening, settled down to about the same figure. However, the number of reminders, or repeat orders, issued by the project office was running at less than twenty per week within two months of opening of the depot compared with fifty when the project began.

Major improvements are proposed for some of the blocks in the project area and demonstrate the difficulties facing tenant participation. In the past the improvement programme has always been managed on the basis of liaison between management and individual tenants. This has been successful in smoothing the progress of the work and reducing the upheaval for individual tenants. But to change from this approach to one of encouraging the tenants to take a more active part in deciding what work will be done, and how, would involve a complete change of attitude. Just how difficult this would be is indicated by a recent event in one tenement block. During the summer of 1975, environmental improvements were planned for the internal hallways and staircases of several local blocks as part of a city-wide programme. All tenants were invited by letter to attend a meeting so that they could be consulted by the officers concerned but only a handful turned up. At the meeting, officers explained to tenants what could be done but the choice of options was extremely narrow because of cost constraints. Work began shortly after the consultation, with no further opportunity for tenant involvement. The tenants were not particularly interested, at that stage, in the external space. Their priority was to have their flats improved. That there may have been technical and financial reasons why one thing was done before another does not alter the fact that the tenants' priorities did not coincide with those of the local authority.

Another great difficulty in encouraging tenant participation was the weakness and scarcity of tenants' associations in the project area. There were four local residents' associations, only one of which appeared to have a stable membership of any size, and none of which had the experience or will to take up direct involvement in management. The high turnover of tenancies (up to fourteen percent) in most of the area and the dissatisfaction which many tenants were known to have had with their own dwelling suggested that community interest was weak. The level of overcrowding which existed and the lack of opportunities for transfers had led to frustration. Half the tenants involved in the housing maintenance project had wanted to move. And the apathy and disillusionment generated by high levels of unemployment and concentrations of vulnerable families, coupled with extremely low environmental standards, formed the worst imaginable circumstances under which tenants might be more directly involved in the running of their estates.

Housing management in the inner areas

Housing officials, councillors and residents alike, confirmed that housing conditions in the project area were typical of other inner city council estates. But the project area lacked the scale and monotonous uniformity of the larger dockside council estates and also the particular type and intensity of problems associated with high density, high-rise maisonette blocks in Everton and Netherley. In addition, the quality of the surroundings, particularly in high density areas, can be as important as conditions inside the dwellings, and are often equally neglected. For example, the Environmental Health Department isolated over twenty separate items which needed attention in their environmental care trials in an area of council tenements near the south docks. These included litter, street cleaning, carriageway repairs, vacant land, derelict buildings, noise, atmospheric pollution, house repairs and street furniture.[1] The problem is the extent to which the local authority in Liverpool is capable of dealing with the decay of its older inner area estates and the complexity of their physical and social problems.

The Housing Management Division of the Housing Department deals with the administration of the waiting list and allocations; the management of council dwellings, including rent collection and planned maintenance, and the improvement programme in council housing. A separate Maintenance Division handles the day to day maintenance of all dwellings.

Housing management is decentralised into seven district offices, each responsible for approximately ten thousand dwellings, although the areas are at present under review. Each district manager is responsible for the implementation of policy in his district. Because the practice of estate management necessarily has to incorporate visible direction at a local level (all the sorts and conditions of men and their housing could never be completely legislated for) the district managers appear to people in their districts to be more powerful than is really the case. This view is often encouraged by councillors, some of whom send people to the district offices with requests that they should know are not within the managers' discretion. The district managers work in a web of constraints of differing strengths which cover both policy and procedure. Potentially, they have the strength to influence changes, but perhaps because of the differing characteristics of districts across the city, they do not appear to realise their corporate strength and tend each to relate strongly to the centre rather than to each other. The lack of a strong information system for the district managers also weakens their position. Although, through their joint management meetings and their contributions to committee reports, they are made aware of what is happening, they do not receive full copies of committee agendas, reports or city-wide information.

(1) Lees A M, *Environmental Care: The Raising of Environmental Standards* (City of Liverpool Environmental Health and Protection Department, 1971).

Although district officers have an area-based responsibility, it is only at the level of housing area liaison officers that the area covered is small enough and the responsibility general enough for any personal identification with tenants' problems. But the liaison officer's job description lists sixteen separate duties. Their main job is to develop contact between tenants and the district office and to help tenants with problems. But each is responsible for more than a thousand tenancies, and they have not sufficient status, time, or information to give sustained help to tenants or in any way influence policy from their local knowledge.

In the face of this weakness at the ground level of housing management, tenants tend to go first to the district office with their problems. The two inner area district offices are under extreme pressure. There are queues at the counters, each of which deals with a separate type of enquiry; rents, repairs, and general tenancy matters. Constant arguments appear to be in progress as tenants try to break the nerve of the counter staff. The apparatus of security grills and screens needed to protect rent money adds to the feeling of remoteness and mistrust. For those tenants who persevere at the public office or who write in, home visits or interviews with the liaison officer or one of the specialist staff will usually provide the advice and help needed. However, in these conditions it is doubtful if many tenants will seek advice during the early stages of a problem.

The average cost per dwelling of improving the communal areas in the maintenance project, excluding time spent consulting tenants and discounted over the Corporation's current planned maintenance period, was about double the normal level of expenditure. Part of the higher cost could be attributed to the small number of dwellings involved. But they were high mainly as a result of including items which ought to be done as part of planned maintenance, the attention to detail, the response to tenants' wishes and the completeness of the work, none of which are apparently achieved in current programmes.

Consultation with tenants' associations at city level is through the Amalgamated Tenants Associations Coordinating Committee (ATACC). This committee has representatives from fourteen tenants' associations of whom half are in the inner area, and helps to form new tenants' and residents' groups. Consultation with councillors takes place formally in a coordinating committee comprising ATACC and members of Housing Committee, and covers all aspects of housing management policy and practice. ATACC's main efforts have been in trying to establish tenants' rights (for instance, security of tenure), to gaining acceptance of a tenants' charter, and to strengthening its influence as a city-wide tenants' body. As yet, ATACC has shown little interest in promoting schemes for local tenant management. Rather, it believes that the council should use its resources to carry out properly its statutory obligations.

The estates with the most problems present the least favourable circumstances for tenant participation in management. Nevertheless, there could be some advantages to tenant involvement in the situation of decline found in the pre-war tenement blocks. For if tenant participation could be used as a vehicle for placing decision-making at a level which is comprehensible to tenants and directly related to the particular needs of a single black of flats, it may be possible to retain housing which would otherwise almost certainly continue to decline until demolition was the only possible choice. But it is clear that this would not become possible without the local authority better meeting its own part of the landlord/tenant agreements. The events described in chapter four on page 53 amounted virtually to an avoidance of responsibility by the local authority. It would be unfortunate if well-meaning attempts at tenant participation came to be seen as, in effect, an evasion of responsibility. Neither significant improvements in living conditions in the worst inner council estates, nor any well-founded opportunities for tenant participation can be created without major changes in allocations policy and in the level and methods of management; and these must be the responsibility of the local authority.

9 Growing up in the inner city

Work and training

Getting a job[1]

Leaving school is one of the most crucial times in any young person's life. But getting a job or training when leaving school in Liverpool is more difficult than anywhere else in the country. Currently Liverpool has more young people out of work than any other city in the country, over six thousand in the summer peak of 1976. Chapter five showed that unqualified school leavers were most at risk of being unemployed or being forced to accept very low-grade, unskilled work. While high levels of youth unemployment were found throughout the city, over twenty five percent in many areas, young people in the inner areas left school earlier, gained fewer qualifications, had fewer training opportunities, faced a lower grade of job and changed jobs more frequently than elsewhere in the city.

The Employment Training Act of 1973 obliged local authorities to provide a careers service for young people. At the same time those under eighteen were given a choice of registering for unemployment at either the Careers Service or the Employment Services Agency (ESA); and the Careers Service was relieved of the duty of paying unemployment benefits. The role of the Careers Service is to provide careers guidance to young people, to place them in their first job, and to offer assistance at a later date if requested. The Liverpool service is currently organised in five area teams, the two inner area teams operating from headquarters just north of the city centre.

Careers officers spend something over half of their time giving vocational guidance in schools to those in their last year, as much as a full day each week in many schools, especially those in the poorer districts. They aimed to interview each pupil in his final year, and in this they were largely successful, although a quarter of those in our Edge Hill school leavers' survey said they had not seen a careers officer. Of those who had, more than half said they had not found the interview helpful, in the majority of cases, because of lack of time.

The service thought that careers provision in the inner area schools needed improvement. Few schools had a well maintained information display and library facilities; even some with good reputations fell short of adequate careers instruction. Only two of the fifteen secondary schools in our study area had a full time careers teacher, although a further nine did have a part time one. The majority of teachers interviewed felt that attaining the standards set in Department of Education and Science guidelines was probably the limit of what could be expected

(1) This subject is discussed more fully in IAS Liverpool, *Getting a Job: The Training and Placement of Young People* (Department of the Environment 1977).

of the schools without placing undue pressure on the curriculum.[1] However, several head teachers and a majority of those interviewed in the school leavers' survey thought the schools should do more to prepare pupils for the realities of poor job prospects and social security.

Jobs are found for approximately a third of school leavers in Liverpool, although this figure would be increased considerably if account were taken of all cases where officers had put young people in touch with the employers. The placement rate has tended to be slightly higher for more skilled jobs and statutory age leavers. But of the Edge Hill school leavers only twenty two percent found their first job through the service, compared with thirteen percent who contacted employers directly and eleven percent through advertisements. Most of those in the group interviews got their first jobs through friends or by going round local firms.

Although the Careers Service recognised that some groups of people had particular difficulties, it claimed it could do little for them. There was no attempt to allocate resources systematically to areas of high unemployment or to concentrate attention on particular schools. Instead a limited number of experimental schemes had been run from time to time, in particular Out of School, Out of Work courses at further education colleges and outward bound schools. However these special initiatives were very limited and the Careers Service was sceptical of their value. They had not succeeded in getting through to some of the more difficult unemployed young people, amongst whom they claim there is resistance to training or any form of further education which is far stronger than that found elsewhere in the country.

The Careers Service makes its greatest effort in the schools, and gives a limited amount of advice to all school leavers in the city. To this end, its structure and organisation differ little from that in other parts of the country, despite the exceptionally large numbers of young unemployed in Liverpool, concentrated among those with few qualifications. It is thus difficult either to give special assistance in the schools to those likely to have employment problems later, or to pay special attention subsequently to young people who become unemployed in the first two or three years of their working life.

Now that young people can make use of ESA facilities they can apply for vacancies advertised in a job centre, or, where no suitable position is available, be interviewed by an employment expert, or referred to an occupational guidance expert. The Liverpool Job Centre in Leece Street has a youth section, with a separate youth register and an employment officer. However, this does not replicate the vocational advice of the Careers Service, and the employment officer has no specific training and experience for dealing with young people. At present, the impact of the ESA is marginal. For instance the Youth Employment Officer at Leece Street was, in 1975–76, achieving no more than five placements a week on average, despite having access to a wider range of vacancies than the Careers Service. Young people

(1) Department of Education and Science Education Survey No.18, *Careers Education in Secondary Schools* (HMSO 1973).

in the group interviews which we carried out were very critical. They felt that customers were treated in a very impersonal way; the staff did not try to match the person to the job; the method of sending people to jobs was inefficient and often involved inaccurate information; and the jobs on offer were low-paying and dull. One of the groups said:

> 'the Employment Exchange never tries to find out what you're good at or what would suit you. They just send you anywhere. So you can often take a job that's unsuitable because you need it, and so you soon jack it in. When you go back on the dole they want to know why you left the job.'[1]

In general, ESA policy has been to avoid detailed discussion with applicants concerning personal or domestic matters. These are considered irrelevant to placement, and cannot be properly understood by employment officers who are trained only in counselling and interviewing techniques. Furthermore, the weight of recent reforms within ESA has been in the direction of 'a policy of letting economic and accounting considerations override any others.'[2] Providing above all a service to employers represents a change from the original concept of the service of bringing assistance to the unemployed.

South Liverpool Personnel provides an example of an independent employment agency set up to represent the interest of a certain group. About half of their clients were black, eighty percent of them Liverpool born. The operation is a relatively small and localised one. In 1972 and 1973 an average of four applications per week were received, although this varied widely from almost nil in the autumn to eight or ten towards the end of the school year. Virtually all the clients were under twenty five years old and three quarters came from Liverpool 8 or surrounding districts. The agency identifies strongly with the interests and attitudes of its clients, most of the staff being past clients of the agency. The work extends beyond a straightforward placement service and includes personal counselling, representation on tribunals and help with social security problems.

Training opportunities

The availability of apprenticeships is of central importance to boys leaving school, especially to those with less than five O levels for whom clerical jobs will not normally be open. For this group there are very few other opportunities for jobs offering any well organised training. The situation is less serious for girls: even though the number of apprenticeships is very small, confined virtually to hairdressing, there is a much greater supply of clerical jobs with some opportunity for acquiring skills.

Between seven hundred and a thousand boys a year take up apprenticeships in Liverpool. The number of places shows strong cyclical fluctuations, but has been diminishing overall, declining by half between 1966 and 1973, the last year for

---

(1) Interview reported in IAS Liverpool, *No one from Liverpool 8 Need Apply* (unpublished discussion paper 1975).

(2) Hill M J *et al*, *Men Out of Work* (Cambridge 1973).

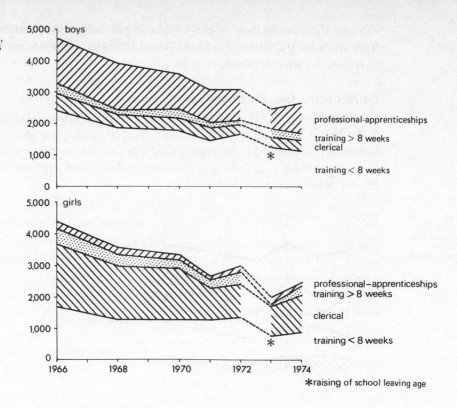

Figure 41
First jobs entered,
Liverpool 1966–74

boys

- professional–apprenticeships
- training > 8 weeks
- clerical
- training < 8 weeks

girls

- professional–apprenticeships
- training > 8 weeks
- clerical
- training < 8 weeks

1966 1968 1970 1972 1974

∗raising of school leaving age

which complete figures are available. They are concentrated in the engineering, metal goods, construction and distribution trades. Their volume, rightly in the view of the Training Services Agency (TSA), is governed by the existing and foreseen needs of industry in the area. But apprenticeships have disappeared from declining sectors of industry, and not been replaced by new firms coming to the area. A graphic illustration is provided by the closure of the English Electric, Netherton plant, which took some eighty apprenticeships a year; but the motor industry, one of the growing sectors in Merseyside in the last ten years, takes few apprentices. New apprenticeships have been located in the new industrial estates and new towns but these are not easily accessible to residents of inner Liverpool.

The quality of training offered through apprenticeships has been improved considerably as a result of the Industrial Training Act 1964. Industrial Training Boards have encouraged the establishment of systematic programmes, often involving initial periods at college for off-the-job training, followed by planned job experience and periods back at college. They have also acted as the stimulus for Group Training Schemes for smaller firms. For example the Merseyside Training Council was set up in 1962 to provide and promote training in the engineering industry. By 1967 they had some two thousand five hundred apprentices. Until 1968, first year off-the-job apprentice training was carried out either by large companies or Colleges of Further Education. The Speke Training Centre, built to replace these courses, was then the most advanced in the country and provided one hundred and fifty places. A second centre has since been built at Bootle. The Construction Industry Training Board works in a similar way to the Merseyside Training Council. It oversees the training of one hundred and fifty apprentices, although in this case they receive their off-the-job training at colleges. Apprentices receive help from specialist training staff, and the Board attempts to place those laid off at times of recession with other firms.

Careers Service records show that only about a third of boys leaving school obtain apprenticeships. This is lower than the national proportion, and is much less than in the North West region where the high rate reflects its predominantly industrial structure. The demand for apprenticeships far exceeds the numbers available, which vary considerably each year with economic cycles so that applicants have a better chance of being taken on in a good year.

**Figure 42
Take up of
apprenticeships,
Merseyside
Training Council
1968–74**

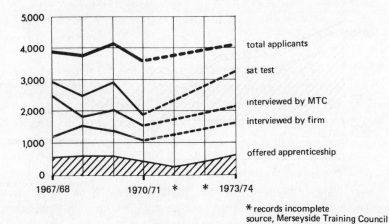

* records incomplete
source, Merseyside Training Council

Records kept by the Merseyside Training Council show that demand far exceeds supply. The number of new apprenticeships in 1973–74 was only six hundred and thirty from an application list of four thousand of whom over half went forward for interview having passed the preliminary tests. A firm manufacturing printing equipment in inner Liverpool received two hundred applications in one year but had only three places available. Similarly, Plessey, a major inner area employer, receives approximately four hundred applications each year for apprentice training. In a normal year they offer around thirty places; in 1975, it was only three.

In these circumstances many who would be able to find an apprenticeship almost anywhere else in the country fail in Liverpool. A recent survey of youth employment[1] concluded that, while the most able boys have as good a chance of obtaining an apprenticeship in less prosperous areas as elsewhere, many of the less qualified fail in their efforts. This is certainly true of Liverpool. Employers have a wide choice of candidates and can pick out the best. The requirement for O levels is steadily increasing and many academically qualified young people end up looking for semi-skilled or unskilled jobs and thus make the position of the unqualified even more difficult. Given the low academic performance and early school leaving in inner areas relatively few boys find their way into apprenticeships. A quarter of the Edge Hill school leavers had taken apprentice or equivalent training. In Vauxhall only six percent had taken an apprenticeship. The Merseyside Training Council and the Construction Industry Board said they had taken only a

(1) National Youth Employment Council, *Unqualified, Untrained and Unemployed* (HMSO 1974).

very limited number of apprentices from Liverpool 8. Furthermore no firm interviewed in our industrial survey employed a black apprentice, despite their being in the area where most black people lived and between them employing more than two hundred apprentices.

One paradoxical result of the decline in numbers of apprenticeships in Liverpool has been that training places have gone unfilled. The one hundred and fifty training places at Speke Training Centre were all taken up between 1968 and 1970. Since then, they have often been difficult to fill, and in 1972, only eighty four places were taken by employers, some of the remainder being taken by people on TSA apprentice award schemes. Some courses providing the off-the-job planned training at colleges of further education were no more than half full at the beginning of 1976.

Liverpool has benefited from a recent attempt to reduce the impact of cyclical factors by providing a number of government financed apprenticeships in years when the number of private places fell. This apprentice award scheme was first instituted in 1971. It enabled thirty apprentices to be taken on by Merseyside Training Council and placed at Speke for the initial forty eight week training; and a number of others to go to technical colleges. The scheme met the full cost of first year apprenticeships, and placed trainees with employers for subsequent training. It worked well, and all apprentices from Speke were placed. Plans have been made to reintroduce the scheme in 1976 with sixty places at Speke, and a further thirty in employers' establishments with associated day release.

A similar scheme operates in the construction industry under the aegis of CITB, and has been established on a semi-permanent basis in view of the collapse of apprenticeship and planned training schemes in the industry. Of the twenty seven apprenticeships taken on without sponsors in 1974, twenty three had been placed with firms to finish their training by the beginning of 1976. The 1976 intake has been considerably enlarged, and it is likely that over a third of the one hundred and fifty apprentices taken on will be award boys. A small, private initiative has recently been taken by the John Moores Trust so that training may be given to five young people each year; mainly from disadvantaged or minority communities from inner city areas. The results to date are rather mixed but it is too early to draw any firm conclusions.

Opportunities in Liverpool for non apprentice training are even more limited. Only seven percent of boys and eleven percent of girls in 1972 entered jobs with planned training of more than eight weeks. Both proportions in Liverpool were lower than the corresponding national ones. However little information is available about the quality of the training offered. That for boys was chiefly in electrical engineering, construction, distribution and public administration; and for girls in textiles, leather goods, clothing and footwear.

The only other planned training available for young people is provided through Short Industrial Courses organised by TSA at employers' establishments. These are necessary because there is a minimum age of nineteen and a half for admission to the Training Opportunities Scheme (TOPS) offered at skillcentres and further education colleges. The Short Industrial Courses last for thirteen weeks and give trainees an introduction to a broad area of work and to work discipline. On Merseyside they are currently run at Plessey, English Electric, Unit Construction and Cammell Laird, among other firms. The majority of applicants are unemployed and the courses apparently do improve a young person's chances of finding a job. However, many people have failed to complete the courses and there is a need for more personal support and advice than is currently provided. Between five hundred and six hundred places are provided on these courses in a year, mainly for young people. There is a waiting list.

A recent TSA discussion paper[1] gave detailed attention to induction training for young people at their place of work. At present it is usually limited to a general talk and a tour of the work place. Too often it is seen merely as a way of providing the new entrant with only what he has to know to become an effective worker as quickly as possible. The paper asserts that as many as sixty percent of all new entrants to the labour force below skill level receive little or no training from their employers. The TSA considers

> 'that properly conceived vocational preparation would raise substantially the ability of many ... young workers ... The importance of "learning to learn" things relevant to work would help them to adapt to change more readily and therefore work more effectively throughout their lives. Proper training for young people would in fact raise the whole potential of the workforce.'

The TSA considered that proper induction and basic vocational training was unlikely to be forthcoming under existing institutional management. It therefore proposed the introduction of gateway courses, to a recognised national standard, available to all young people as pre-entry courses, or as part of initial training given by an employer. No information was collected about the availability or standards of induction training in Liverpool. However, of the young people in the Edge Hill survey not taking apprenticeships, less than twenty percent were attending further education, and a large proportion complained of the inadequacy of their initial introduction to work.

Despite extremely high levels of youth unemployment, there is very little special provision for young people out of work in Liverpool. However three special schemes have recently been developed: Community Industry, the Wider Opportunities Scheme, and the Job Creation Programme. Community Industry was established by the National Association of Youth Clubs in 1971 but is now largely financed by the Department of Employment. Projects undertaken by Community Industry need to be those which would not otherwise get done and which are of value to the community. Work in Liverpool has included decorating, working in play groups, helping in theatres, helping community groups with their administration and supervising exercises with spina bifida children. The primary aim of Community Industry is to employ youngsters who would not otherwise find work and, through

(1) Training Services Agency, *Vocational Preparation for Young People* (1975).

a realistic work situation, prepare them for other jobs. The method appears to work. Few leave or are dismissed and the young people may stay as long as they like, although they are encouraged to move when a suitable opportunity for work is found. Individual counselling is built into the scheme and each employee's progress is reviewed quarterly. Although one hundred and fifty places were available in Liverpool in 1975, demand exceeded supply. Current estimates are that this number could be quadrupled from existing sources alone. The majority of those leaving Community Industry take up semi-skilled work in industry and commerce. A few have been placed in apprenticeships, and some go on to further education.

The second project open to the young unemployed was the Wider Opportunities Scheme. Experimental courses were organised by TSA, one of them at the Aintree Skillcentre offering about twenty places, the majority for young people. They were aimed at the unemployed; adults and young people with little clear aptitude or known preference for a particular occupation; and those with literacy or numeracy problems or who had difficulty in dealing with people or getting on in work. The courses were intended to develop the participants' self-confidence and awareness of their own capacities, rather than to train in specific occupational skills. Placing those completing courses has been difficult. Adults have progressed to full skills courses, but these are not open to people under nineteen and a half. Thus many young people have returned to the unemployment register. It has also been difficult to find the right kind of instructor, able to communicate skills and act as a good counsellor. The course at Aintree is relatively inaccessible to many parts of Liverpool with severe unemployment problems.

The Job Creation Programme announced by the Manpower Services Commission in September 1975 aimed to support labour intensive projects, particularly for young people, in areas of high unemployment. Wherever possible, the jobs were intended to provide some vocational training and be linked to appropriate forms of further education. The programme was intended to be a temporary measure, to provide short term jobs. Individual proposals for projects were made by a variety of sponsors including local authorities, other public bodies, private firms, voluntary organisations and community groups. The projects were sifted by a local committee on Merseyside. Early in 1976 a total of one thousand five hundred and forty six jobs had been created in Liverpool of which one thousand two hundred and seventy two were for young people.

At present training opportunities for young people on Merseyside depend not on an intelligent assessment of labour needs over a period, but the annual fluctuations of regional or even local economies which reflect its historic industrial structure. In Liverpool where there is an endemic weakness in the whole economy opportunities for training are correspondingly reduced. But suitable training should be available as of right, as in higher and further education, to those who are capable of completing it. Control over the supply of training places to fit the demands of industry should be done nationally and over a long period, free from the direct control of individual employers or the immediate fortunes of the local economy. The arguments that such an approach produces too many graduates and

156

would do the same for skilled manpower are not easy to sustain. With skill comes adaptability. Workers with basic skills are more likely to be prepared to retrain or move than those without. Raising the general level of skill in the work force as a whole needs to be seen as an investment which can in itself stimulate economic activity.

Many young people in Liverpool have for too long been forced into low grade, badly paid and unskilled jobs because they have not had the opportunity to acquire any skills. But the ability to compete for training opportunities is impaired by the failure of many to obtain suitable qualifications at school. A vicious circle is set up: shortage of jobs and training opportunities affects attitudes to school and examinations, and so on. We must now look to the earlier years of full time education. Our discussion in this field is necessarily more tentative as we carried out no action project or research but draw on the finding of others.

Education

Educational priority

It is now widely accepted that influences other than the school have the greatest impact on educational attainment. A great deal of experiment and analysis has been carried out in America.[1] The Coleman Report found that in order of importance, the factors which most affected attainment were neighbourhood and home background; characteristics of fellow pupils; and characteristics of the school, including teacher quality, curriculum content and physical facilities. These findings were confirmed by Jencks who also took into account the effects of heredity, environment and economic status. He concluded that, of the three, heredity had the most impact on attainment, followed closely by the home and school environment and the influence of other children. Economic status was found to make only a very small impression.

The research in Britain being conducted by the National Children's Bureau[2] has shown that children's attainments in reading and arithmetic are lower for those from large families, from households where the wage earner is an unskilled worker, from single parent families and from families who live in overcrowded conditions or who lack basic amenities in the home. Other factors which also appeared to affect attainment were the interest taken by the parent in the child's education, and whether the child's mother was working after the child went to school.

A Labour Party document on the deprived child[3] refers to the importance of pre-school education in removing children temporarily from a home environment which may be devoid of stimulus culturally and physically. It refers also to class

(1) Coleman J S, *et al*, *Equality of Educational Opportunity* (Government Printing Office, Washington DC 1966); and Jencks C, *Inequality* (Peregrine Books 1975).

(2) Davie R, Butler N and Goldstein H, *From Birth to Seven* (National Children's Bureau and Longmans 1972).

(3) *The Deprived Child* (Labour Party Research Department 1973).

divisions in language whereby middle class children are aware through books of the vocabulary of literary language as well as the colloquial speech which may be the sole achievement of the working class child. Middle class children are already familiar with the formal language required of them at school. Working class children with few toys, little space and busy parents face early disadvantages.

Chapter four showed the inner areas of Liverpool to be the low status part of a basically working class city and an increasing polarisation of social class between rich and poor areas. And chapter five showed concentrations in certain parts of the inner areas of those whose children would be most likely to fail at school; large and single parent families, unskilled workers, those in poor quality, overcrowded housing. It was a recognition of disadvantages associated with family and neighbourhood which prompted the Plowden Committee's recommendations for programmes of educational priority which would concentrate on specific deprived areas.

The Liverpool EPA experiment which ran from 1968–71 covered a large part of inner Liverpool, although not all the schools were included.[1] A particular contribution was alternative teaching material for inner city schools and the fostering of links with the community. The Liverpool team concluded that in EPA schools the balance of curriculum should change from academic to social, be based on the realities of the immediate environment, and that there should be an increase in the time spent on creative pursuits involving the parents. They also thought that social and environmental studies should concentrate on skills rather than information and that teaching attitudes and the atmosphere in schools needed to change. The main legacy of the Liverpool project has been the continuation of the EPA programme itself, and its extension and adoption in other schools and other parts of the city. In addition the Priority Centre was set up to continue work started by the EPA team. And the first community school in Liverpool is now operating in Netherley, a new council estate on the outskirts of the city.

The extension of positive discrimination and the associated social priority programmes to schools elsewhere in Liverpool is a realistic one. It reflects the widespread occurrence across the city of many of the social characteristics associated with low achievement. However, it seems unlikely that the slightly higher level of expenditure in EPA schools on staffing and materials alone can compensate for the extra amounts that richer families can spend on books or games equipment for their children, let alone for the disadvantages of poverty and overcrowding. The Plowden Committee recommended too that all EPA schools should make sufficient provision for nursery education to allow all children between four and five to attend part time and half of them full time.[2] American experience in the Head Start compensatory pre-schooling programme suggested that a slight initial advantage had disappeared by the end of the first year of school.[3] But parents face real difficulties in bringing up children in cramped

(1) Midwinter E, *Priority Education: an Account of the Liverpool Project* (Penguin Books 1972).

(2) Central Advisory Council for Education (England), *Children and Their Primary Schools* (1967).

(3) Jencks C, *Inequality* (Peregrine Books 1975).

houses on low incomes and the value of play group and nursery school as an opportunity for social contact for children and a break for mothers should not be minimised. However, it needs to be seen as a preparation for school for parents and children alike, in which parents should be involved as actively as possible.

At primary school, formal education starts to becomes more important than social contact and it is at this stage that many parents who lack confidence, are overworked, or who failed at school themselves, start to feel they have little or nothing to contribute to their children's education. A recent survey suggested that an apparent lack of interest in school by many parents was caused by their assumption that all responsibility for their children's education now lay with the school. They felt that they would be interfering if they went to the school uninvited; and lacked the confidence to have a satisfactory discussion with the teachers if they went.[1]

School achievement

Some figures of educational achievement were obtained during the course of our area resource analysis and in the City Planning Department's social malaise study. In 1974 the percentage of fourth year primary children in District D with verbal reasoning quotients less than ninety was fifty percent, compared with thirty eight percent in the city as a whole, which itself scored badly against the rest of the country.[2] The social malaise study showed concentrations of educationally subnormal children in parts of the inner areas, particularly the wards forming a tight ring around the city centre. In the two areas of most extreme social malaise, the inner council estates and the worst parts of the rooming house area, both educational subnormality and low reading ability were found to be between one and a half and two times the city average.

Children from District D took up seven percent of secondary school places in the city in 1974. But they formed only five percent of those taking CSEs, two percent of those taking O levels and one percent of those taking A levels. In that year only thirteen children from the district with a population of sixty thousand sat A levels. Over half the Edge Hill school leavers had left school without taking any O levels or CSEs.

The figures show that levels of formal educational achievement in at least this part of inner Liverpool were substantially below the average for the city. In a sense, they were predictable, given the importance attached to the home environment and social characteristics of the catchment areas from which the schools draw their pupils. The consequences are serious, for employers place an ever increasing emphasis on academic achievement and, in a declining labour market, are able to pick and choose those school leavers with the highest qualifications. The social

(1) Morton-Williams R and Finch S, *Young School Leavers: Report of an Enquiry carried out for the Schools Council by the Government Social Survey* (HMSO 1968).

(2) IAS Liverpool, *Area Resource Analysis District D Tables 1973–74* (Department of the Environment 1976). The verbal reasoning quotient was a national test, standardised so that the average score was one hundred and that twenty five percent of children would score less than ninety.

polarisation of the city referred to in chapter four creates single class schools, primary and comprehensive secondary alike, which still further reinforce the importance of the social factors and home environment referred to earlier. Formerly, a few children of real ability would overcome the difficulties, gaining admission to one of the city's grammar or direct grant schools. Now, parents who are ambitious for their children and able to choose where to live take great pains to select neighbourhoods where their children can attend schools with a good academic record.

Further education

Higher educational achievement is strongly associated with social status. In parts of the high status area in outer Liverpool those with HNC or degrees formed up to one third of the population, nearly three times the city average. This compared with less than one percent in some of the inner council estates. Not only is achievement lowest in further education in the inner areas but also participation. The social malaise study showed the take up of higher education grants from the inner area wards to be about half the average for the city.[1]

An analysis of college records showed that twelve hundred residents of Liverpool 7 and 8 enrolled in Liverpool colleges of further education in 1974–75, forming seven percent of the city total. Yet these two postal districts contained about fifteen percent of the city's population.

One in five of those from Liverpool 7 and 8 who enrolled in colleges in 1974 were on full time courses, mainly academic subjects for which previous qualification was necessary, about a quarter of them O level courses. Only five percent of those on full time courses were on secondment from employers, but of the large majority taking part time courses, over half were already employed. The Edge Hill school leavers' survey gave a similar result in which two thirds of those taking further education courses were sent by employers. Having a job is clearly an important motivation in taking up further education, whether from personal impetus or pressure from the employer.

Altogether one third of the Liverpool 7 and 8 residents were taking courses which required no previous educational qualifications. The majority of these were taking vocational subjects which would better equip them for a job, for example, typing or catering. Others were trying to gain qualifications which they did not get at school. Central College, which specialised in O and A level courses and also had a pre-TOPS course, had fourteen percent of its intake from the study area, near whose boundary it lay.

The low take up of adult and further education not only reflects the under achievement at school but, like it, has its causes in the home and social environment. But other factors are at work. It becomes increasingly difficult both intellectually and financially to take up courses long after leaving school. A full

(1) Amos F J C, *Social Malaise in Liverpool* (City Planning Department 1970).

grant is not awarded to people under eighteen for full time college courses in subjects which could have been taken at school. The local authority has the discretion to award small grants but these compare unfavourably even with social security. However, special grants are available for those on courses sponsored by the Training Services Agency. Furthermore, the strong social pressures to leave school early are themselves partly financial. In addition, many young people had been bored or disillusioned by their school experience. The opinion of many of the two thirds of the Edge Hill school leavers who had not taken any kind of further education was that school had 'turned them off' and that further academic training should be part of work.

However, efforts by the Workers Educational Association and Educational Priority have shown that interest among those not normally expected to participate can be stimulated by varying the content and organisation of courses in response to local differences.[1] As a result, nearly a quarter of the WEA enrolment in 1974 came from Liverpool 7 and 8. In addition, a number of special projects have been run in inner Liverpool, for instance the adult literacy project started by the Liverpool University of Settlement and a community workers' course at the Institute of Extension Studies at Liverpool University.

The Adult Education Centre described in chapter three is another initiative designed to test whether attitudes to further education can be changed, principally serving Liverpool born blacks who appeared to be particularly alienated. Those applying to the centre were predominantly young men from the locality, about half of whom were black. Over half were unemployed, and slightly less than half wanted full time courses, most of the remainder being available for evening classes only. Two thirds of the group had left school at fifteen, and over two thirds had no educational qualifications. A quarter wanted English language classes and a further third academic subjects, usually at O level standard. Thus the clients were a group who had largely missed out on school and jobs and who would not usually have taken part in adult education in a formal setting, especially one where basic skills were assumed. Yet, within six months, forty people had been helped to start on training courses at colleges and a further two hundred had attended one of the centre's own courses. These included a full time pre-O level course set up in conjunction with Central College and the Training Services Agency.

The Russell Report advocated an area office approach to the provision of further education.[2] But whether the example of the Adult Education Centre could have wider application is difficult to assess. It is unique in that it caters for, and advocates on behalf of, a highly localised group with particular problems. Similar schemes in other areas, equally well tailored to local life styles and attitudes of small, identifiable groups might be equally successful. But it is likely that more fundamental changes in the content and provision of further education as currently practised would be required if it is to reach a significant working class audience quite apart from minority and deprived communities.

(1) Lovett T, *Adult Education, Community Development and the Working Class* (1975).
(2) Department of Education and Science, *Adult Education: A Plan for Development* (HMSO 1973).

Research carried out in an inner London EPA has shown that special programmes for schools in so-called disadvantaged areas did not reach more than a quarter of those children who were actually disadvantaged.[1] The real problem was to identify pupils who were not achieving their full potential in whichever school they were. The underlying question of the whole EPA approach for Halsey was 'whether, and if so under what circumstances, education can change society'.[2] His conclusion was that it could only become an important element of change in conjunction with other more fundamental ones. It can be argued that in any society, educational policies reflect its dominant system of values. Jencks argued that 'schools serve primarily as selection and certification agencies, whose job is to measure and label people, and only secondarily as socialisation agencies, whose job is to change people. This implies that schools serve primarily to legitimise inequality, not to create it.'[3]

Given a universal system of education, the aim of inner city schools can be no different from those elsewhere; that is to provide an equality of opportunity in education measured by the achievement of its pupils. For the inner cities, education becomes the means of social mobility. Those who are able gain qualifications which place them on the path of progress leading to secure jobs. They eventually move away from the inner city for many reasons, but an important one is to find a home where the prospects of their children succeeding in school are enhanced, thus reinforcing social polarisation. Yet the opportunities for inner area children to progress in this way are diminished by that very social polarisation. When education forms such an important element in aiding individual social progress, it is difficult to reject positive discrimination even though the evidence suggests that it can play but a small part in compensating for the obstacles in the way of educational achievement.

The real obstacles to educational achievement lie in the home and social environment and in the polarisation which reinforces attitudes to schooling. But the purpose and methods of secondary education in the inner areas need to be examined to ask whether its main aim should be to provide for the academically able or to accept the reality of the social environment within which it works. This clearly is a false dichotomy. Concentrating on those pupils with obvious academic inclinations can mean that the majority of children will pass away their secondary school years in boredom, aggression or truancy. But the other course can risk providing no one at all with the qualifications which are one of the few avenues of social mobility for inner area children. The answer may lie in combining with academic education a real alternative which is accorded the same status and respect both within the school and outside. The non-academic alternative needs to open new avenues of achievement to young people which are useful and worthwhile and which, whilst aimed mainly at those who are not academically inclined, can be

(1) Barnes J and Lucas H, 'Positive Discrimination in Education: Individuals, Groups and Institutions' in Legatt T (editor), *Sociological Theory and Survey Research* (Sage Publications 1974).

(2) Halsey A H (editor), *Educational Priority, Vol. 1: EPA Problems and Policies* (HMSO 1972).

(3) Jencks C, *Inequality* (Peregrine Books 1975).

respected, and even followed, by those who are. Efforts have been made to raise the status of alternative directions through sport, community service, craft training. In theory it has been the aim of secondary education since 1944. It has not yet been achieved.

Authority and conflict

The chapter so far has looked at work, training and education, the institutional aspects of growing up in the inner city. But a theme to emerge with great force from our projects was the wide differences in attitudes between young people in inner Liverpool and those running the services set up ostensibly to serve them. The social expression of these attitudes could be found in truancy, delinquency, crime and vandalism. At their most extreme they were expressed in behaviour which was disturbing or frightening to others but often taken for granted among those involved.

In his study of an inner city tenement estate in Liverpool, Howard Parker suggested a development of delinquency which started at about eight years of age, rose to a peak of organised theft from sixteen to eighteen and then tailed off with girlfriends and marriage.[1] But he was at pains to point out that this pattern of delinquency applied to identifiable groups of boys at clearly defined times. The youngest were found to graduate from acceptable naughtiness to petty pilfering in a social environment where the availability of stolen goods was taken for granted, yet theft as such was frowned upon. By the time they were ten or twelve the group had become local hard-men and moved easily from theft from cars to joyriding and shoplifting. By their late teens most of them had begun to withdraw into the more normal social structure of the neighbourhood; leading to fairly regular work, marriage and a nearby council flat.

The social malaise survey showed particularly high levels of truancy and delinquency in the inner council estates and the worst parts of the rooming house area, between one and a half and three times the city average in each case. In addition, parts of the outer council estates showed levels slightly above average. Howard Parker thought that many boys were truants simply because they saw little value in school, but the Vauxhall CDP concluded that truancy was a more complex and individual response which varied from school to school.[2]

The problem of police records preventing their getting jobs was brought up by the young people in the inner city and employment group discussions. Most of the boys in the group had been in trouble with the police. One, when asked, told a prospective employer about being arrested and felt it unfair that he then did not get the job. Another had a certificate in electrical engineering from a prison, but feared showing it. The Leece Street survey showed that of those under thirty from the study area who were registered unemployed, one fifth had a police or prison

(1) Parker H J, *View from the Boys: A Sociology of Downtown Adolescents* (David & Charles 1974).

(2) Jones P, Smith G and Pelham K, *All Their Future: A Study of a Group of School Leavers in a Disadvantaged Area of Liverpool* (Department of Social and Administrative Studies, Oxford University 1975).

record. This compared with only one tenth of those over forty. The young age at which young people get involved in serious crime is confirmed by the 1974 police statistics for Merseyside which show that forty three percent of all indictable offences were committed by ten to sixteen year olds. Less than a quarter were committed by those over thirty.

Crime was virtually accepted as a way of life among the discussion group on employment. Most of them regarded stealing as acceptable for an unemployed person; a way of topping up income from unemployment benefit. They seemed very lenient towards lawbreakers, even though some said they would never steal themselves. They were also fatalistic about anything new coming into the area, shops, factories, and the like. These would be robbed before they even got under way. The experience of Stopover, the hostel for young people at risk, brought out the relationship between homelessness and crime. A majority of early referrals, prior to the opening of a bail hostel in Liverpool, were from the Probation Service. And a recent report on unemployment and homelessness, among young blacks, concluded that homelessness, even more than unemployment was likely to lead to conflict with the law.[1]

Vandalism is another form of behaviour closely associated with the inner areas but also with young people and especially boys in gangs. There are various theories about its causes, including an expression of misdirected energy, 'the development of mother-dominated child-rearing in the nuclear family', or the first stirrings of social evil and a prelude to serious crime. David Pullen, following his experiences of the Neighbourhood Projects Group in Liverpool described in chapter ten, saw vandalism as 'a clearer symptom of other, more serious, social problems than a symptom of more serious crime.'[2]

The Liverpool report, Crime in the City, recognised early preludes to trouble. Children spend much of their free time in the street, block and city centre. With big families, 'Mum (was) fully occupied by the baby of the moment (with) little choice but to allow her children this freedom'.[3] The Neighbourhood Projects Group felt that children's summer holidays become a major problem in the big cities for both parents and local authorities.

> 'Their play becomes uncontrolled and destructive because it does not relate to anything that adults are doing, and present economic conditions do not often allow parents the time to channel their children's activities fruitfully.'[4]

These comments allow many vandalistic acts to be summed up as simple bad behaviour. But the vandalised objects have usually already been neglected or abandoned. Colin Ward claims that local authorities are often primarily responsible for the neglect and by implication, that neglected, decaying or damaged

(1) Community Relations Commission, *Unemployment and Homelessness* (HMSO 1974).

(2) Ward C (editor), *Vandalism* (The Architectural Press 1975).

(3) Report of the Steering Group, *Crime in the City* (Institute of Extension Studies, University of Liverpool 1974).

(4) Neighbourhood Projects Group, *A Statement* (Liverpool 1974).

property deserves to be vandalised.[1] Property which does not suit its inhabitants and is poorly looked after, in which all decisions about its use have been taken independently of the users, is likely to be attacked.

At the time when we started work late in 1972, Liverpool was still smarting from a much publicised, discussed and misrepresented riot. A riot can combine elements of crime and vandalism, but is a rare occurrence. The Neighbourhood Projects Group, active in that area, described the events of the summer:

> 'The riots, although they received much lurid publicity at the time, were a tempest in a teapot compared to their American ghetto counterparts. Still, they were extreme manifestations of violence that was usually contained or rationed out in small skirmishes between rival gangs. Basically, the riots were fights between two young local gangs, one mainly white, the other mainly coloured, on a site between their two territories'.[2]

Two years later, those in our employment discussion group who had been involved looked back at the events as very exciting, more so than other experiences, before or since. *New Society*, in a special article on the riots, thought that though the 'actual situation may change ... it will not disappear until the community realises that the ingredients of violence are poor houses, high unemployment, no community involvement, and poor community resources.'[3]

Young people tend to come into contact with authority very early in life in a way which does not fit their own experience. Howard Parker cited the staff of the local primary school who argued that standards inside the school demanded conformity and produced consistency and security which the children enjoyed. This was in contrast with ambiguous standards outside the school. Our discussion groups and the Edge Hill school leavers' survey both suggest that the young peoples' attitudes hardened as they moved up the school and became more directly aware of their own lack of opportunities. Many were cynical, both of the attitudes of those running the school and of outsiders towards it: 'I went to St. X's; it's known as a trouble school.'

Nor were the young people under any illusions when it came to getting a job. Although many of those interviewed had ambitions beyond the unskilled labour they knew would be, or had been, their lot, they seldom stretched beyond perfectly reasonable expectations of apprenticeships or some form of skilled or community work. No evidence of any local tradition of taking up unskilled work was found. Rather, aspiration was rapidly brought down to earth by the reality of available work. One girl in Vauxhall described her interview: 'you couldn't really call it an interview. I walked in and she looked at me and said: Unsuitable ...'. A young person's attitude, as reflected by appearance and manner was clearly a major influence in getting a job, possibly of greater importance even than qualifications.

(1) Ward C, *op. cit.*
(2) Neighbourhood Projects Group, *Annual Report 1974*.
(3) 'Anatomy of a Riot', in *New Society* 17 August 1972.

This too was the view expressed in a report in the National Youth Employment Council, only regional factors being of greater importance.[1]

Careers Service officials seemed most aware of the difficulties faced by young people in some areas, but felt they could do little for them. They acknowledged the existence of particular areas of very high unemployment as a serious problem. But they suggested that the roots lay in the character of some closely-knit communities, and the resistance of some young people within them to travel any distance to work. It was often difficult to persuade young people to work when wages were little more than the level of unemployment benefits. The low aspirations of many young people, and the tradition of casual work on Merseyside, were also seen to be relevant.

The question of how to deal with difficult cases was brought up at every meeting with ESA and Department of Employment officers. Reactions varied from one of considering the socially disadvantaged 'a marginal problem to be treated with polite indifference', to one in which a good deal of personal prejudice against their more trying clients was allied to classifying them as 'very poor placing prospects'. Liverpool was thought to present employment officers with a more difficult problem than anywhere else in the country, a circumstance attributed to a 'lack of importance attached to work in some communities of extreme poverty', the large numbers of 'problem youths', and a 'high reliance on benefits'.

The consistent observations by officials of anti-authoritarian attitudes was an accurate reflection of reality among a small minority of young people. What was more disturbing was the readiness of many officials to generalise from particular bad experiences. Often the thinly-veiled contempt appeared to have a strong class, and occasionally racial, basis. The extreme attitudes of the small minority of young people loom large in the official conventional wisdom and affect the way in which everyone from those areas is treated by those in authority. In discussing delinquency and the boys' relations with the police in particular, Howard Parker observed that the rules of society did not seem to benefit them. They were left uncommitted to a social order of which they are meant to be a part.

Our own conclusion is that institutions providing for the needs of young people are not relating to a large and almost certainly increasing minority in inner city, and possibly other, areas. This should not detract from the remarkable achievements of some individuals within these institutions, nor condone the extreme attitudes of others. But the corporate values in too many cases, do not fit the reality of life for many inner city young people. Many institutions, above all, perhaps education and the law, reflect a social order, a hierarchy of manners and behaviour which, to many young people from poor inner city areas, appears designed to ensure that they keep their place. The traditional means of breaking away, through education and employment, are not succeeding, partly because of a failure of communication, and partly because they have little to offer at the end of it.

---

(1) National Youth Employment Council, *Unqualified, Untrained and Unemployed* (HMSO 1974).

10 People and government

Them and us

The relationship between people and government emerged early in the study as a key issue. While the investigation of this theme through area management was a main part of the brief, it also became quickly apparent, through consultations in the study area, that many residents and local organisations were particularly concerned about the level and effectiveness of local authority services.

Running right through their responses was a sense of alienation from the activities of authority in general and the Corporation in particular. There appeared to be deep-rooted mistrust of the activities of officials and councillors alike and a cynicism about the likely results of their efforts. Many felt that officers did not understand or respond to local needs and that members were forced by the party line to ignore local needs. Others found it impossible to get the specific services they asked for or were unable to find their way through what appeared to be an impenetrable maze of different departments, divisions and levels of responsibility.

These initial impressions were reinforced by our experiences both in the action projects and in continuing consultations with local authority officers and civil servants on one hand and neighbourhood and residents' associations and many members of the public on the other. If a theme can be extracted at all from the preceding chapters it is that, in inner Liverpool at any rate, there was an enormous gap between 'them and us'. But it was not merely an information gap; that those in authority did not know what those on the receiving end wanted. Nor was it simply a failure of administration to deliver the right service in the right place at the right time. More seriously, there appeared to be fundamental differences in attitude between provider and consumer.

The basic machinery of local government has remained broadly similar for nearly a hundred years.[1] The committee system and functional departmental structure, adopted by all local authorities, is an inheritance from the ad hoc local government boards of the nineteenth century and remains the means of perceiving and meeting needs. But two major developments have put a great strain on this method of working. First, local authorities, largely by statute, have been given responsibility for a much wider range and larger scale of services. Second, they have expanded their original function of maintaining standards and providing services by taking a major role as developers, particularly of housing. The most important recent development of the basic machinery in response to these extra responsibilities has been the imposition of a centralised coordinating and finance allocation structure

(1) See, for instance, Hill Dilys M, *Democratic Theory and Local Government* (George Allen and Unwin 1974).

which, in Liverpool and other authorities, takes the form of a Policy and Finance Committee and a Chief Executive.

The system has drawbacks, of which local authorities are well aware. The scale of operation needed to provide a full range of social, education, housing and environmental services, makes local sensitivity and personal attention on the part of the authority more difficult to achieve. A complex and centralised hierarchy of officers tends to make administration and day to day decision making appear remote to the general public.

This chapter looks at selected aspects of these problems. It examines firstly the gradual development of area-based initiatives by the city council through administrative delegation and special projects. This is followed by an assessment of the impact on the people of the inner area of the local authority's major development programmes of recent years. Then there is a discussion of community action seen as a response to increasing government intervention. Finally the effectiveness of local authority decision-making is considered in relation to the inner areas.

The development of area perspective

Expenditure and need

Area resource analysis of the council's expenditure for 1973–74 in District D, provided some disturbing results.[1] The City of Liverpool spent nearly five million pounds on services for the residents of District D, some 9·6 percent of the total population of the city. The expenditure was divided among a number of services and the meaning of the analysis can best be understood by looking at them individually.

In primary and secondary education, for instance, despite an established positive discrimination policy, expenditure was only slightly above average. Yet the discussion in chapter nine showed school achievement for the area to be very much lower than elsewhere in the city. And the take up of further education, at only six percent of the city's total, was much below average. In an area of low social status, this low figure might be explained by people opting for training rather than further education. But later work showed that training opportunities in the inner areas were also much fewer than elsewhere.

Expenditure on social services in the district varied little from the city average. Expenditure on highway maintenance was above average but that on libraries and leisure was low, mainly because of a very low proportion per head of maintained open space included under this heading. Sefton and Princes Parks lay just south of the district.

(1) IAS Liverpool, *Area Resource Analysis District D Tables 1973–74* (Department of the Environment 1976).

168

The low level of expenditure on housing was largely due to the small proportion of the city's council housing in District D. The area had been little affected by major inter-war redevelopment programmes and although the slum clearance programme had recently reached the area (a fifth of all demolitions in 1973–74 was in District D), little rebuilding had taken place at the time of the analysis. Despite high densities, overcrowding and the relative age of council housing in the district, the proportion spent on repairs and maintenance was slightly below average. However, investment in the private sector was considerable with forty one percent of the value of improvement grants being directed to District D. This was partly a consequence of the most successful of the three major general improvement areas then declared being in the district, and partly to a residue of large, old houses suitable for conversion and improvement.

Expenditure in District D was clearly very near to the city average for most services mainly because it was usually determined by average per capita standards of provision. When it differed from the average this could usually be attributed to simple variations in the base population or in the particular aspect of the physical fabric to which that service referred.

Conditions in District D however were, in some respects, significantly worse than the average for the city; in the quality of its housing stock and environment, or in the incidence of certain indicators of deprivation. Its needs were greater than its share of the city's population would suggest, at least for some services. The distribution of total resources within the district poses the same question in another way. Of a total expenditure of just over five million pounds over half was spent on education, sixteen percent on housing, twelve percent on social services, and fifteen percent on environmental health, libraries, leisure and highway maintenance. By definition, this pattern of expenditure corresponded closely with the distribution for the city as a whole. Yet the character of District D would suggest that a different pattern might more closely relate to its needs, for instance a greater expenditure on social and environmental services.

Administrative delegation

Larger local authorities have devolved much of their administration of services, chiefly for administrative convenience. Most departments in Liverpool had some form of area administration. Yet the form and extent of delegation differed greatly in each case, both in the size of population served and the degree of responsibility handed down to local officers. Only four departments, Social Services, Environmental Health, the City Building Surveyor and Planning had a common boundary system. Each department has developed its own system independently. The results, in terms of that particular department, often makes sound administrative sense. Some, such as Social Services, need to have local offices, easily accessible to residents. In other cases, for example Environmental Health, it is perhaps more important for the district officer to get out into his district than for large numbers of people to be able to get easily to him. But the result, in conjunction with various central government functions such as probation, police, social security etc, is a complex network of at least fifteen administrative boundary systems, overlain by yet another system of political ward boundaries.

Whatever may have been suggested by the existence of area systems in different departments, a strongly hierarchical tradition had been maintained. One had only to attend meetings at which both district officers and their superiors were present to appreciate this, often in sharp contrast to the informal and questioning relationship which representatives of different departments profess to have with each other. Experience of setting up and running projects in the study area suggested that there was little real delegation of authority to district officers. An important example was that of the district housing managers who had, in theory, complete control over all aspects of management except allocations. Yet their scope for responding flexibly to local issues was slight. Centrally determined policy decisions had built up a complex system of rules and regulations which effectively ruled out any real decisions at district level. Furthermore, each district manager had a responsibility for between ten and twelve thousand tenancies; equivalent, in effect to a sizeable town.

The same impression was gained of the district personal social services officers. Their range of authority covered little more than the day to day deployment of their social work teams. Even the district environmental officers, who had been put into a particularly privileged position by the first chief officer of that department, had no money to spend directly. Their limited financial discretion had to be formally approved by the chief officer in each case.

Special projects

The matter of coordination is more complex, though closely connected with that of the delegation of authority. Local authorities have been well aware that strict departmental divisions of services and programmes may not always exactly fit the reality of problems to be solved, and that more than one department is likely to be involved in many issues. A number of attempts have been made in Liverpool to coordinate services for certain areas or to take a new approach to their provision. The Vauxhall CDP, the Shelter Neighbourhood Action Project (SNAP) and the City Council's Brunswick experiment deserve special mention here as they each had a strong local flavour.

Although set up to improve local conditions through community action, the Vauxhall CDP like the others elsewhere, rapidly turned its attention to the organisation of local authority services. One outcome has been the Vauxhall mutli-service centre which combines the local offices of social services, probation, education welfare, information and the neighbourhood law centre. Yet bringing together services does not mean that they necessarily become more effective or responsive. Their proximity might mean that gaps in services, or duplication of services might become more readily apparent. But the centre implies no increase in the limited delegation to local offices, which has already been noted. The Vauxhall Steering Committee, set up to give local residents a voice in decisions about the project, is a purely advisory body and, although able to exert considerable influence on the City Council, does not make any financial decisions about local services.

It has little real power, being not unlike a more formal, though more effective, version of the district forum in the area management experiment.

SNAP raised many hopes. A New Town for Granby was the ambitious slogan of an exercise in community participation and housing improvement which, in practice, underestimated the difficulties both of generating mass interest in a very poor area and stimulating any kind of effective response by the local authority. It had some real achievements but in retrospect there appears to have been little impact on methods of operating within the local authority. No changes in management or administration have resulted from the SNAP exercise other than the housing aid centre.

The same conclusion could be drawn from the Brunswick experiment. Using money from the Urban Programme, a list of improvements for one area of council tenement housing was drawn up. The programme was coordinated by the City Planning Department and run by a working party chaired by an official from the Town Clerk's department. No doubt the various initiatives were better coordinated than each had been when carried out as a separate departmental initiative and a degree of community representation was achieved. Yet, despite attempts by the City Planning Department to widen its scope and take a fresh look at local needs and objectives, the programme which resulted was not much more than a combination of bids for capital expenditure put in by each department. The weaknesses of this approach can be attributed to some extent to its artificiality. Government had made available a fixed capital sum provided it could be spent quickly. This became the chief constraint on the choice of action, rather than the development of a total approach to genuinely local issues.

Area management

Area management was designed to take these experiments a stage further. Its origins and structure were described in chapter two. In practice, its role became initially that of bringing to bear an area perspective on the activities of the Corporation, using District D as the case study for showing how focussing on needs and issues in a single area in a non-departmental way could give fresh insights. In a sense, area management was doing what the Inner Area Study itself had been doing through action research and policy reviews, but from within the Corporation.

Its activities covered a number of issues, for some of which resources were available to mount an action project but for others, the method of working had to be through the preparation of reports for the District Committee. An example of the former is given by the Birchfield pre-school project. Pre-school provision had been identified early by the Area Management Unit as an important element, as they saw it, in breaking into the cycle of deprivation through selective provision in needy areas. A petition from local residents had been put forward asking for a nursery class at Birchfield School in District D. A rapid assessment of the Education Department's policy on pre-school provision showed that decisions were being made in an arbitrary manner. The area management staff working with the City Planning Department quickly produced a simple method based on 1971 census data for assessing priorities for pre-schooling between small areas. Using this method it was clear that Birchfield school did warrant priority provision. Consequently a scheme was put forward for an extended day nursery class and an outreach worker and was approved by all the necessary committees. But administrative delays in the Education Department have persisted and the project is not now due to start until 1977.

Another example of an action project was that on housing mangement, worked out jointly with our study team and the Housing Department and described in chapter eight. An experimental multi-purpose form for claiming certain local authority benefits was designed and tested, and a project under the Job Creation Programme supported. A further project is currently being developed on clearance and redevelopment.

But in many ways it can be argued that the policy reviews carried out by area management may have been more influential in their effect on the central decision making machinery of the Corporation. Three have been particularly significant, bringing to light local issues of considerable importance and revealing failings of local coordination or sensitivity.[1] One was a problem of derelict, dangerous and decaying houses in a street near Lodge Lane where the then current practice of using closing orders was itself leading to the deterioration of other, occupied houses. A second concerned industrial development in District D. And a more recent example concerned the problem of vacant land in the District, particularly the future use of sites reserved for education and open space uses. In each case, although the initiative, and the examples, came from District D the analysis and recommendations had a wider applicability for they related to problems experienced in much of the inner areas.

But even these action projects and policy reviews have as much demonstrated the strength of departmental viewpoints at all levels in the official hierarchy, often against strong evidence for local coordination or adjustments to programmes, as they have shown a non-departmental organisation can stimulate new initiatives in policy or the delivery of services.

Part of the problem is that it was clear from the start that there was no strong political backing for the experiment in Liverpool. Senior politicians were prepared to tolerate it, particularly as central government was paying three-quarters of the cost. But there was no way in which the caucus of the major parties can yet be thought to have regarded area management as a significant experiment in the development of local government in Liverpool, with the possibility of its becoming an important element in the fight against urban deprivation. Members of the District Committee were hesitant and, despite its status as a full committee of the council, were not prepared to support overtly an area interest against departmental

(1) Area Management Unit reports to the District D Committee, *Derelict Houses in District D* (January 1976); *Land and Buildings for Industrial Development in District D* (December 1975); *Procedures for The Development of Vacant Land in District D with special reference to the Problems of Education and Open Space Uses* (June 1976).

172

policy. Furthermore, the lack of correspondence between District D and the six wards, none of which was located entirely within the district, may have contributed to this hesitancy. Possibly premature attempts to exercise a more specifically local interest in the allocation of resources to the district were rebuffed. Power and authority has remained firmly with the main service committees and departments. The case for local initiative and coordination has been demonstrated and accepted only on an experimental basis in a limited number of specific cases, notably the housing management project. It remains to be seen whether arguments and evidence for a wider, area perspective can find their place within the Corporation.

The local authority as developer

Since their inception local authorities have gained ever more control over the physical environment: nineteenth century public health improvements, the extensive inter-war housing estates, the comprehensive renewal schemes of the sixties and early seventies. Liverpool now owns much land in the city, particularly in its inner area and about a third of the housing stock is in public ownership. Effective implementation of an extensive programme of housing improvement will involve even more council ownership of land and buildings. To this must also be added the extensive ownership of land by statutory bodies.

The major local authority programmes have involved complex planning and management. Coordination has been achieved in two ways. The Housing Department's Programme and Redevelopment Divisions were responsible for the coordination of slum clearance and housing redevelopment across the city; and the City's development plan provided the framework within which all major programmes were to be co-ordinated. The programmes were ambitious but, despite real achievements, a number of things went wrong. The reasons were changes in central government policies; the lack of government resources for many of the public uses other than housing; unwillingness to invest on the part of the private sector. But the failures were also within the local authority itself, in particular the rigidity and inflexibility of the planning and development for many years during the 1960s and early 1970s. These failures can now be seen with hindsight but, as with the case of slum clearance discussed in chapter eight, the consequences of those failures are still being felt and need to be reviewed briefly for the lessons which they may still hold.

A comprehensive system of urban motorways and primary distributor roads was the chief proposal of the 1966 Merseyside Area Land Use and Transportation Survey. Most of it would pass either through older commercial property on the fringes of the city centre or rundown residential areas in the inner city. The proposals were made during a boom on Merseyside in the late sixties when the prospects for economic growth were good. But ten years later, apart from the completed Mersey Tunnel approaches, the M62 as far as Broad Green, Scotland Road, Rice Lane and other isolated sections, little of the original scheme remains, the remainder having been dropped by the Merseyside County Council, following a major review in May 1976. Some of the proposals in fact would have been abandoned two years earlier, by the City Council, but for local government reorganisation and the consequent delays.

The development of district shopping centres has been affected by the same rigid planning. Although based to a large extent on existing shopping patterns the proposed network of centres emerged as an abstract system based on theoretical catchment areas over which the local authority had only partial control. The intention was to create opportunities for new investment in shopping and civic and welfare uses. One centre, Belle Vale, has now been built by the Corporation. It is an attractive, covered complex, easy to get to by car and is clearly popular and successful. Yet it is located some distance away from the new Netherley council estate which it was designed to serve, to be near a proposed new railway station probably not now to be opened. The Wavertree Road centre in our study area provides a stark contrast. Its centrepiece was to have been a large, popular department store, then co-existing with a large number of small shops on a crowded shopping street. The new centre was to include local offices for council departments. Many of the smaller shops were included in slum clearance schemes and the remainder declined steadily over a period of years as delay mounted. But the department store itself closed, thus sealing the fate of the district centre as a major shopping attraction. It remains to be seen what can be salvaged in practice from the original concept but the revised planning brief shows little change. Meanwhile an informal market operates daily on the cleared land as the remaining shops continue to decline, much of their passing trade lost by closure of the department store.

One of the most obvious results of over-ambitious planning has been the huge amounts of vacant land reserved for future developments and scattered throughout the inner areas. In March 1975, eleven percent of land in the study area was found to be lying vacant.[1] More than three-quarters of this was owned by Liverpool District Council, most of it reserved for future public uses. About half had been vacant for at least two years and as much as three-quarters was likely to be still vacant in 1980. This pattern was confirmed by a report from the City Planning Officer[2] which identified some one thousand two hundred and fifty acres of vacant land in the city in October 1975, mainly owned by the city or county councils, unlikely to be developed in any way before 1980.

The chain of events leading to vacant land started when sites were cleared of slums. New uses were proposed, many either housing or social uses needed to meet general standards of provision for the predicted future population; for instance, space for school playing fields or open spaces as well as highways and new council housing. But procedures for redevelopment, other than housing, were slow and inefficient or resources were not available and the land lay idle and blighted.

(1) IAS Liverpool, *Vacant Land* (Department of the Environment 1976).
(2) *Vacant and Unused Land in Liverpool*, Report of the City Planning Officer to Policy and Finance Committee (October 1975).

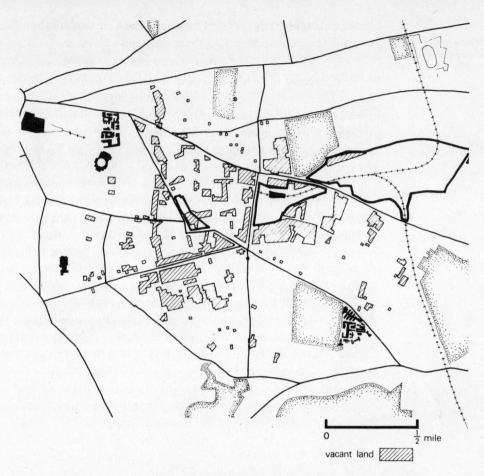

Figure 43
Vacant land, study
area 1975

0   ½ mile

vacant land ▨

Some attempts have been made to counteract the blighting effect of land
reservation. In 1969 a working party was set up to examine the scope for
temporary uses or landscaping of vacant land, pending its permanent development.
Although it was decided that large scale temporary use was uneconomic, a certain
amount of landscaping has been done, either under the Department of
Environment's Special Environmental Assistance Scheme or the Council's own
programme. However, despite the persistence of vast amounts of derelict land, the
Estates Department does not maintain a comprehensive or up to date record of
vacant land in the city. Nor is the City Estates Surveyor charged with assessing the
economic or social costs of holding land vacant. His brief is to 'obtain the
maximum benefit to the Council out of its land holdings', a brief which is given a
strictly commercial interpretation. Furthermore, no single department was
responsible for vacant land, other than those sites which had been given some
form of temporary treatment.

There appear to be a number of reasons why these and other plans were allowed
to drag on so long before being revoked. They formed an integral part of a
complex end-state plan whose success depended on their construction. Also, like
other elements of that plan they became the measure of success or failure of the
Corporation. Furthermore Liverpool rate payers did not have to face the full
economic costs. Grants from central government contribute to the cost of major

175

road schemes, and to the cost of holding large quantities of slum cleared land vacant. For too long, little mitigating action was taken. It was assumed when the proposals were made that resources would come available, the programmes would proceed smoothly, and no machinery would therefore be needed to cope with anything that went wrong. The extent and impact of the blight was hardly realised, the proliferation of vacant sites being seen almost as the result of unconnected events for which little could be done except treat each one as a separate eyesore.

Thus, apart from the so far limited amount of good new council housing in the inner areas, the major public developments of the last ten years have not brought the benefits that they should have done to inner city residents. A combination of over-ambitious planning, cumbersome and centralised management and ineffective monitoring has resulted in a depressing state of physical chaos. Planners have neither given sufficient heed to economic reality nor accepted fully that only those things over which the local authority has any control and for which it has resources can be planned with precision. New questions are beginning to be asked: who benefits from planning and development? The real or potential impact of urban motorways, for instance, highlights vividly the polarisation of the inner city in benefiting those whom affluence, technology and mobility have freed at the expense of those whom economic stagnation and social premises have trapped. The main sufferers were small businesses in cheap old property and poor communities in old housing, both less likely to use the new motorways than larger firms and car owning commuters who not only would travel on the roads but would also not be affected by their construction.

The problems for local planning in inner cities are many. There is the extent to which the local plan must follow the structure plan, that it cannot be adopted until the structure plan has been approved. There is in any case the length of time which it takes actually to prepare a local plan with due process of public participation. More fundamentally there is the matter of whether a land use local plan on an ordnance survey base map is the appropriate means of expressing policy in an inner area as large as that of Liverpool's with its diversity of conditions. In certain areas of immediate and firm change there is an obvious need for specific plans, action plans and design briefs, part of the design process leading to immediate development or change in the physical fabric of the area. But in other, very large areas there is no such certainty as to when change may occur, what form it could take or indeed whether it will occur at all in the foreseeable future or the period for which resources can be firmly committed.

In such areas there may well be conflicting demands placed on the plan making process. On the one hand, local plans need to retain sufficient flexibility to be able to respond easily and swiftly to changing circumstances, and fresh opportunities as they develop. It means for instance being able to vary the allocation of land from, say, residential to industrial use as the pattern of demand changes and new trends emerge in consequence either of policy changes or economic forces. But on the other hand, the planning system must not become so flexible as to remove all protection of the rights of individuals and existing communities against unfavourable development. It means ensuring that change will not occur without due warning and consultation. It means too, recognising that the reservation of land for public purposes should be made only as and when there is both a clear need in terms of local conditions as well as national standards, and a firm commitment of public resources.

This criticism suggests that local planning policy for the inner areas of a city as large as Liverpool should be couched in terms similar to those used for the structure plan, that is written statements of policies and criteria for development control which stress flexibility within broad limits and give assurances of a more meaningful consultation than is strictly required by statute. But the planning policy should be fleshed out only as and when the need arises by action area plans and design briefs. In all respects, local planning should closely integrate plan making and development control with each other and with other land management programmes of the local authority, with economic development, social, housing and environmental policies.

Community action and participation

Community action in Liverpool

It is difficult to see the growth of community action in Liverpool as anything other than a response to trends in local authority activity. Virtually all the organisations which we consulted in and around the study area were set up as a result of some conflict with authority, usually over a housing or environmental issue. Although there are references to the activities of residents' groups just after the war, events have taken place largely since about 1960.[1]

By 1969 there were fifteen community councils in Liverpool, all but Toxteth having been set up in the space of three years. All were modelled on Toxteth with a model constitution drawn up by the then Liverpool Council of Social Service, which also set up a Neighbourhood Organisation Committee (NOC), helped with administrative costs and funded two full-time community development officers. In some cases too, the growth of the community councils was actively encouraged by the Corporation, chiefly through the City Planning Department. The councils which survived remained centralised, involving mainly professional people. An analysis carried out by Liverpool University during 1970 and 1971 showed that half the items discussed were organisational or about the involvement of local people and organisations rather than about real issues.[2]

Another important independent development was the growth of tenants' associations. By 1972 there were about sixty in Liverpool, mostly in council estates and involved in the Amalgamated Tenants' Associations Coordinating Committee (ATACC). Despite its initials, this organisation has developed very much as a liaison committee through monthly meetings with the Housing Department and

(1) Frankenberg R, *Communities in Britain* (London 1966).

(2) *Community Councils in Liverpool*, unpublished report by Department of Political Theory and Institutions, University of Liverpool (c1972).

committee, although there was open conflict with the local authority for a considerable period over the Housing Finance Act.

Perhaps the most influential of the later organisations has been the Southern Neighbourhood Council, set up in Toxteth in 1972 in a high density area of council tenements. The significance of this group lies in its formal pattern of election on lines recommended by the Association of Neighbourhood Councils. These were to have been forerunners of a third tier of local government. A government consultation paper subsequently suggested that statutory status be given to neighbourhood councils in 'unparished' areas in England.[1] Such a move had been strongly resisted by many members of the Neighbourhood Organisations Committee. Currently the issue appears to be dormant although, in 1975, proposals were put forward by the Southern Neighbourhood Council for 'priority area development', to include area and neighbourhood councils with area managers responsible to them, and teams of officers at both levels to provide services. However, it was conceived more as an alternative bureaucracy than alternative democracy, as the City Council's service committees would remain in being.

The extent to which any of the local groups could be considered representative is difficult to assess. Active membership was small, although probably no smaller than active ward party membership, but on certain occasions large numbers of people could be assembled. As pressure groups, they have not had marked success in influencing council policies, although several significant battles have been won, mainly in getting areas switched from slum clearance to improvement. Nor has any real movement developed capable of seriously influencing policy. With the possible exception of ATACC and NOC and, in a different field, the Merseyside Play Action Council, the tendency has been towards fragmentation and parochialism rather than federation or concerted effort. Most groups have been formed in response to a specific issue. When that was resolved they have either disbanded or turned to other issues and usually changed in the process. But their independence and fluidity has proved a real strength. Such groups form the only representation of disparate local interests to counteract the move towards centralised politics in the City Council. Over specific issues and for limited periods many of these groups can be considered to have been truly representative of the interests of at least a majority of residents in their areas.

The community in action

Two outside events instilled new directions into community action in Liverpool. The first of these was the announcement of the Urban Programme, and the second was a local scheme, the Neighbourhood Projects Group, inspired by the Chief Executive as a means of combating increasing vandalism and violence. Although the Urban Programme was originally aimed at areas of racial tension (in which Liverpool was included) it was welcomed by local authorities and the voluntary sector alike as a useful source of funds for a large number of activities outside

(1) *Neighbourhood Councils in England*, Department of the Environment Consultation Paper, 30 July 1974.

normal local authority programmes. This was especially true in Liverpool. Of the total allocation of just over twenty one million pounds in the first seven phases, nearly seven percent went to Liverpool, the majority of it to voluntary sector applicants.

The application procedure for urban aid was later institutionalised in a unique but shortlived exercise in cooperation. A Priorities' Committee was elected from voluntary organisations and community development interests to assess both local authority and voluntary schemes and list their priority. The list was then approved virtually verbatim by both the City Council and the Home Office. In 1975 the same procedure was followed and thirty six schemes put forward by the Priorities' Committee, only to be replaced at a late stage by a short list of local authority projects, none of which had been on the original list. This revised list, defended on the grounds of generating more jobs against strong opposition from the voluntary sector, was approved by the City Council and in part by the Home Office. Thus the Council, which came to power only two years previously on a community politics platform, appeared to have dealt a body blow to any effective cooperation in community development between the voluntary sector and the local authority, at least for some years to come.

By 1970, it had been estimated that malicious damage was costing the local authority some nine hundred thousand pounds annually. In that year the city offered twenty five thousand pounds for use by youth and community organisations to find new solutions. Following the appointment of a Vandalism Steering Committee, the Neighbourhood Projects Group (NPG) was set up. Playschemes, youth centres and neighbourhood centres were run by workers all living locally and many born and bred in their areas. NPG was bolder and at times more radical than residents' associations, aiming at those for whom the more traditional youth and community provision had proven useless. The project leader saw the real fight 'not against vandalism but against established traditions and organisations, particularly where these were defended by an entrenched bureaucratic or professional group.'[1] After a brief flowering of independence in which the scheme, although still fully funded by the local authority, was run as a cooperative by the workers themselves, relations with the Corporation became increasingly strained. NPG was taken on by the newly appointed Community Development Officer early in 1974 and axed in April 1975.

During this period in the 1970s, in parallel with the growth of residents' and tenants' associations and other independent neighbourhood activities, the City Council was considering its own position. In 1970 the Liverpool Council of Social Services had seen that there was 'a long way to go before we have a genuine participant society and many adjustments to be made. The City Council has yet to decide and declare a policy on community development. Its eventual attitude will determine whether Liverpool is to have consensus or the conflict community development approach widespread in the United States of America'.[2]

(1) Pullen D R, *Memoirs of a Vandalism Officer* (Neighbourhood Projects Group 1974).
(2) Poole H R, *March of the Reinforcements* (Liverpool Council of Social Service 1970).

G

In 1972 the Council appointed a Community Development Officer, with direct responsibility to the Chief Executive. He was to be the focus for the development of community development policy within the local authority and a reference point between different council departments and community groups. However, his independence was short-lived. He took over direct control of NPG early in 1974, became a central figure in the assessment of urban aid applications and, when the Liberals came to power in April 1974, became the principal officer of a newly formed Community Development Committee. This committee was vague about its intentions and had a limited budget; the community development section became confined by departmentalism as much as any other. By the end of 1975, the Community Development Committee had been replaced by an advisory committee of the chairmen of those service committees most directly involved in community work. The Community Development Officer had already left for another job elsewhere and the section has since remained a small unit in the City Solicitor's Department.

Our own experience of the community in action came chiefly, though not exclusively, through our play action projects. They showed us the problems faced by small voluntary groups in running independent activities and about the confused and difficult role of the local authority in funding them. The most successful was the Dove Street playground. A strong management committee already existed and had been running play activities on a small scale for several years. The playleader, a massive and well-respected father figure, had been working with youngsters in that area for over ten years. What was being funded was thus not merely an idea but a soundly based, if impoverished, voluntary group which needed little assistance in rapidly expanding once money was available.

The other two playgrounds were a different matter entirely. Both the Kinglake and Falkner Playgrounds were to be run by a committee of professional workers already active in the area. Although competent, the committee did not have strong roots in either locality. During the building of these two playgrounds, attempts were made to set up local committees. Kinglake was taken on by a residents' association operating in a large tenement block overlooking the playground. An entirely new committee was set up to manage the Falkner playground, following a public meeting of local residents. In each case playleaders were appointed and the playgrounds struggled on for a year. Finally the Kinglake playground was closed down by the local authority, mainly because of poor management. The death of a child climbing on the wall of the Falkner playground one December evening brought to a head the local factions which had already split its management committee. A temporary Steering Group was appointed and, at the time of writing, the playground had been handed over to the local authority to be run by them with the funds remaining from the Inner Area Study and the Urban Programme for both playgrounds.

Perhaps the major lesson to be learnt from setting up the three playgrounds was that running an adventure playground is a complex task, not to be undertaken lightly. There is a world of difference between the commitment and expertise required to run a summer playscheme, itself no mean task, and that called for in setting up and running a full time adventure playground with paid playleaders and expensive buildings and equipment. A strong and experienced management committee with good support from local residents appeared to be an important pre-requisite to setting up a voluntary adventure playground.

The whole complex world of play in Liverpool involved up to six departments of the corporation (although chiefly the Education Department), a host of voluntary groups and the Merseyside Play Action Council, the coordinating committee which the groups had formed to represent them in their relations with the corporation. Our surveys demonstrated the useful role which voluntary groups could undertake in complementing and extending the services of the local authority. But we concluded that a fruitful partnership required an organisation like the Merseyside Play Action Council to liaise with the local authority. At the same time however the local authority needed to focus its own complex organisation onto specific projects, change its own patronising and sometimes destructive attitudes towards the voluntary sector and operate in a spirit of active support and encouragement rather than the current one of grudging acceptance. If necessary the local authority should consider setting up schemes in some areas with the intention of handing them over later to a residents' committee. However, there were, in Liverpool at least, fundamental divisions between departments and levels of organisation which would make such an outcome almost inconceivable.

Who makes the decisions?

For more than two decades after the war, political control in Liverpool was held in turn by the Labour and Conservative Parties, each with big majorities and strong leadership. The main outlines of the policies whose effects we now see in inner Liverpool were laid down in this period: the slum clearance programme, housing redevelopment, the motorway proposals, comprehensive education. The policies were politically inspired although, even then, the ways in which needs could be assessed and met by the local authority were complex.

Local authority services and programmes represent an amalgam of past decisions overlaid by a continuous process of assessment, mainly financial, and incremental change. Decisions are not so much taken as generated and confirmed. The formal decision at the City Council to change an existing service or set up a new one represents the ratification of months of discussion and consultation which might have been started by an event, a survey, by the observation of an officer, by a point raised by a member in committee, or following pressure by an outside body. But at some point during this process an attempt will have been made to assess the need for a service; to justify provision; and to assess the extent and nature of that provision. An increasingly sophisticated range of techniques has been developed to measure and assess the need for services. William Duncan's attempts in the 1840s to relate mortality rates to housing conditions by plotting their incidence was the impetus for much of the local authority activity in Liverpool which followed. A clear line of descent can be traced thereafter down to the City Planning Department's social malaise work in the 1960s and the social area analysis which has formed part of this study.

As the services provided by local government have become more numerous and complex, so methods of assessing need have become more technical and less intuitive. The professional side of local government has grown rapidly in relation to the political side. Members have had to rely increasingly on an interpretation by their senior officers of a mass of information collected in their departments about the needs that are to be met by certain services. As councillors they have neither the time nor the training to cope with the vast amounts of technical information circulating through the committee cycle alone, itself only a synthesis of that actually collected and analysed.

Then in 1970 came the McKinsey reforms which crystallised and formalised the trend towards the growing professionalism in local government. Their aim was to achieve a greater centralisation and coordination of the control of the local authority's services. The technique was to make local government more business like, government by objectives based on the collation of information and an evaluation of progress. The number of committees in the Liverpool Council was reduced from thirty three to nine, with a corresponding reduction in the number of departments. At the same time corporate management was introduced into the committee and officer structure in three ways. A Policy and Finance Committee was to make major city wide decisions about policies which cut across or surmounted departmental issues. Here the priorities for the city as a whole were to be debated and established. A Chief Executive was appointed, here, as in other authorities, by raising the status of the old-style post of town clerk. His duty was to develop a corporate approach to city-wide problems through a management team of chief officers of the major departments. To ensure that this approach filtered down through the departmental structure a new Programme Planning Department was set up, in which officers loosely attached to each of the departments would separately prepare detailed annual programme statements which would, in total, present a corporate budget.

But almost before the McKinsey reforms had been put into effect, the political backlash started. The reforms had been couched too overtly in terms of administrative structures, substituting rational thought and objective measurement, as it were, for political priorities. Members felt they were losing political control of the processes of government, not only in the Labour and Liberal Parties but in the Conservative Party which had brought the reforms in. The process of retrenchment started very quickly. The Chief Executive and his management team and the Policy and Finance Committee have remained. But the Programme Planning Department was quietly wound down and, after local government reorganisation in 1974, disbanded. The number of committees and chief officers have increased though to nothing like their former size. And, for several years, the new style of corporate budget was replaced by the traditional line budget.

Other changes were occurring in the 1970s. The polarisation of politics between Labour and Conservative was breaking up in Liverpool as it was nationally. The period of big party majorities and strong political leadership has been replaced by minority control of Council. A number of factors have contributed to this locally. Traditionally, a large proportion of council members in working class areas have been from working class backgrounds. However, a recent analysis of the workings of Labour ward parties in Liverpool suggests that there have been significant changes in the local ward party machinery.[1] Active Labour Party membership has increasingly been drawn from those of a more educated background and in working class or deprived inner city areas has lost touch with the mass of its electorate.

This can be illustrated by differences in polling between the poor wards and the more affluent ones, which have consistently recorded turnouts perhaps one and a half times those in the former. Those wards within which the local authority is most active and where the need for services must be greatest, show the lowest turnouts. The successful candidate at a municipal election in an inner city ward who gains a small majority in a twenty percent turnout can claim to have been elected by only about one in ten of those eligible to vote. Also the traditional voting patterns of inner Liverpool have been largely broken up since the war by slum clearance. The traditional Catholic/Protestant polarisation has disappeared except in one or two staunch Catholic areas like Vauxhall, although even here in 1972 the then Labour leader of the Council only narrowly defeated a residents' representative emerging from the work of the Community Development Project.

It is these changes that must partly account for the recent rapid rise of the Liberals in Liverpool. They have gained most of their support in older areas of private housing; respectable working class and lower middle class areas comprising the 'outer inner city' and inner suburbs. They were the areas most threatened by encroaching slum clearance. They were also the areas where council services were largely confined to the environment and education. Furthermore they had been the scene of a considerable amount of successful community action. The Liberal Party was able to find a sufficient number of young, enthusiastic candidates who concentrated on a large number of small environmental problems, which they picked up through a revitalised local surgery system, got corrected by enthusiastic pressure on the relevant officers and publicised through newsheets. In this way they were able to convince a sufficient proportion of the electorate that they had something to offer.

Paradoxically, though, this apparent rise in local interest on very specific matters can be seen as part of the continuing erosion in the role of local councillors resulting from the centralisation of power in the strong party leadership of the 1950s and later in the McKinsey reorganisation. Few councillors can sustain an effective balance between their local advocacy and their policy-making role in committee. Members themselves see their surgeries and local contacts to have little bearing on their policy-making role. One study area member, although very active on the City

(1) Hindess B, *The Decline of Working Class Politics* (MacGibbon 1971).

Council and a committee chairman, described his local role as that of a 'glorified social worker'. Another wanted to 'go back to school' in order to understand fully the business of the City Council. Several admitted that the only way they could cope with the complexity of council business was to skim agendas and reports for anything that pertained to their ward and to merely vote with the party line at committee, thus further abrogating responsibility to the party caucus.

The most persistent complaints received at local surgeries were about the maintenance of council housing. Councillors had a special form which they filled in for the housing managers who then ordered the work. In this way the pressure for any significant change in administration to cope with a situation that was clearly unsatisfactory, was effectively removed. The administrative failures were institutionalised and tenants merely jumped the queue by going to their councillor. The problem was contained through ad hoc action but never solved by basic changes in policy. If members had had any faith in their local role and if there were a proper transfer of information upwards, the obvious widespread concern over housing management would have been translated into effective changes in policy by the Housing Committee. Instead, councillors appeared unable or unwilling to translate their individual local experience and observation into collective political action for change.

The McKinsey reorganisation explicitly increased the centralisation of authority in Liverpool. By introducing corporate management effectively only at the most senior levels it still further increased that tendency. The status and effectiveness of officers at more junior levels, in local offices and the like, has been eroded, their power to make decisions diminished. Combining a number of small departments into single large ones was part of the action, placing more authority at the centre but not necessarily achieving a greater coordination at the local level between the separate divisions of the new department. By paying too much attention to the structure of the Corporation and its administrative efficiency and having insufficient regard for the needs and wishes of people and communities, the consumers of its services, the remoteness of the local authority as a whole from its public has been increased. The subsequent modifications to the original reorganisation did little to change this; rather they confirmed the basic strength of the departmental system and the powerful partnership of committee chairman and chief officer.

But these changes have occurred at a time of weakening political authority as the days of big majorities have gone. They have come too in a period of ever increasing control by central government of the actions required of local government as the Report of the Layfield Committee has shown,[1] only partly offset in theory by the greater financial autonomy introduced by devices such as the transportation policies and programmes. The result has been for the solutions to problems, the very identification of issues, to become more technical and less political; for services to become universal, city wide in their application with insufficient regard to variations in local conditions and circumstances.

(1) *Local Government Finance: Report of the Committee of Inquiry* (Cmnd 6453, HMSO 1976).

Local government in the inner areas

If local government is to become effective in the inner areas, three main questions must be faced. Firstly, how can a flexible and coordinated response at the local level be reconciled to the demands of city-wide political control and corporate management? Secondly, how can resources be effectively channelled to those in greatest need? Thirdly, how can distinct, minority views be given adequate expression within a local democratic system based on consensus politics?

Area management could provide some answers to the first question. But effective coordination and direction of programmes at the small area level would require much greater political backing than has been given to the Liverpool experiment. It would require real changes in the ways in which power and authority is exercised within the service departments for these are the fundamental constraint on local action. It would mean a delegation of responsibility to area-based officers such that, within the resource limits set, they are able to take full responsibility for services and programmes. A certain capacity is needed for making local decisions which requires recourse neither to programme committees nor senior officials.

But delegation in itself cannot achieve positive discrimination. A real redistribution of resources to the areas of greatest need would require an act of political will which could well risk electoral support. This would be true particularly if the scale of action was greater than the token discrimination which has hitherto been the practice. Under current constraints on local authority spending, extra resources for inner city areas would have to be found by reducing expenditure elsewhere and probably cutting services in more affluent areas. Such a decision would be most unpopular. Yet it would only be a way of putting into practice vaguer and more generally acceptable objectives such as 'a redistribution of resources'. There are two possibilities; visible redistribution locally, carried through by a strong, idealistic political lobby, or extra resources from central government to clearly defined areas.

The achievement of an adequate expression of minority views must be a major objective of any political system which calls itself democratic. That objective is not being met for large numbers of people in inner Liverpool. A combination of poverty and apathy among the electorate, an erosion of local party democracy and an increasingly remote administration has meant that the special conditions of the inner city have been insufficiently recognised other than in housing. The reality of the inner city is not reflected in council policies, because members are out of touch, whether with black, Liverpool 8 or white, Catholic Vauxhall; because the demands of city-wide corporate planning rule out the expression of local differences in Corporation programmes; because local officers have little scope for independent action; and because key sectors lie outside its responsibility, with other agencies, or levels of government. The only democratic reforms to have been discussed seriously have been neighbourhood councils.

Enabling legislation for elected neighbourhood councils was built into the Local Government Acts for Scotland and Wales, but not for England. But such councils, even if introduced, would be unable on their own to come to grips with the basic lack of power of inner area residents. As envisaged they would be purely advisory, or, at best, as in the Southern Neighbourhood Council or the Vauxhall Steering Group, have limited resources sufficient only for small scale supportive services – community workers, youth clubs, information services and so on.

The questions posed in this last section go to the heart of the relationship between people and government in the inner areas. But before taking the discussion any further, we need to arrive at our final statement of the issues which face local and central government in the inner areas, drawing on the description of the last six chapters. We shall return to the three questions in the last chapter of the report.

11 The inner areas: issues and policies

Concentrations of deprivation

The inner areas

We described the inner areas of Liverpool in chapter four, showing them to be on average of lower social status than the rest of the city. They contained the great majority of the remaining pre-1919 housing in the city, particularly its private rented housing, and an increasing proportion of the city's council dwellings, chiefly flats and maisonettes. Above all, we showed that the inner areas of Liverpool had been losing population at an increasing rate for half a century, so that by 1971 their population was about three hundred and thirty thousand or just about half the total in the city.

**Figure 44
Deprivation and the
inner area 1971**

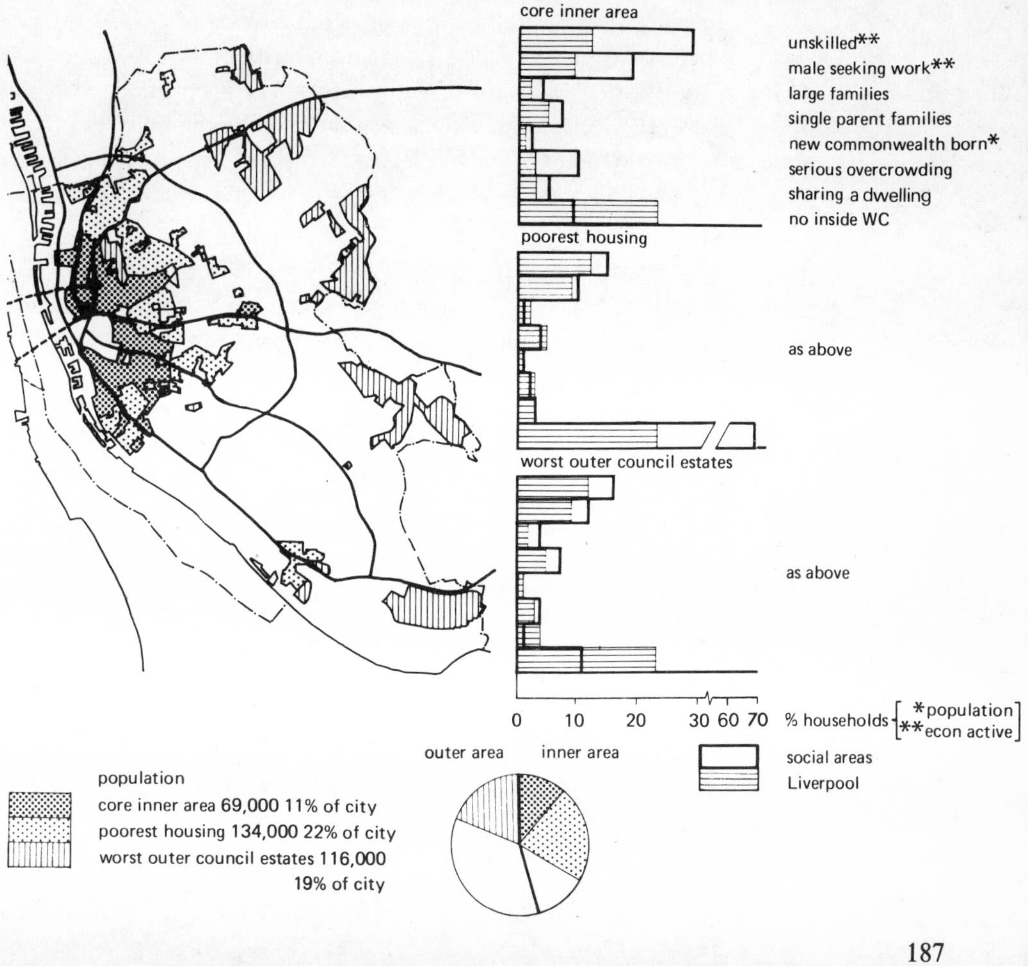

core inner area

unskilled**
male seeking work**
large families
single parent families
new commonwealth born*
serious overcrowding
sharing a dwelling
no inside WC

poorest housing

as above

worst outer council estates

as above

0   10   20   30 60 70   % households ⎡ *population ⎤
                                         ⎣ **econ active ⎦

outer area   inner area   social areas
                                          Liverpool

population
core inner area 69,000 11% of city
poorest housing 134,000 22% of city
worst outer council estates 116,000
                        19% of city

187

But our description revealed too the wide variety of circumstances and conditions in inner Liverpool. This ranged from the stable working class communities in older terraced housing, the newly converted flats in the large villas around Sefton Park and at least some of the more recent council estates, to the poverty and deprivation of multi-let houses in the rooming house areas, the worst of the remaining (and deteriorating) terraces ripe for slum clearance and many of the older council tenements from before and since the war.

Although the population of the outer areas of the city was still increasing it was no less varied, the affluent high status suburbs around Calderstones and the respectable interwar garden suburbs built by the Corporation contrasting with conditions in some of the more recent council estates.

But chapters five, six and seven demonstrated the major issue for government concerning the inner areas of Liverpool. This was the presence within inner Liverpool of areas where concentrations were found of groups of people most at risk of poverty and deprivation and the extent to which social and economic malaise were found in these same areas. The area of most extreme concentrations in 1971 was comparatively small, a population of about seventy thousand, not more than a quarter of the total living in the inner areas, or eleven percent of the total population of the city. Although no more than a quarter of the inner city, these areas nonetheless need to be seen as the poorest of a continuous gradation of social conditions in which the great majority of the population of the inner areas is comparatively poor and of low status. The proportion of population in these areas of concentration is illustrated for 1971 in the following table, compared with the proportion in the city at large. The table shows, too, the proportion of all those in the city who are in these groups who live in the concentrations.

The concentrations are found in two types of area, the worst areas of multi-let housing and overcrowding in the rooming house areas of Abercromby, Granby and Princes Park; and the inner council estates. The former were characterised

	Average % for city	Average % in area of concentration	% of city total in areas of concentration
Unskilled workers/all workers	12	27(33)	25
Male unemployed/all male workers	9	18(22)	23
Unemployed unskilled/unskilled workers	18	28(51)	39
Large families/all households	2	4(6)	20
Single parent families/all households	5	8(15)	19
New commonwealth born/total population	1	3(11)	36
Households over $1\frac{1}{2}$ persons per room/all households	3	10(15)	40
Households sharing a dwelling/all households	3	5(19)	17
Households lacking an inside wc/all households	23	9(30)	4

Note: Figure in brackets is highest % for small areas within general area of concentration.

Source: IAS Liverpool, *Social Area Analysis 1971* (Department of the Environment 1977).

especially by a high incidence of black people and new commonwealth immigrants, unskilled workers and single parent families. Above all, they contained many people who had moved recently to Liverpool. They had the highest levels in the city of unemployment, serious overcrowding, shared household facilities, poor health and family instability. Unemployment was much higher even than the generally low level of skill would indicate. The concentration of new commonwealth immigrants combined with the incidence of poor health, family instability and bad housing conditions suggested that here disadvantage is rooted in social pressures and personal and family circumstances rather than just a lack of qualifications or skills. Some of the conditions described here are found also in nearby council estates which have been used to rehouse people from slum clearance in these areas.

The older council estates, found mainly north and south of the city centre near the docks and, to a lesser extent, in Everton, Edge Hill and Old Swan, showed more straightforward, though only slightly less extreme, concentrations of deprivation. Unemployment was severe, but no greater than the high proportion of unskilled workers would suggest. There were no large concentrations of vulnerable familes and little evidence of family instability. Movement of population into these estates was small and there were very few new commonwealth immigrants. Indeed, such estates contained almost exclusively poor, stable, white, working class communities. Deprivation had a clear economic foundation in lack of skill and unemployment.

The remainder of the inner areas, consisting almost entirely of older terraced housing shows evidence of deprivation chiefly in the quality of the housing itself, the lack of amenities. The population itself has a lower status and a degree of poverty only a little less below the average for a generally poor city.

Outer Liverpool

Chapter five, and some of the later chapters, showed that deprivation was not confined to the inner areas of Liverpool. Concentrations of groups of people at risk

	Average % in area of concentration[1]
Unskilled workers/all workers	16(19)
Male unemployed/all male workers	12(13)
Unemployed unskilled/unskilled workers	17(31)
Large families/all households	4(10)
Single parent families/all households	7(11)
New commonwealth born/total population	0(1)
Households over $1\frac{1}{2}$ persons per room/all households	4(5)
Households sharing a dwelling/all households	1(1)
Households lacking an inside wc/all households	11(30)

Note: Figure in brackets is highest % for small areas within general area of concentration.

Source: IAS Liverpool, Social Area Analysis 1971 (Department of the Environment 1977).

189

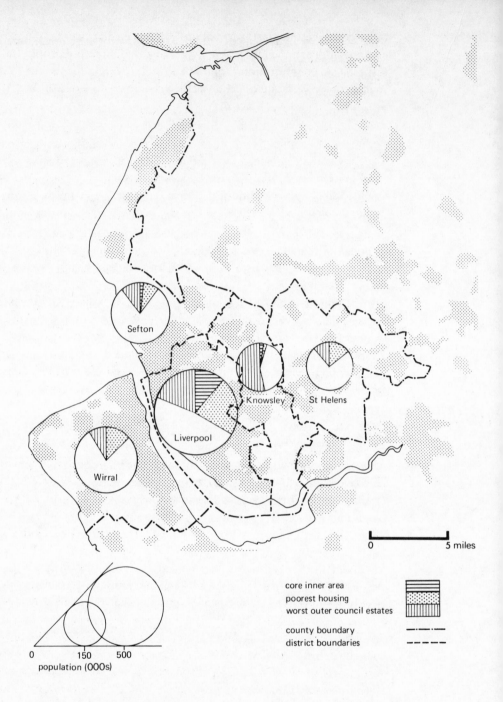

**Figure 45
Deprivation,
Merseyside 1971**

Sefton

Knowsley

St Helens

Liverpool

Wirral

0   5 miles

core inner area
poorest housing
worst outer council estates

county boundary
district boundaries

0   150   500
population (000s)

of poverty were to be found in many of the outer council estates in 1971. The estates most affected were in Speke, Gillmoss, Netherley and Cantril Farm, built mainly during the post war period to rehouse families moved from the inner city after slum clearance, firstly from the oldest terraced housing and latterly from the stress areas of multi-let housing. The total population living in these poorest of the

190

outer council estates in Liverpool in 1971 was greater than that in the worst concentrations in the inner area, over a hundred thousand people. But in most respects, the concentrations, though above the average for the city, were not as high as in the worst inner areas, as the accompanying table shows.

Merseyside

A comparison for 1971 between Liverpool and the other four metropolitan districts in Merseyside shows that the concentrations of deprivation associated with the worst rooming house areas are found exclusively in inner Liverpool, as are three quarters of those in the older council estates of the inner areas, small examples being found elsewhere in Birkenhead. The characteristic features of the older parts of Bootle, Birkenhead and St. Helens correspond much more closely to the older terraced areas of inner Liverpool where the problems chiefly are those of housing.

But the other noteworthy feature in the rest of Merseyside is the presence of areas similar in their social and economic characteristics to the poorest outer council estates in Liverpool described above. These are located chiefly in Knowsley; the main areas are Kirkby and Cantril Farm, local authority estates built by the Liverpool Corporation before local government reorganisation to rehouse families from the slum clearance areas of inner Liverpool.

Great Britain

A similar pattern is found nationally according to an analysis of census data for parliamentary constituencies. Inner urban areas in Tyne-Wear, West Yorkshire, Greater Manchester, West Midlands, Nottingham, and Hull show broadly similar conditions of economic, social, and housing stress to those of inner Merseyside although Liverpool is worse off than most.[1] The extremes of deprivation shown by inner Clydeside are unique in their intensity except for the worst part of inner Liverpool, the Scotland-Exchange constituency. Every indicator is present to a serious degree, but particularly those relating to low skill and unemployment, to large and single parent families and above all to overcrowding. Sixteen percent of all households were living at more than one and a half persons per room, eight times the national average and partly the consequence of the high proportion of council tenancies. Inner London is characterised mainly by housing stress, particularly sharing, and a high proportion of new commonwealth immigrants, seven times the national average. Unemployment however was not much greater than the national average and substantially less than in inner Clydeside or the inner provincial cities.

The combined population of inner Clydeside, inner London, and the inner areas of major provincial cities is about 3·8 million. Some seven percent of the country's population is therefore involved. Yet these areas contained in 1971 above average

(1) IAS Liverpool, *Social Area Analysis 1971* (Department of the Environment 1977).

191

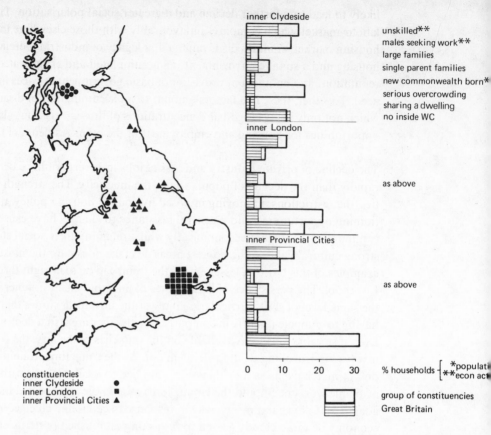

Figure 46
Urban stress,
Great Britain 1971

inner Clydeside

unskilled**
males seeking work**
large families
single parent families
new commonwealth born*
serious overcrowding
sharing a dwelling
no inside WC

inner London

as above

inner Provincial Cities

as above

0   10   20   30   % households { *populati
                                     **econ act

constituencies
inner Clydeside   ●
inner London   ■
inner Provincial Cities ▲

group of constituencies
Great Britain

proportions of every vulnerable group and every form of deprivation which we have discussed; ranging from, say, thirteen percent of male unemployment, or housing lacking basic amenities; to thirty percent of all serious overcrowding, or new commonwealth immigrants.

Thus, in both the nature and concentration of deprivation, inner Liverpool is more akin to the inner urban areas of other major cities than to other parts of Merseyside, suggesting strongly that its major determinants are not local factors but relate to a particular stage in urban and industrial development in this country. While the extent of economic deprivation depends on the decline of the traditional industries of the city concerned, the degree of social deprivation appears more closely related to the size of the conurbation and to past patterns of population migration and adjustment within the region. However, there are sufficient differences between each inner city area to suggest that local factors are also important.

Accumulated disadvantage

The concentrations of deprivation in the core of the inner city are the result of five major factors associated with its location, population and housing stock, which are mutually reinforcing and which, without strong government intervention, are likely to lead to a further decline and a greater social polarisation. They are a labour market which compares unfavourably with those elsewhere in Merseyside; a housing market similarly disadvantaged; a legacy of industrial dereliction, decaying housing and a squalid environment; an accumulated and exaggerated bad reputation; and an unequal provision of basic government services in relation to need. Together, these five factors amount to an accumulation of disadvantage which not only brings together concentrations of those at risk but also affects the opportunities for housing and employment of the other residents of the inner city.

The decline of private industry and loss of jobs in Liverpool have occurred more rapidly than the decline of population in the inner city. The strength of community ties, the restrictions on moving imposed by council housing policy, the lack of training opportunities, and a general resistance to change, have caused some communities to stagnate economically whilst retaining their social stability and strong cultural values. The poorest areas near the docks are the most extreme examples of this but to a lesser extent the trend can be seen right through Liverpool. The persistence of higher rates of unemployment in inner Liverpool for the same level of skill, particularly amongst the unskilled, shows that workers are having to compete unfairly in comparison with other areas in a depleted job market. Even if suitable jobs were available on the outskirts of the city, the cost and time involved in travelling would rule them out. At the same time, training opportunities do not match needs as they themselves are tied to available jobs rather than available workers. Should the labour force as a whole be expected therefore to adapt its life style and move away in response to economic change, or should the economy be more closely geared to respecting established patterns of community life?

Population, migration, both voluntary and forced, has already done a great deal to reduce the effects of economic decline. The removal of large numbers of people to the outskirts of the city may have improved their economic chances slightly but did not pay due regard to the social and community strains involved. Voluntary migration has left behind in the inner city a higher proportion of the unskilled, elderly and least adaptable.

For those who remain there exists not only the kind of economic trap described above, but also a housing trap. Those at the bottom of the market who do not benefit from slum clearance have little chance of bettering their housing. The poorest, ineligible, or desperate often end up with the worst housing which nobody else wants, whether it be multi-lets in the private sector or hard to let council tenancies which may further be unsuitable or overcrowded. As housing policy is based on a close match between numbers and overall demand, the housing opportunities of those at the bottom become severely constrained. As the worst quality and least desirable housing are concentrated above all in the core of the inner city, this adds an area dimension to the basic lack of housing opportunities. To find a better house, even if the need can be adequately established or the money found, often means moving away from the inner areas. This area-based disadvantage will persist until housing conditions in the inner areas can be brought to compare more favourably with those elsewhere.

This residual older housing is accompanied by a further legacy of industrial dereliction and a decaying environment. The private sector has been allowed to despoil or abandon large areas of industrial land without being held responsible for the resulting dereliction. But public agencies have been equally culpable. British Rail has retained large stretches of land which it is unlikely ever to use again, and failed to keep it in decent order. The local authority has made mistakes over shorter periods by over-ambitious planning and insufficiently frequent policy reviews. There is thus a combination of industrial decay and dereliction, blighted land, and crumbling housing inherited by the present population of the inner areas, for which they were in no way responsible. Yet this dereliction discourages potential employers from investing in new jobs, has a depressing effect on residents, and, as a social cost, is handed on from one generation to the next.

The sum total of these trends and the resulting combinations and concentrations of decay, stagnation and social breakdown, have an impact on people's attitudes. People in the most affected areas, whether they be Liverpool 8 or the council estates of say Edge Hill or Vauxhall, become alienated and react with either aggression or apathy. Attitudes held by people living elsewhere harden in response and whole neighbourhoods acquire bad reputations. Putting a large number of antisocial or dirty families in one estate gives that estate a reputation which discourages socially ambitious families from moving in and makes it more difficult for existing families to move out. Areas where a combination of clubs and cheap flats allow prostitution to flourish develop a reputation out of all proportion to the events actually taking place, a reputation which reflects on residents rather than those who use the clubs or prostitutes. Particular schools acquire reputations which can damage the chance of their pupils finding a job. Codes evolve which, to the initiated, carry a wealth of meaning and prejudice. Liverpool 8 becomes a postal district to be shunned, not to be used in applying for a job, and where it is almost impossible to obtain a mortgage. Those who prefer to live in the stigmatised areas, and they are probably the majority of those actually living there, face the prospect of a permanently low status in the eyes of the rest of society, based to a great extent on the area in which they live. This may not bother many people living there but a bad reputation is one of the most difficult things to change as it will outlast the circumstances which give rise to it. As such, it stamps the seal of disadvantage on inner city areas in a very powerful and intractable way.

Finally the trend towards centralised decision-making in local government has meant that services increasingly have been delivered according to average levels of provision and by standardised methods. Such an approach effectually discriminates against deprived areas where more people are in greater need and the pressure on services organised on a per capita basis is such that different methods need to be found for providing the services. Local authorities find it difficult to discriminate heavily and overtly in favour of particular areas. There are limits to the proportion of scarce resources that the Council can allocate to combatting the effects of inherited disadvantage when their impact is felt severely only by a small minority of the city's population.

The Council is further hampered by a lack of rate income in poor areas, the vagaries of the rate support grant, and the burden of being already a relatively poor city. Many of the more affluent of those who earn their living in Liverpool live outside the city. Most of those whom the city has to subsidise live inside, in the inner areas and the new outer estates. But the rate support grant which is designed to overcome these and other disparities is based chiefly on past spending policies and other factors, and only to a limited extent on the greater need of such areas. Furthermore, the rate support income declines with falling population without the costs of providing services and an infrastructure for those who remain decreasing to a comparable extent. We return to this matter of resources in chapter thirteen.

Thus, while the existence of poverty and social stress in parts of the inner areas and elsewhere result from wider inequalities in society, there are factors peculiar to inner Liverpool, but similar to those in other inner cities, which add a further element of disadvantage to the problems of poverty and discrimination. Only a minority of those living in the inner areas are actually deprived. But the lack of nearby jobs and decent housing, the decaying surroundings, the bad reputation and the unequal provision of services between them impose a cumulative disadvantage for all those living in the inner city which is self-perpetuating. It is felt most severely by those living in the area who are actually unemployed or seriously overcrowded or actively discriminated against, but is shared in by other residents who, even though not living in personal poverty, face the same job market, the same decaying environment and the same stigmatising attitudes held by outsiders. The enduring poverty of inner Liverpool not only represents a tragic waste of human and land resources, but also erodes the quality of life and government in the city as a whole. By degrees, the credibility of the local authority is put in jeopardy and its financial resources severely restrained.

It would be wrong to leave an impression so bleak that it deepens the despair already felt by many residents and public servants. Such a view ignores many good things: access to the city centre, fine parks, cheap housing, a strong sense of place and community, a toughness and loyalty to friends and employers not always found elsewhere. Above all it tends to exaggerate the extent of disadvantage through sheer weight of words. The areas of most severe economic and social stress contain only about eleven percent of the city's population and in these areas only a minority can be described as being deprived as individuals through unemployment, overcrowding or family breakdown. The vast majority of those living in the inner area, whilst poorer than most and by no means facing easy lives, have values, hopes and satisfactions which are broadly the same as those shared by people living in other parts of the country. Broadly the same, but not identical. Inner city communities are shaped by a unique set of economic and cultural forces which gives them a special flavour.

Our main concern for the future is not the alienation of these communities from government and society but the alienation of government and society from the inner city. Studies of this kind concentrate, by definition, on problems. They hark back to the past, to the things that have gone wrong; to the policies which have turned sour. But such an approach has, in itself, served consistently to support the conventional wisdom that inner cities are intrinsically bad places. A growing awareness of the inherent value of strong community ties might have come too late. But even that awareness does not necessarily acknowledge value in the differing attitudes and culture of that community, however it may be expressed. The reputation rather than the reality has too often shaped public attitudes and government policies.

The trend towards decline

There can be little doubt that regional economic policies have been of great advantage to Merseyside. They have brought nearly a hundred thousand jobs to the region since the war, and injected large resources into the local economy which have had their own multiplier effect. The new towns have been profitable developments and other peripheral expansion has proved generally attractive and successful. Despite the depressed state of the Merseyside economy, there is little to distinguish the new development from similar schemes elsewhere in the country. Some of the outer districts of Merseyside have an unemployment rate only slightly above the national average, although conditions can quickly deteriorate as the recent example of Skelmersdale shows. Many agencies have combined effectively in this huge investment which, while by no means overcoming all of Merseyside's problems, had provided residents of the new areas with generally better physical surroundings and a wider range of opportunities for home and work, and subjected to less social stress than that faced by their counterparts in the inner areas.

The considerable economic and social success of most of the new towns and peripheral developments, however, must be contrasted with the failure to date of much planned overspill from Liverpool to produce successul communities. It could be argued that the pioneering spirit associated with voluntary movement out of the older urban areas has produced better results than the element of compulsion inherent in a policy of large scale relocation following slum clearance. What seems more likely is that the new towns and the new private developments have attracted, or selected, young, relatively skilled, populations; those most able or determined to achieve material success and adapt to new surroundings. In contrast, much of the overspill development in the outer council estates has, at best, provided better housing and schools and an improved physical environment. But the social and economic circumstances of their residents have changed little in comparison with their former lives in the inner areas.

By contrast, the redevelopment and latterly the rehabilitation of the inner areas has focussed almost exclusively on housing and related social investment without any effective policies for its economic development. This failure can be attributed partly to the division of responsibility for different aspects of policy between different levels of government, and partly to the lack of monitored and coordinated action in housing and economic development in the inner area. At the simplest level, it is only necessary to compare the current physical chaos of inner Liverpool with the well-ordered pattern of development in a new town such as Runcorn to realise how devastating the impact has been. It may be argued that the programme in the

196

inner area started later and will work itself out in time and that it cannot be evaluated at its present stage. However, the evidence of severe economic and social disadvantages facing all residents irrespective of the quality of their housing, makes this view difficult to sustain. There have been no convincing strategies to offset the disadvantages of poor job and training prospects and social disadvantage. The continuing decline of private investment will be very difficult to stem. If regional policies continue in their present form, the high unemployment areas will continue to be largely without government economic aid as this stimulates, but also responds to, the level of private investment.

Thus government policy has tended to concentrate on the weaknesses of the inner city, rather than the strengths. The most basic arm of policy, to disperse population from the most congested areas, aimed to overcome the disadvantages of overcrowding and high density. But the ways in which such a policy was interpreted showed scant regard for the people involved. Clearance and rehousing programmes were autocratic and insensitive. Much of the earlier new housing was of poor quality, high density and inhuman in design. Furthermore, the new housing and economic opportunities made available outside the city have drawn off many young, skilled families who might have been prepared to invest money, time and energy into their homes, their communities and their surroundings. An attitude that the inner areas are not good places to live has been reinforced by government policy for good but insufficient reasons.

The choices for policy

Government today faces the fundamental question of whether there exists sufficient political and administrative will to make significant inroads into the concentrations of poverty that persist in the inner areas of our larger cities, by tackling the sources of the accumulated disadvantage which bring about these concentrations and add to the deprivation experienced within them. Our experience in Liverpool demonstrates this. It should be the priority task for urban policy making by reason of its scale in Liverpool and the relative degree of deprivation experienced within the inner areas, greater than in any other parts of the city. It is clear that concentrations of deprivation are forming in certain outer council estates but their level of intensity is not as great as in the inner city, and therefore are of lower priority than the inner areas.

But we are reasonably sure that neither the concentrations of deprivation, nor the accumulated disadvantage, are unique to inner Liverpool. The statistical evidence and the experience of other inner area studies suggests that they are to be found in the inner areas of London, Clydeside and the larger English provincial cities, albeit in different forms in each. It is for this reason that the question is fundamental not only for local government in Liverpool and Merseyside but for central government.

The responses to this question span the whole spectrum of political philosophy and administrative experience. At one extreme is the attitude enshrined in such cliches as 'the poor are always with us', that 'people like living in slums', or that 'people are without jobs because they do not want to work'. In a more respectable form, this attitude says that poverty, inequality, and their manifestations in such places as the inner areas, are inescapable facets of our society. The duty of a humane and caring government is then to provide a safety net of minimum standards below which individuals are not allowed to fall, while giving major emphasis to ensuring adequate opportunities for people to improve their lot through their own efforts. Inevitably, the purity of such a vision is unattainable in a society as complex as ours, in the aftermath of nearly a century of evolution towards a welfare state and an even longer history of intervention by local government in so many of the conditions of urban living.

Another response may be paraphrased from the report of the Coventry CDP[1]. The team described the evolution of their own approach to these issues. Simplifying their ideas, they started by accepting the pathological view of poverty inherent in their brief; that it is the result of personal inadequacy on the part of individuals and families and that its impact can be reduced by self-help and community development. The next stage in their thinking was that much of the poverty in society was made worse, if not caused, by adminstrative failure. Local and central government was unable adequately to identify needs and incompetent in delivering the services. But, in time, they jettisoned this view as well and moved to their final position; that individual poverty, although having elements of the two previous ideas, is fundamentally the result of the distribution of political and economic power in society, itself largely a function of the control over wealth. In its most extreme form, not necessarily espoused by CDP in practice, this view says that anything less than a frontal assault on power and wealth will not only be ineffectual but may be positively harmful through diverting attention and resources away from the main issues.

A contrasting argument is that little more needs to be done. 'Provided we had the resources we could do the job' is the belief of many people, particularly in government agencies. Others argue, with equal sincerity, that it is already being done. But the trends belie such optimism. The material circumstances of most working class people in this country have improved so much over the last thirty years, even relative to most professional and managerial incomes, that those who are really poor no longer form a democratic majority. The new poor are those trapped at a low but not always uncomfortable level of material welfare, but bound about by rules of elegibility for income, housing and other services. They form a substantial but often forgotten minority, the economic and social misfits or failures.

Current changes in policy

The policies of central and local government have in fact been changing at an accelerating rate during the period of our study, particularly since the summer of 1976, although the changes had started earlier. The most significant has been the

(1) Bennington J, Bond N and Skelton P, *Coventry and Hillfields: Prosperity and the Persistence of Inequality* (Coventry CDP Final Report, part 1 March 1975).

appointment of the Secretary of State for the Environment to take special responsibility for urban affairs and to chair a cabinet committee to coordinate the work of all departments in this field. The first public intimation of this news was given in the speech at Manchester Town Hall in September 1976 referred to in chapter one.

But there have been other indications. The Strategic Plan for the North West was completed in July 1973 and the response by Government in December 1975.[1] The Plan was expressed in very general terms but said that 'the improvement of living and working conditions in the towns and cities (is) the predominant issue in the North West.' The poor urban environment, it said, was largely contained within the Mersey belt and included the inner areas of Merseyside and Greater Manchester where 'people . . . are underpriviliged in their quality of life compared with elsewhere.' The government response accepted these principles, though with provisos about resources.

The Stage One report of the Merseyside Structure Plan, published in 1975, was based on a strategy which would:

> 'concentrate investment and development within the urban county and particularly in those areas with the most acute problems, enhancing the environment and encouraging housing and economic expansion on derelict and disused sites. It would restrict development on the edge of the built up areas to a minimum'.[2]

More recently, the policies and actions needed to achieve this general aim have been spelt out in more specific detail, with estimates of the resources necessary for the economic development, in a report by the County Planning Officer to the Policy, Planning and Resources Committee of the County Council.[3]

The Department of Industry, the County Council and the City Council have given increasing regard to the industrial development in the inner areas of Merseyside, including the small rolling programme of advance factory units and industrial land referred to in chapter five. The Job Creation Programme and initiatives by the Training Services Agency have begun to tackle the problems of unemployment. And the Manpower Services Commission is setting up an experimental pilot project for tailoring training and other manpower services on Merseyside to meet the special needs of the area.

Policies have been changing too within Liverpool City Council. The major development has been the new policy for the improvement of the pre 1919 housing described in chapter eight, closely followed by the revisions to the methods for determining priorities in the allocation of council tenancies. But industrial land policies and land use requirements for the inner area are also being reviewed.

(1) *Strategic Plan for the North West: SPNW Joint Planning Team Report* (HMSO 1974); and statement by the Minister for Planning and Local Government, December 1975.

(2) *Merseyside Structure Plan, Stage One Report* (Merseyside County Council 1975).

(3) *Targets for Merseyside for the 1980s*. A Report by the County Planning Officer 17 December 1976. The proposals for economic development and training closely parallel in many respects our conclusions and recommendations on these subjects in chapter twelve.

Separately and together these changes represent a fairly significant change of direction in the intentions of both central and local government towards removing some of the cumulative disadvantage specifically associated with living in Liverpool's inner area. Yet there must still be real cause for concern. It was almost precisely these same disadvantages that post-war regional and urban policies sought to overcome. The dispersal of population and the rebuilding of the inner areas were designed to counter economic decline and remove the disadvantages of bad housing. The failure of this approach occurred not because of the dispersal of population, but because central and local government together had neither the breadth of vision to coordinate economic, social and physical programmes across Merseyside, nor the precision of focus to take special action where the broader policies were failing to take effect.

There is a real danger that the current debate over policies for the inner areas is becoming polarised between the choice of new towns or inner cities and will perpetuate the same narrow vision and partial approach. It is the lack of comprehensive and effective regional policies by central government which allows such a polarisation to occur. Regional industrial investment, new towns, and urban renewal have been run as programmes inspired and mainly financed by separate government departments and divisions. The separateness within central government, and the division between it and local government, has been most apparent in economic development, for at least there was a measure of planning and cooperation in the housing field between Liverpool and its overspill destinations in the town development schemes and new towns. Yet each programme represents a selective central government initiative with broadly similar aims; to counter the impact on the conurbation of the long term decline of its traditional industries and to renew its physical fabric.

A more effective approach would have been to give real authority for the planning and executing of strategies for appropriate geographical areas in which new towns, the renewal of inner cities and regional economic development can be seen for what they are, integral parts of a single programme for the future prosperity of areas such as Merseyside. Polarisation between new towns and old cities would have become irrelevant. The debate could have centred on firstly the national balance of special assistance to the conurbation, and secondly on the right balance of different initiatives within it. Such an approach would not remove imbalances altogether. Programmes develop a momentum of their own (eg. slum clearance) which need strong political pressure to reverse. But it would remove the worst effects of the massive, blunt, uncoordinated programmes so much in evidence in today's inner areas. It would avoid the consequences of shifts in policy which may now be seen merely as a cut-back in the national new towns programme coupled with a corresponding transfer of resources in favour of inner area. But the danger of placing too much faith solely in regional coordination is that it would miss much of the strength of the argument in chapter ten concerning the overcentralisation of authority, its exercise through technical rather than political decisions and the consequent remoteness of government from people.

200

Regeneration: the choice for policy

Inner Liverpool has the worst concentrations of poverty and social stress on Merseyside, and probably in England, though not Scotland. It exhibits an accumulation of disadvantage which threatens the future of all residents of inner Liverpool, not only the most deprived, and to some extent the future financial capacity and public credibility of the local authority. Equity alone demands action to counteract the backlog of disadvantage that exists; a backlog which means that equality of opportunity as a national principle is seriously threatened.

The disadvantages directly associated with living in the inner areas are such that any policies for the inner areas, even if they are part of a wider, regional strategy and even though they may operate at different levels, are bound to select certain areas and groups of people for special attention and additional resources. But, apart from the clear demands of equity, there are further justifications for positive discrimination in favour of the most deprived inner areas. First, by focussing on the needs of deprived people where they are geographically most concentrated, it gives the possibility of a greater effectiveness in the use of scarce resources, a greater take-up of benefits and a greater demonstrable effect. Secondly, provided the approach is sufficiently wide, it gives the basis for a serious attempt at compensatory provision in a number of fields to overcome the effects of accummulated disadvantage. Finally, by focussing on the total provision of services for specific areas and communities, it offers the prospect of more radical reform in the administration of services, and the opportunity to recreate a viable local democracy. It lays the foundation for reforms in the administration and provision of services and relationships between government and people which would have wider applicability in areas of future priority action such as the outer council estates.

Regeneration, the policy of positive discrimination towards the worse concentrations of deprivation in inner Liverpool and Merseyside, would have four aims:

to enhance the status of the inner area, recognising local values, and giving to the people who live, work and invest there a greater commitment to its future;

to raise standards of material well being and widen the choice of home, work and life style for its residents;

to improve conditions of housing and environment;

to foster economic development for the inner city.

In a sense these are aims which could hold for urban policy in any part of Liverpool or indeed in any other city in the country. Their significance for inner Liverpool lies in the current failure for them to be fulfilled to a greater degree than anywhere else in the city. But broadly similar conditions are to be found in other provincial conurbations, London and Clydeside. To that extent, policy should be for the regeneration not only of inner Liverpool but for the inner areas of all those cities which contain substantial concentrations of poverty and deprivation in their midst, a national policy for regeneration.

Regeneration does not imply a return to some past vision of a tight-knit city of traditional working class communities. Wider social changes make that impossible, even were it desirable. Nor does it imply any future vision of the city beautiful. The consequences of such well meaning impositions in the past are all too evident today. And it does not necessarily imply substantial economic growth in the inner city. Rather it would aim to generate selective growth in the city in favour of those most affected by its decline. The search should be for policies which would at the same time allow more of those who want to leave the inner city to do so and provide better opportunities for those who wish to stay.

It must be accepted too that residential densities should probably continue to decline though not if this was by keeping land unnecessarily vacant. One of the strongest components of urban stress is lack of space. In the past, expectations of population growth and fears of land scarcity led local authorities to pursue high densities with some unfortunate and unforeseen results. The significant decline in population in the inner city has not resulted in very great reductions in the density of residential areas as housing has competed with other uses whose demands for space have increased much more. It seems very unlikely therefore that reasonable living conditions will be possible in the inner areas without further reductions in living density and an inevitable moving out of population. But the migration should not need to be as selective as in the past, either into or out of the inner area; and the social, economic and physical conditions in the inner areas should compare more favourably with those elsewhere in Merseyside.

Regeneration would not be for the benefit of existing residents only. It would seek to reestablish the necessary elements for inner city communities to be economically and socially viable. It would create the conditions under which a greater variety of social classes might choose to live in the inner city, reversing the longterm trend towards polarisation. But a stable community also needs a capacity for renewal, physically and socially. Young people need to be able to settle locally or new families to come in as older generations die off or move away. Even to move towards some of these elements in inner Liverpool needs a great opening up of opportunity in areas where few have existed for many years. Communities need to be told they have something to offer, and not be rejected. Such rejection can only further demoralise those who remain and increase their feelings of uselessness. A fierce pride would not allow such sentiments to be expressed directly. They show forth in a smouldering resentment of authority, crime, vandalism, and intensely parochial attitudes. Regeneration, on the other hand, argues that many inner city communities have much to offer but for this to achieve expression the backlog of decline will have to be made good. Ironically, the objectives of planned dispersal which sought to remove the physical aspects of inner city disadvantage, may best be served by a policy of regeneration in the inner areas themselves, through which more people are able to decide their futures from a base of economic and community stability, rather than one of decline and despair.

But however successful a regeneration policy may be in improving opportunities and raising the status of stable inner city communities, a small minority would still be in need of care and support. Many of the ingredients of regeneration would favour those who are now currently socially disadvantaged; not least a generally higher level of economic activity for those who can take advantage of increased opportunities. Improved status for minority groups such as blacks or single parent families would go some way to improving their opportunities but extra support would need to be provided for the most vulnerable in any group. But many of the most disadvantaged are now living in the inner areas because of social rejection or discrimination. Part of any policy of regeneration must be to make society accept responsibility for its rejects. The care of ex-prisoners and mental patients, for example, should be undertaken within the fabric of rich communities as well as poor. New towns, the suburbs and private estates should take responsibility for more social casualties, not just by paying more taxes but by direct caring.

In summary a policy for the regeneration of inner areas would be an exercise in selective discrimination in favour of those in poverty and of the areas within which they are most concentrated. Growth in certain economic and housing sectors, and in selected parts of the inner area, would be achieved by selective industrial development; increased opportunities for training and education; improvements in housing and environmental conditions, including a reduction in densities; and some local institutional reform. In essence it would follow a principle that opportunities need to be offered to people in ways which respect their existing community and social ties rather than assume they must necessarily be broken by moving away to seek new opportunities. If many people then choose to move away because they have saved money, gained qualifications or been trained, then so be it. But by offering greater economic opportunity and improved housing conditions locally, and respecting local communities by offering them more responsibility, a policy of regeneration would lead to many people choosing to enhance their skills and find their homes in the inner city.

We recommend in chapter twelve a set of four programmes through which the policy for regeneration should be carried out. They are:

promoting the economic development of inner Liverpool;

expanding opportunities for training;

improving access to suitable housing for those most at risk in the housing market;

chanelling resources to areas of greatest social need.

The programmes do not constitute a plan in the generally accepted or statutory sense, but more a set of economic and social programmes, each pointing in a similar direction. Together they recognise a need to improve opportunities for those who can take advantage of them and to increase support for those who cannot. They recognise that developing industry and raising job opportunities needs to be carried out in conjunction with raising the skills of the work force and with realistic housing policies. They accept that regeneration is a dynamic process, that there will be a coming and going of population and changes in social and community structures to which all policies will need to respond.

Rather than attempt to predict targets for each programme or the total package, a political and administrative framework should be created which would maintain the whole programme and its constituent parts moving in the required direction with regular reviews of priorities in the confident assumption that circumstances will change, that the outcomes of policy cannot be foreseen with any clarity. But we have referred many times in this report to the problem of attitudes; the insensitivity and remoteness of government; the failure to recognise, let alone tolerate, different values; the uncertainty, fear and anger and the deep seated and growing sense of alienation from government on the part of many residents of the inner areas; the failure of elected representatives to do more than speak for a few individuals across the barrier between governors and governed.

The political and administrative framework for regeneration must therefore seek to counter the entrenched attitudes in the rest of society towards so many of its residents; to do this will require strong, central authority to achieve the necessary degree of positive discrimination. Yet at the same time, the need for central authority will have to be reconciled with the equally pressing need for effective local responsibilities within the inner areas for the execution of policies. The problems of achieving this reconcilation, the institutional problems of regeneration, forms the subject of the final chapter in our report.

12 Regeneration of inner Liverpool

Halting the economic decline of the inner area[1]

The visible impact of Liverpool's economic decline on the inner areas is in empty shops, warehouses and factories, abandoned docks and railway sidings, vacant land and unemployed people. A major aim of regeneration should be to bring these resources into productive use by stemming the loss of jobs from existing firms and by increasing as far as possible the inflow, or creation, of new jobs and new workshops, factories and warehouses. This process forms a counterpart to the training programmes described in the following section. However, the aim should not be to provide an artificial balance between training programmes and the number of new jobs which might be attracted to the inner area. Indeed, a programme aimed at halting economic decline cannot be readily expressed in quantitative terms. It is much more a matter of using techniques of economic planning and management in the public sector to attract private investment back into the inner area. Accordingly, the figures we do quote are intended to give an indication of the scale of effort required, rather than precise targets to be achieved.

Most of the tasks involved can be seen as a continuation of current policies by existing agencies. However, the scale of effort required, the perspective and attitudes to be adopted, and to some extent the tasks themselves represent a break with the past, and require a new approach to their totality.

Industrial promotion

Both Merseyside County Council and Liverpool District Council have industrial development offices, though none of the other metropolitan districts are similarly served. The main activities are the promotion of the county to outside industrialists, supported by the provision of sites and advance factories by the city. These activities form an essential part of any economic strategy and should be further extended. In particular, the different, but complementary, services offered to local industry by the two authorities could be strengthened in a number of ways. The capacity register of local firms being built up by the County Council should be regularly updated. Detailed advance knowledge should be collected of the needs of new companies coming to the area. Further use should also be made of special marketing campaigns to identify growth sectors and firms seeking to expand. Firms willing to resettle locally could be found by establishing links with planning authorities in those parts of the country where growth is restrained by government policy.

(1) For further details, see IAS Liverpool, *Economic Development of the Inner Area* (Department of the Environment 1977). The recent report by Merseyside County Council, *Targets for Merseyside for the 1980s*, also gives further details (see footnote, page 199).

But the activities of local authorities in fostering economic development need not be confined to such work. The authorities are major commercial undertakings in their own right, through their purchases, their investment funds and as employers. These could be used to the advantage of the inner areas, and to a certain extent already are, for instance, by giving preferential treatment to Merseyside firms in tendering for contracts, possibly fixing a price margin within which local firms would be preferred. Other examples could include local sub-contracting on major contracts awarded to firms from outside the county, making purchases from local shops, wholesalers, and agents and using building contractors who employed local workers for developments. Consideration should be given to the use of their investment funds in the local economy. A range of possibilities could flow from this type of initiative. For instance the local authority might establish a trust to invest in Liverpool companies. Or a new institution might be set up to channel the savings of local people into the regeneration of their economy.

Finally, local authorities should adapt their own personnel policies to giving priority to recruitment of suitably qualified residents of Liverpool; ensuring that recruits are drawn from all districts and communities of the city; and reserve some posts for applicants from communities in which work is being carried out. In particular they need to ensure racial equality in job opportunities.

Industrial land

Very recently the availability, condition and location of industrial land in inner Liverpool has been reexamined, and a start made on a small programme of advance factory building. This work has involved both local authorities and the Department of Industry. But it will only partially redeem the scarcity of industrial sites. Accordingly, a five year rolling programme for the supply of industrial land in the city should be prepared, including the provision of advance factory units. A minimum target should be two hundred and fifty thousand square feet of floorspace annually, sufficient for about eight hundred jobs. It should include variously sized units, particularly smaller premises. In preparing this programme and marketing these sites consideration should be given to other incentives to attract firms to inner locations who might otherwise prefer greenfield sites on the periphery. These might include preferential rent terms such that the price of inner area sites on offer would be lower than those elsewhere; and special grants for landscaping, environmental improvement and protection.

The scope for rapid and flexible site preparation and the reclamation of semi-derelict industrial areas can be shown by recent proposals in Rochdale. A large area of industrial land in mixed ownership was made a general industrial improvement area. A rapid sketch plan of possible environmental treatment of the site was prepared to attract prospective industrialists rather than to direct development. Flatted factories were provided and environmental improvement carried out under the Job Creation Programme and using local amenity groups and small task forces specially set up for site improvement and landscaping.

206

Town planning also exerts an influence on economic development through the allocation of sites for industrial and commercial purposes, and through large scale redevelopment. The development control system in particular should be used as a positive aid to economic development, by favouring applications for industrial or commercial developments unless they present very serious, local environmental problems. Applications received should be given special priority and prompt attention within the statutory period. Planning applications should be treated as an important source of information concerning industrial demand. Where consents are not granted the applicant should be assisted in finding an alternative site.

These proposals reflect our view that greater priority should be given than in the past to industrial development compared with other land use allocations in the preparation of local and district plans. The precise quantities and locations of industrial land will remain a matter for the local planners but overall quantities and broad locations need to be determined much more than at present by overall economic strategy. Greater attention should be given to assembling sites of an appropriate size and shape for industrial development and ensuring that land use allocations are not so rigidly defined that it proves impossible to vary them where appropriate, or to permit so called non conforming uses under certain circumstances. The recent consultation paper put out by the Department of the Environment for changes in development control might point the way in its concept of local special development areas.[1]

Finally, there is the special question of the docklands, particularly the South Docks. Even now, in the north especially, they provide some jobs which are easily accessible to the inner areas. But the derelict dock lands cover a large area which has many potential advantages of sea and rail access, space, little environmental conflict and proximity to local labour reserves. As a matter of prime urgency, a detailed review should be made of the feasibility of industrial development in the dock areas, including a possible major new industrial estate or sites for larger industries. The area represents probably the only major potential asset of a size that, if capable of industrial development, could reverse the falling levels of employment in the inner area. But it is unlikely to present a straightforward commercial proposition. The choice may well be accepting the costs of renewing a decayed and probably obsolete infrastructure; or facing a continuation of the present stalemate into the foreseeable future and the chronic dereliction and unemployment with which it is associated.

Major industrial enterprise

The Department of Industry is the main government body administering regional policy. It is unlikely to be possible to vary the level of capital grant within the special development area to give greater priority to high unemployment areas. However, permanent extension of the temporary employment subsidy for such areas should be considered.

(1) Circular letter from the Department of the Environment, 23 July 1976.

Many parts of inner Liverpool are dependent on a few large employers and their future prospects should be cherished for they have an impact on the inner city much greater than their number would suggest. In cases where the maintenance of existing employment is particularly important, large plants should be made the focus of planning agreements under the 1975 Industry Act, taking into account the desirability of encouraging local employment growth. The National Enterprise Board should be encouraged through its regional office in Merseyside to negotiate with the regional headquarters of companies located in Liverpool. Such firms might also be considered as a priority for selective financial assistance under the Industry Act 1972.

Consideration should be given to evolving management, marketing or production services for larger firms. Teams of business experts employed by government or the local authority could be used to plan future growth with existing firms in a selected area following the laying off of workers by a major employer. This approach has been used in Northern Ireland and Scotland. Where relevant the assessment could be extended to the fields of production engineering, product innovation, finance and marketing; and on advice covering the availability of government services, land and premises, training, industrial mortgages, capital grants and export services. The work of such a team could contribute to the general strategy for economic development.

Local enterprise

On past record, the industrial development policies of either the Department of Industry or the local authorities through their existing institutions would be unlikely to bring sufficient new investment to inner Liverpool even if it were given full priority over other areas. The difficulties of attracting industrial investment into the inner area are sufficient to require a special approach designed to supplement the work of the existing policies in central and local government. The aim would be to stimulate and promote industrial investment within inner Liverpool by assisting in the creation of new enterprises; and by maintaining employment and encouraging growth among existing firms. Our experience in the inner area suggests that the most promising field would be smaller firms of up to about a hundred employees. The methods required to promote the growth and establishment of such firms would differ from those for larger companies. New and small firms are less likely to have settled markets, established sources of finance or well organised management.

Stimulating local enterprise should include offering financial incentives to new or existing firms in the forms of loans, grants, guarantees and equity capital; providing advice and support to new and existing firms in the fields of production, management, finance marketing and premises; developing and promoting new ideas for business opportunities; and encouraging new and expanding firms from outside the city to locate in or near high unemployment areas.

Eligibility for financial assistance would depend on a firm's potential commercial viability given adequate finance and management. Priority for financial assistance,

208

advice and support should be given to manufacturing and construction firms; to labour intensive firms offering training opportunities for unskilled men; to firms locating in, or employing people from, areas of relatively high unemployment; and to firms set up, owned or managed by residents and workers in the inner area. Interested firms would mostly already be on Merseyside and either expanding or developing new products. But there have been instances of enterprises not set up for commercial purposes which could, with the right financing and assistance, become viable firms. Recent examples from inner Liverpool include projects organised through the Job Creation Programme and Community Industry, including the manufacture of fibre glass boats and the fitting of motor caravans, setting up a community group to make toys and running a building cooperative to fit alarm systems to council flats.

Each of these activities is small. But on the basis of similar experience in Northern Ireland they could nevertheless amount to the creation of as many as a thousand new jobs a year. This might involve a total investment of the order of two million pounds per annum including finance for equity and loans and grants for capital investment and for promotion and advice. This of course would include payments under existing policies for financial assistance and money raised in the private sector. But the special approach which we are describing would need to be one of the channels through which this investment could be realised. It is very doubtful if such an approach could be carried out by local authorities as presently organised insofar as it would require entrepreneurial attitudes and the power to take equity in selected firms where necessary. But it is precisely these powers which make the special approach an integral part of our economic proposals. How best to achieve such powers will be considered in the next chapter.

Raising levels of skill[1]

High unemployment, particularly amongst unskilled men, young people, immigrants and the black population is endemic to inner Liverpool and therefore requires basic changes in attitude and approach for any impact to be made. At present training opportunities depend almost entirely on the supply of jobs. Therefore the worse the labour market the less chance anyone has to break out of it by obtaining a skill. Those involved are faced with a stark choice, to go away from Merseyside and seek work elsewhere or to court long term unemployment. Many have already taken the former course. It is nevertheless a difficult decision to make, particularly for someone who is lacking a basic skill, has his roots on Merseyside, may be a council tenant with few prospects of a transfer, and has felt his self-confidence ebbing as unemployment lengthens. This is not just a personal tragedy. It represents a waste of labour resources.

A long term objective of training policy should therefore be to provide opportunities according to the wishes and capabilities of the work force and not according to the

(1) This subject in general is discussed in IAS Liverpool, *Economic Development of the Inner Area* (Department of the Environment 1977).

number and type of jobs available locally. Of course control would be required over the total provision nationally. But this should depend on overall manpower forecasting and not on the annual requirements of individual employers. In the shorter term, the basic objective of overall training strategy as it applies to the inner areas should be to make training opportunities available at least the equal of those elsewhere, and aimed at the specific needs of the local workforce. Our proposals for action cover the broad fields of manpower planning; training and placement for adults; training and placement for young people; work preparation schemes for the long-term unemployed; and employment transfer schemes.

Manpower planning

A comprehensive approach to manpower planning in Liverpool and Merseyside should be developed to include placement, training and worker mobility. It should be based on the principle of creating a skilled work force for future industrial development and not be limited to meeting the requirements of existing employers. It would involve all agencies and departments active in training, placement and provision for the unemployed, and should be exercised at a county wide level or for the Special Development Area. The Manpower Services Commission would probably need a Merseyside office to prepare manpower forecasts and assess training requirements based on the needs of local industry, the characteristics of the unemployed, the problems of the areas of high unemployment and the groups at greatest risk of unemployment.

Training and placement for adults

Placement services provided by the Employment Services Agency should be reorientated, within existing budgets, to give greater priority to the needs of the unemployed rather than, as now, mainly providing a service for employers. The live register should be reviewed regularly for each individual to establish whether he or she could become suitable for employment with the aid of a refresher course, needed retraining, or expert occupational guidance. The aim would be either to place the individual in a job reasonably quickly or direct him to an appropriate form of training. In addition the current, experimental Socially and Occupationally Disadvantaged Scheme (SODS, but with a change of name), should be extended on a permanent basis to help the hard core unemployed, if it proves successful. If not, an alternative should be sought.

Sufficient training places should be made available each year to accommodate at least a quarter of the unemployed. This would mean increasing the number of training places in government skill centres by providing a new centre or centres in inner Liverpool. In addition existing training courses which currently have long waiting lists should be expanded including Short Industrial Courses, similar initiatives offering training below skills level and courses specifically for the unemployed. But a small proportion of places on courses should be reserved for people with special priority including men from high unemployment areas, unskilled workers, and men over forty five or young people under twenty five. New courses should be provided which would be better equipped to meet the needs of

210

firms with special training requirements, needing closer contact with local employers. Finally, a more flexible approach to the qualifications required for entry to courses should be adopted, and more personal support given to those on courses, to reduce wastage.

Training and placement of young people[1]

Within the general requirement for a coordinated approach to manpower planning, special priority should be given to the training and placement of young people in Liverpool, in which the main emphasis should lie in increased provision for training. We have worked out our detailed proposals only for Liverpool but, in practice, the same principles should be extended to the rest of Merseyside. The bulk of our proposals form, in effect, a local application of suggestions made by the Training Services Agency.[2] The exceptional shortage of training places in Liverpool suggests it should be given priority in any national programme.

The number of apprenticeships available for suitably qualified young people should be increased, initially by four to five hundred a year, to bring the proportion up to Merseyside standards. This could be achieved by extending permanently the apprentice award scheme; by encouraging local authorities and other public agencies to increase their apprenticeships; and by increasing training grants to private employers. A programme of gateway courses should also be set up, covering induction and vocational training below craft level, and providing a thousand places for those in work or unemployed. Training and work schemes for unemployed young people should be extended by making available a proportion of the proposed gateway courses; making permanent, and extending the range and character, of Short Industrial Courses, and the 'Out of School, Out of Work' scheme of the local authority; expanding Community Industry; providing places in the work preparation schemes described below; and encouraging the creation of privately sponsored and community based training schemes.

Careers advice and job placement do not directly contribute to increasing the levels of skill. Accordingly, only relatively minor changes in emphasis are proposed in this field. Raising standards of careers teaching in schools should have priority in areas with high youth unemployment and special programmes for early school leavers should be developed in such areas. The Careers Service should give priority to those areas and people with most severe employment difficulties. The development of independent employment agencies and training schemes serving well defined neighbourhoods should be encouraged.

An underlying issue is the pronounced difference in attitude between the young unemployed and many of those in government services. The initiative for change should come from those with responsibility for services by becoming more responsive to the needs of different communities. One important step would be for

(1) For further details, see IAS Liverpool, *Getting a Job, The Training and Placement of Young People* (Department of the Environment 1977).
(2) Training Services Agency, *Vocational Preparation for Young People* (1975).

the trade unions to examine the case for some form of special representation for all young people under eighteen who are not studying, whether working or unemployed.

Work preparation

A work preparation programme should be set up to employ workers from areas of high unemployment on integrated work schemes and training programmes. Again, our proposals are for Liverpool, but the same principles are applicable to the whole of Merseyside. The programme would aim to raise the levels of skill and confidence among those who had lost, or never had, experience of regular work or modern industry. Its workers would be recruited from two groups, the largest concentrations of whom are found in the inner city and neither of whom have benefited significantly from current Job Creation Schemes. They are men with a history of insecure, casual unskilled work or who have been unemployed for long periods, roughly a third of the total unemployed in the city; and young people with a record of excessive job changing, frequent unemployment, or failure to find a first job soon after leaving school, roughly a tenth of all school leavers.

The scale of programme required would fluctuate with levels of unemployment and should diminish in size as the numbers of hard core unemployed were reduced. At present, it should cater for five hundred to a thousand workers annually, of whom at least a tenth should be young people under eighteen. The aim of the programme would be to meet the special needs of its work force by providing closely related work and training schemes. The work schemes would be carried out for local authorities, voluntary and community organisations and, where appropriate, for private organisations; the training schemes would include on the job training as part of the work schemes, secondment of workers to training courses and colleges, and new forms such as block courses and team training.

This concept of work preparation is derived in part from Enterprise Ulster and the current Job Creation Programme. However, it would differ from the latter in having a longer time horizon, in being orientated more to the needs of adult hard core unemployed and unqualified or disadvantaged school leavers, and in having the duty to seek out and promote work schemes rather than relying on the initiative of others. It should have a strong local management, representative of the many relevant interests in this field.

Employment transfer

An important complement to increasing local training opportunities will be assisting those who wish to move elsewhere to work or train. The current Employment Transfer Scheme covers resettlement expenses and relies on individual initiative in finding a job and a house. It tends to favour workers who are skilled, unmarried or not in any way disadvantaged, for instance in living in an unpopular council estate from which a transfer would be difficult. The current scheme should therefore be extended to make special provision for unskilled workers and young people by

212

offering a combination of training schemes and housing to them and their families in areas where the economy is more buoyant.

To achieve any success, such a scheme would need to be advertised in ways which could get through to those involved; television, local commercial radio and local press; local DHSS, housing management and social services offices and employment exchanges. If successful it would form an important element in adjusting the balance of advantage between the inner areas and other parts of the city and county. It would need to operate in close conjunction with proposals outlined in the next section to allow easier council housing transfers between one authority and another.

Improving housing opportunities[1]

To improve the chances of those at the bottom of the market getting decent housing requires changes in city-wide housing policy. Although such an approach may have an inner area element, for example adjusting the points system in response to local differences in demand, it would be aimed mainly at those who were disadvantaged in the city's housing market, wherever they live, now or in the future. Those currently most at risk in Liverpool include the homeless; single people living in hostels; families living in overcrowded or unsuitable council property; subtenants and the adult children of existing council tenants; single people in general; childless couples; poor and single parent families; and those living in multi-let houses or at risk of eviction. But the problem is a dynamic one. Those most at risk are continually changing in their numbers and composition. Spending power, social patterns and fashions change in ways which continually influence demand. Individual's needs and preferences change with their age, job, marital status and children.

Review of housing for the disadvantaged

The Housing Department should prepare regular reviews of disadvantage in the housing market. These should cover those who are most at risk of poor housing and the personal circumstances, and the extent to which they are or are not being met, either in the public or private sector. It would cover aspects of allocations policy, management procedures, tenant welfare arrangements, hard to let property etc in the public sector; special provision by housing associations and use of nomination rights; multi-occupation in privately rented furnished houses; and the poorest conditions in the remainder of the privately rented market. The reviews would allow programmes to be adjusted regularly on the basis of sound local knowledge.

Within this overall perspective three main policy changes are required to improve the opportunities for suitable housing for those now suffering the worst conditions. Firstly public responsibility should be extended to those for whom council housing

(1) For further details of some aspects of this subject, see IAS Liverpool, *Single and Homeless* (Department of the Environment 1977). Recent changes in allocations policy by the City Council have introduced some of the recommendations in this section (see footnote, page 121).

is currently unsuitable or not available and who are at risk in the private sector. This applies particularly to some single people and smaller, younger, more mobile households generally. Secondly, a stronger social needs element should be introduced into council allocations policy to avoid pushing the most vulnerable into the worst housing. Thirdly, the opportunities for transfer within the public sector need to be improved, both within the city and to and from other parts of Merseyside and elsewhere.

An extension of public responsibility

The extension of public housing responsibility to those not curently eligible could be achieved by better use of existing council stock as well as by new provision. There is a demand, partly hidden by sharing, sub tenanting and under occupation for small units, some of them furnished and quickly available but for limited periods. Much of the older inner city stock which is no longer suitable for family use would be suitable for single people. Indeed a start has already been made by turning over some blocks in the north end of the city to housing associations for student use and by restricting the use of high rise flats to households without children.

There is also scope for direct provision by the authority of good quality furnished accommodation. But a localised, imaginative and flexible approach is required to the management of property where there might be a high turnover. Different kinds of services might be needed, furniture and household equipment for instance, or clothes washing facilities on the premises. And, this kind of provision can function adequately only if there are no waiting lists. Access should be quicker and therefore vacancy rates higher in this kind of property than in that for long term family occupation. Access to such property would need to be separated from normal waiting list procedures, possibly by setting up housing associations within the local authority structure.

Whilst most of those at risk need nothing more than suitable housing, there are some who will continue to need extra care and support. Much has been done for the elderly; more attention should be given to other groups needing small scale, supported housing; drifting alcoholics, young drug users, discharged psychiatric patients. The total numbers are small, a few thousand in Liverpool at most. But their needs are particular and diverse. Their demands, too, are hidden by the existence in Liverpool of poor quality bedsitters, lodging houses and hostels and, at the end of the road, plenty of derelict houses for dossing. A limited amount of specialist supported housing should be provided for those groups both by the council and housing associations.

The rapid decline of the private rented sector, particularly the loss of the oldest and cheapest property through clearance, has seriously diminished the market in property available to young families for their first house. Given improvements in fitments, repair and surroundings, there is no reason why many tenement blocks should not continue to be suitable for young couples, even those with young babies, if lifts exist and work. But at present, once into a flat of this kind it is very difficult to get out again. The better opportunities for moving which are discussed below would be needed before the present policy of placing young couples in small flats could become acceptable.

Despite their rapid growth, housing associations are still relatively small organisations, able to operate flexibly at a neighbourhood level. When demand is not extreme they should be able to re-introduce the advantages offered by some old style private landlords in giving priority to young couples who wished to take a house near their parents. But they now have long waiting lists and the demands of equity reduce the scope for such informal methods. Housing cooperatives can offer advantages here. By operating only at the neighbourhood level, they allow very localised placing.

More people should be able to become owner occupiers. Reference was made in chapter seven to the restrictive practices of building societies and the withdrawal of local authority housing advances, with cutbacks in public spending. Such a withdrawal does not seem in keeping with the most recent government policy of concentrating housing resources in areas of greatest need, and should be reintroduced as soon as possible. Those in insecure employment or even out of work should have the same opportunities as anyone else, within their more slender means, of owning a house. It is still possible to buy a small, unimproved terraced house in parts of Liverpool for under a thousand pounds. Priority should be given to increasing owner occupation; by reintroducing council mortgages, by government pressure on building societies and by experimental equity sharing, the use of government guarantees, or by other methods.

A social needs policy

To avoid concentrations in the worst council houses of those who are most vulnerable, it is necessary to discriminate in their favour. A social needs category would allow priority to be given to those who are most at risk and most in need of decent, secure housing. To the current medical criteria might be added long term unemployment; large or single parent families; a history of institutional care; sub-tenanting or a risk of eviction. The danger is in creating a stigmatised group. However the present, informal arrangements for introducing an element of social need by offering hard to let property to needy but non priority cases have created stigmatised areas. The important thing is to create a special group only as far as assessment of need goes and not in the direct provision of housing.

A social needs policy would reduce the need for crisis intervention and temporary accommodation. Much of the excess demand for temporary accommodation which leads to the use of hotels and boarding houses for homeless families, is caused by the Council's unwillingness, gradually being eroded, to give priority to those who are homeless or in danger of becoming so. For example, to introduce the risk of eviction or living in unsuitable temporary accommodation (including council provision) as criteria for priority on the waiting list, would itself act to prevent homelessness. Thus the housing aid and homeless services need to have direct access to sufficient, good quality tenancies to cover emergencies. And the points system needs revision such that the Homeless Service and the Social Services Department can make a case on social grounds comparable to that which can now be made by the Medical Officer of Health on health grounds.

Council transfers

One of the reasons why many families are apparently trapped in the older council estates is that they are unable to move anywhere else. Not only are there strong social pressures to stay, but the places where some work might be available, say the West Midlands or the South East, are those where housing pressures are greatest and the chances of another council house remote. The previous section included a recommendation to extend the Employment Transfer Scheme which included the provision of council housing elsewhere in the country. But others who are now effectively trapped in inner city council housing may wish to move away without taking advantage of such a scheme or may not be eligible.

There is thus a need for making separately available, a limited amount of good council housing in other, more affluent parts of the country, for those from the most deprived parts of the city. It may be necessary to compensate the receiving authority.

But it is also necessary to make movement within Liverpool much easier. In a small way the housing management project showed that more sensitive local management can improve the opportunities for local transfers and reduce the length of time a flat stays empty. The same opportunities are required for movement between districts. While many people prefer to settle in one place and stay there, there is an increasing tendency for people to move house more frequently. In the extreme of economic decline by inner Liverpool this is even more important. Job opportunities, while bad by any standards, are better anywhere else in the city than in the inner areas for those who need unskilled work and cannot afford to travel very far. Alternatively, some suburban couples whose children had moved away and who had more space in their council house than they needed, might welcome a return to a flat near the city centre, provided the living conditions and surroundings could be made suitable.

However, in order to achieve greater mobility, not only would transfers between districts have to be given greater priority, but also more vacancies would have to be retained than may be politically acceptable, and not only allowed to occur in unpopular estates where no one wants to live, but also deliberately maintained on popular estates to allow greater freedom of movement for poor families from other council property. If more opportunities to move could be found, particularly if priority were given to disadvantaged groups, then more of those now restricted to the most unpopular flats or maisonettes would be able to live elsewhere. The demand for them would decrease further, particularly if the other requirement of not putting homeless or social need families into hard to let flats, were also met.

Thus the true demand for these properties, possibly nil, would be allowed expression and fundamental decisions could not be avoided about their future. They could then be made attractive by being improved or adapted; someone could be found to take them on their own terms; or they could be demolished.

Channelling resources into areas of greatest social need

A priority area approach

The chief lesson from the detailed examination of inner Liverpool in the earlier part of this report is the existence of parts of inner Liverpool where social needs of a great variety are most intense, yet current provision does not successfully provide for people living in these areas either by discriminatory programmes designed to compensate for their poverty, or by methods of delivering services sensitively attuned to the values of these communities.

Chapter ten suggested that a trend towards centralised decision-making and a decline in local democracy were increasing the alienation between people and government. Decisions were being made on the basis of increasingly sophisticated methods of supposedly objective measurement. But these methods were not really objective at all, and tended to support the values of a professional elite of senior decision-makers, both officers and members, not those of field officers or ward members and certainly not those of members of the public from working class areas or minority groups. The growing centralisation of power in government has made many people feel alienated from its mysterious deliberations and apparently random and often irrelevant decisions and frustrated them in attempts to influence events in their own neighbourhoods.

The existing structure of the council could not be an effective means of channelling resources into the areas of greatest social need. There is not the political strength to discriminate sufficiently. There is not the political or management structure to undertake a major, comprehensive programme for one part of the city and involving all departments. And there is not sufficient delegation or public involvement to allow adequate expression of the needs and values of inner city areas in local authority services.

The problems raised by this are inherent in the whole of our approach to the inner areas, including the questions of attitudes in government, resources and the responsibility for action. They are properly discussed in chapter thirteen, within the context of a total approach to the inner areas by central and local government. At this stage, we confine ourselves to proposing that a priority areas committee should be set up, responsible to Council but including representatives of whatever government department or departments become responsible for allocating resources for the regeneration of the inner city areas. Such a committee would have two functions. It would be the forum for negotiating the resources of regeneration to be allocated to Liverpool; and within council policy it would be responsible for the broad allocation of those resources to the areas of greatest social need through the local, ward committees described below.

The administration of a number of services, most of them already provided by the Council, should be brought to a more local level and made more amenable to local influences, if they are to reflect the special needs of the most deprived areas. From our experience in action projects these are likely to include at least the following: council housing management and improvement; private housing improvement and environmental care; community based education; community development; income and social support; and planning and estate management. The priority given to each, or even its inclusion at all, would depend on the particular local circumstances in different parts of the inner city. For instance, in some areas there is little or no private housing; in others there may be a great need for particular social services.

Most of these functions are already organised on a small area basis, through various systems of local, public offices. That this form of organisation is currently neither sufficient nor effective has been concluded in earlier chapters. There are at least three factors inherent in any successful programme of local action: geographical decentralisation; local coordination or direction; and some local control of services. At present only the first of these is achieved and in a rather ad hoc way. Isolated attempts have been made to achieve interdepartmental coordination.

The extent to which any or all of these criteria could be met in any programme of channelling resources, would depend on the degree of political commitment given to the whole programme and the extent to which the City Council would be prepared to delegate power to local members or officers. We suggest that there is a real need in the areas of most severe stress to set up small, multi-service centres, similar to that now operating in Vauxhall. Their major purpose would be to coordinate local services and programmes and identify ways in which they could be improved and related more closely to the needs of the areas which they would serve. The centres should also be involved in the preparation and review of local planning, land management and development control. The minimum requirement would be for a locally based form of area management with greater authority than has the Area Management Unit over a clearly defined range of services and programmes.

To make such centres effective requires new life in the democratic machinery. Ordinary people need to be able to feel greater confidence in their elected members, and the role of the members themselves needs to be strengthened. One method could be for the coordinating and management functions of multi-service centres to be placed under the control of committees of local councillors operating for instance on a ward basis. But to make this level of activity effective, there would need to be an equivalent delegation of authority to area officers.

We have only so far considered decentralisation and coordination. Can a degree of local control be achieved? To what extent should the public be involved in tenant management, community centres, playschemes? To move from local coordination, even with area committees, to community control is a big step. But the failure of the area management experiment to reduce interdepartmental separatism or to enable members to have a greater say in the City Council about conditions in their particular wards, suggests that a local approach would not be very effective without

218

a degree of local control. Arguably the most effective way of running locally based services in the areas of greatest social need would be to make them truly autonomous. Thus each ward committee would have full control over a specified range of local services and would negotiate its annual allocation of resources with the priority areas committee. Each multi-service centre, whether or not all the services were actually located there, would be run by a senior officer, responsible only to his ward committee and to no other officer. He would thus be responsible for managing and directing all the programmes and services for which the ward committee was responsible. This development, however, raises even more fundamental questions about the scale and structure of local government as presently constituted. It raises questions about the present dual system and the validity or practicality of what might become in effect a third tier of government. It is to look to the future, beyond what could be achieved through an inner area study alone.

The voluntary sector and community groups and individuals should be involved in this approach through particular functions, for instance housing improvement or community development, or more directly through grant aid. But the centres should involve the public as much as possible in their activities and services and by developing an effective public face through the provision of aid, advice and information services. The aim would be to make each centre a place which truly represented its locality both in the nature and style of its programmes and services and in the way in which it was run.

Establishing the priority areas

An area-based policy of positive discrimination can, at best, reach the deprived only in the chosen areas, a small minority of all those in need. This reason alone reduces the importance of defining their boundaries too narrowly. But there are other more important ones. From a strictly practical standpoint, conditions tend to change more rapidly than administrative boundaries. More seriously, the very definition of deprived areas can reinforce the deprivation itself. The term inner city is already taking on many of the pejorative implications which have, in the past, been restricted to smaller areas such as Maryhill, Moss Side or Liverpool 8. To define an inner core of deprivation could impose a stigma which would be difficult to eradicate. In addition this labelling process can obscure the true purpose of the exercise. Time is spent defining and redefining indicators of urban stress which allow accurate definition of the area of focus, rather than on planning and setting up effective political and administrative machinery to deal with the problem.

The precise boundaries of the areas of greatest social need are not important; the focus of attention is. Once a decision has been made in principle to channel extra resources into needy areas, political decisions about how they are to be used and exactly who is to benefit from them become of fundamental importance. Nevertheless, if services and programmes are to be effectively focussed, some broad definition of areas is required. It is suggested that a number of priority areas be established, corresponding to the areas of greatest economic and social stress, but brought up to date to reflect conditions which exist when the programmes start.

They would thus (in 1971 terms) comprise the inner council estates, the remaining areas of poor quality multi-let housing and the poorest parts of the older terraced areas not affected by slum clearance. Recent changes suggest that the line now needs to be drawn less tightly around the city centre than the 1971 figures suggest.

The choice of boundaries would depend also on the strength of political involvement in the programme. If local centres responsible to area committees of councillors were to be accepted, there would be strong arguments for the areas to correspond to political ward boundaries. These are currently under review but the priority areas would no doubt include the inner city wards which make up the Scotland-Exchange constituency and also some of the adjacent wards such as Melrose-Westminster, Low Hill-Smithdown, Princes Park-Granby and Dingle. The estimated population of the Scotland-Exchange constituency in 1976 was about seventy five thousand. The size of the selected inner city priority areas would thus be between seventy five thousand and one hundred and fifty thousand population, depending on the wards to be included in the redefinition of their boundaries.

The essence of this priority areas approach is that the precise list of activities carried on should be based on local knowledge and conditions, and would vary in detail in different parts of the inner city and at different times. It should be a flexible, rolling programme of intervention rather than a predetermined plan. Nevertheless we give below examples of the types which we envisage would be appropriate for many priority areas, based on our experience in the study area.

Council housing management and improvement

Effective management of their older housing estates is one of the most difficult problems now facing the local authority in the inner areas. Improvements are required in local management and the involvement of tenants; in living conditions inside the dwellings; and in improving environmental standards and facilities on the estates. Local management offices and maintenance depots similar to those in the housing management project would be fundamental to bring management closer to tenants. About ten local offices might be required to achieve full coverage of council estates in the priority areas. They would be responsible for all aspects of day to day management including repairs, maintenance, local transfers and liaison with tenants; for involving tenants in the management of their housing; and for instituting proper schemes of planned maintenance in their areas, once basic improvements had been carried out. Also, schemes for those estates requiring large scale improvement of dwellings should be implemented from the local offices at the same time as improvements to the communal spaces and environment of estates.

In this way a comprehensive local approach could be adopted to the improvement of individual estates, enabling tenants to be involved in the planning and execution of the programme through their contacts with the staff of the local office. More effective use could be made of the existing housing stock, at the neighbourhood level, particularly to meet the needs of those referred to in the programme for housing the disadvantaged.

220

Major programmes of housing improvement would give opportunities for widening local housing choice as well as raising living standards. The large estates of tenement blocks, whatever the strength of community that has been established, provide poor living standards even after basic improvements have been completed. A local approach to the needs of such communities, informed not by a single survey, but the deep knowledge of local attitudes and preferences that a good local estate management team can command, could achieve many additional improvements over longer periods. For example, selective demolition, the provision of ground floor gardens and facilities like nurseries or wash rooms; the splitting up of some flats and combining of others within a single block; the building of some new large family houses and small one person flats on cleared land nearby. Combined with real environmental improvements, these could create satisfactory living conditions over a complete neighbourhood without destroying complex community networks which might have taken years to build. The improvement of council estates should be undertaken with the same objectives of continuous, gradual renewal as are now being applied to the improvement of older private housing.

Private housing improvement

Chapter eight discussed several major constraints on the effective improvement of older private housing commensurate with the scale of the problem. The most important were the scale of the operation required, compared with the likely availability of finance, staff and voluntary housing provision; the degree of political and administrative delegation required to achieve effective local action; and the likely take up of grants in areas of poverty, social stress and a high proportion of privately rented housing. Each of these needs to be overcome to achieve successful regeneration of these areas of housing stress.

Extra resources available for the areas of greatest social need would help to overcome the scale constraint, especially if it were possible to relax constraints on staffing levels in these areas. But, although most of the housing action areas already proposed for Liverpool are likely to fall within the priority areas, there remains a large amount of decaying pre-1919 private housing not so covered both within the priority areas and elsewhere in the inner city. Powers and levels of grant are greater in housing action areas than those elsewhere. If additional resources are made available, it may be feasible to introduce extra housing action areas in the priority areas. But where the level of housing stress does not permit a housing action area approach, but poverty and private renting are still considerable, different approaches would be needed to achieve improvement and encourage the take up of grants. The local authority could purchase privately rented property and either manage it directly or hand it over to housing associations. Housing associations could purchase more properties directly. Higher grant levels could be reintroduced to assist owner occupiers; the difference in response in Liverpool between the seventy five percent and fifty percent grant levels has been sufficient to suggest that in some areas at least the former level should be reestablished. In addition the reintroduction of local authority mortgages and other methods of increasing the level of owner occupation, outlined in the previous section, should themselves encourage a higher rate of grant take-up, particularly if grant levels are raised.

The tasks necessary to improve adequately conditions in the older private housing areas would be wider than those envisaged for the housing action area programme. In particular, much greater attention would need to be given to the environment and infrastructure. In many areas, the whole infrastructure of roads, pavements, sewerage, water, gas and electricity supply needs upgrading or replacing; back lanes widened; walls, paving and drainage rebuilt.

But the greatest priorities are extra resources and local control so that a total approach to a small area can be achieved, rather in the way that SNAP tried to do it in Granby. More imaginative planning and more flexible implementation of local programmes could transform rather than merely improve many neighbourhoods. Selective demolition, small scale rebuilding, traffic management, landscaping and the provision of local facilities and open space in addition to the basic improvement process could achieve far greater improvements in living standards than has been possible in several improvement areas to date. The area teams proposed in the latest council policy are a beginning. But control could more effectively be achieved if the machinery proposed for the priority areas extended in this case to include representatives of residents groups and housing associations and cooperatives as well as members and officers.

Environmental care

Wherever possible the improvement, repair and maintenance of the environment should be carried out as an integral part of other programmes for development or improvement; whether to mitigate the adverse effects of industrial development or to provide more attractive conditions in residential areas or even to set up more parks. But, inevitably some areas will fall through the net; sites reserved for future uses, areas of existing industrial use, roads and railways. If the attractiveness of the inner areas to residents and industrialists alike is to be enhanced, dramatic improvements will be needed.

The need is thus for a sensitive watching brief on environmental conditions rather than immediate widespread and large scale improvements which because they are relatively easy to set up and can achieve impressive results quickly, appear as a very tempting option though the difficulties in their subsequent maintenance can bring other problems. Nevertheless maintenance and minor improvement would be enough to form a major programme of work, including small scale landscaping, treatment of sites, street cleaning and refuse collection; indeed all those activities of environmental care now carried out by the local authority. But these responsibilities need to be extended to the treatment and care of vacant land and improvement of conditions in industrial areas. And more effective powers are required to enforce private and other public agencies to maintain better environmental standards.

Community based education

We concluded in chapter nine that education alone could not achieve social change and that consequently the main purpose of education in the poorest areas could be

222

no different from that anywhere else, that is to enable as many children as possible to benefit intellectually, materially and socially through gaining qualifications and thereafter a good job. But there are major constraints on the equality of educational opportunity for the inner areas in the form of concentrations of physical, environmental and family circumstances associated with educational failure; a resistance in some neighbourhoods to the way in which education was provided; and a lack of training and job opportunities which lowered motivation at school. Some opportunities to counteract these constraints exist at pre and early primary school level, towards school leaving and in adult education.

Parents need to be involved in the education of their children by being made welcome at school, by having mothers' groups at school and the like, and above all being encouraged to take part in school management. A prime objective for the areas of greatest social need, in line with the conclusions of the educational priority project, would be to establish community primary schools. But the development of community schools should not merely entail widening the range of activities to attract parents to the school. It should allow the values of the neighbourhood to influence the running of the school and even the curriculum, as well as allowing the staff to raise the educational aspirations of parents and children alike. Clearly such exposure has dangers, particularly if small groups of parents are allowed to dominate the neighbourhood influence on the school. Success would depend, ultimately, on the attitudes of head teacher and staff, and the education authority, and the degree to which they are able to adjust their methods.

The Adult Education Centre has shown that the right kind of local provision can allow a latent demand from an apparently rejecting group to be expressed. Experience so far has shown not that young blacks in Liverpool lack motivation, but that they need to be given confidence. Institutional provision needs to be organised in ways which can be acceptable to minority groups. The centre is moving, in a small way, towards becoming a fully fledged community college. The interests and values of young Liverpool born blacks may diverge more than most from those of the rest of British society. But alienation in other areas is considerable and, it would appear, growing. The future demand for alternative, independent provision will depend upon the extent to which existing colleges can effectively assess and meet the special needs of such areas. But at least there would appear to be a good case for the kind of area office approach advocated in the Russell Report and for full-time adult education workers, akin to those employed by the WEA, to encourage the expression of local needs.

Finally, the present combination of low achievement, poor job prospects and rejection of education makes necessary some radical rethinking about the role of education in the poorest areas and the status given to academic achievement. But there lies a dilemma between providing special alternatives in a few areas which may be relatively cheap and simple but which risk a further entrenchment of class differences; and making complex, far reaching reforms which may create problems in themselves and whose consequences would be difficult to foresee. However, job opportunities for young people in Liverpool are now sufficiently bad to make the second alternative worthy of serious consideration. The problem is not one of the supply of schools and teachers, for the population of the inner areas is falling. Rather, there should be a major, independent review of the purpose and benefit of education in inner city areas. Its specific purpose would be to explore practical alternatives to academic secondary education which took into account the economic and social circumstances of the inner city. It would look for ways of transcending the often artificial barriers between education, training, work and leisure for those young people faced with the prospect of too little work and too much leisure.

Community development

A strong element in channelling resources to areas of greatest social need should be the wide range of activities falling broadly under the heading of community development. Almost by definition, they are activities particularly appropriate to the principles which we advocate for the whole programme, in devolution and in community involvement. Current local authority activities include the provision of youth and community centres, playgrounds and play schemes, sport and leisure activities. These clearly need to be extended and broadly remain the responsibility of the local authority, though with greater opportunity for their more flexible use by voluntary groups and the public.

But the other main area of community development work lies in stimulating and supporting the growth of self help activities by community groups. The activities can range from sharing a degree of responsibility with the local authority for the provision of services (as in play, or visiting schemes) to the more general expression of community interests. Key features of this type of activity are the grant aiding role of central government, through the Urban Programme; and of local government in its direct allocation of resources and its responsibility in vetting all applications for urban aid. Several changes need to be considered in this field. One would be for a proportion of the Urban Programme to be reserved specifically for voluntary organisations; applications for this could then be vetted independently of the local authority. The other is for central government to give urgent consideration to the difficulties arising from the offer of grant for a limited period of time after which the full burden falls on the local authority which may not be able to respond.

Income and social support

A major purpose of the regeneration programme as a whole would be to reduce the need for income support, welfare benefits and social work support, mainly by improving job opportunities, personal incomes and housing conditions. But if at the same time, the benefits system could be simplified and made less discriminatory, then the take up would increase. And higher incomes and better housing would reduce the need for some forms of social support such as social work and child care.

The Supplementary Benefits Commission has recently said that the present benefit system is too complex and too reliant on means tested benefits.[1] The area

(1) Supplementary Benefits Commission, *Annual Report 1975* (Cmnd 6615, HMSO 1976).

management multi-purpose form experiment was a tacit admission that the local authority's welfare benefit system is also unnecessarily complex. Action which focusses on areas of greatest social need provides an opportunity to make major improvements in the benefit system where they are most necessary. There would be scope for combining many DHSS and local authority benefits, drawing them together under a single administration and drastically simplifying the whole system, with particular emphasis on reducing the reliance on means tested benefits. Some changes in administration could be applied to the areas of greatest need alone. However, equity and the overwhelming case for simplification, demand more fundamental changes of a universal nature.

It may also be feasible to incorporate the provision of existing social services in this general approach to the priority areas. There would be a certain logic in combining material benefits with personal support services, less for administrative convenience than in providing a coordinated service to the public. The combined service would have the single object of providing support in whatever form was necessary and whenever it was needed. The principle of providing care wherever possible from within the community would be easier to develop from a base of this kind. But whether or not this combination were practicable it would be necessary to ensure that all income support, welfare and social services operate more closely together at the local level.

13 A total approach for the inner areas

Style and attitudes in government

The four programmes described in the last chapter are a necessary, but not
sufficient, basis for the regeneration of inner Liverpool. They prescribe what should
be done but not how it should be done, or by whom. Changes in the style and
methods of government are as essential as the new programmes themselves if the
prospects for regeneration are to be achieved. For it was matters of this character
which led to the problems encountered in previous policies, at least as much as
failings in the policies themselves, or in the process by which they were first identified.

The report has shown many instances of where, for every beneficial action by
government, the clearance of slums, the building of new towns, the attraction of
new jobs to Merseyside, there have been others whose impact has been crude and
destructive, their consequences not foreseen. Emerging problems have not been
recognised speedily enough as circumstances changed. Policies were slow to adjust.
Examples include the blighting effect of the pursuit of unrealistic proposals for long
term development or the lop-sided concern with social and housing policies to the
neglect of economic activity. The tendency has been to propose a scale of action
which is either out of proportion to the problem it is intended to solve, or out
of accord with the more delicate fabric of the underlying situation. Slum clearance
was necessary and its effects, in the long term, beneficial. But its darker side illustrates
the problems in the overturning of social relationships and land ownerships over
a wider area and for a longer period than was warranted by the actual incidence of
irredeemably bad housing. Nonconforming industries in general may have been
out of place in residential areas but have often been pursued irrespective of the
real social or environmental damage which they cause. An element of corporate
aggrandisement is manifest in the proposals for the city centre and the urban
motorway programme and some of the more monumental and inhuman new
estates.

Some of these actions and their unforeseen consequences can be attributed to the
scale and nature of government and the degree to which those responsible for
making decisions and formulating policy become remote from those for whom the
policies are designed. The scale of the large local authorities, the functional division
of services, and the centralisation of authority accompanying the new techniques of
corporate management all contribute to this remoteness. At this scale, policies have
to be expressed in abstract terms, in averages and percentages; methods of
delivering services are standardised, whatever the local variations in conditions;
programmes achieve a momentum which becomes difficult to deflect when
circumstances change. Policies do change, but either very slowly, or in an arbitrary
way which illustrates the same failings of over-simplicity and remoteness: for
instance, when the building of high-rise council flats was stopped and the decision

taken that in future all council dwellings in Liverpool should be not more than two storeys high.

Furthermore, career structures in a large local authority reinforce these features. The able person is almost invariably promoted far away from direct contact with the public into posts that are of more relevance to the administrative structure than the outside world. Field staff in direct contact with clients and the public face divided loyalties. This is noticeable in the case of departments like social services or planning where highly qualified but junior staff have begun to question their positions of responsibility without power. And the councillor faces similar difficulties. He is inundated through his case work in the surgery with a multiplicity of individual claims from his constituents. He works as a city councillor on service committees in which his experience of the real world of his ward and its communities is arbitrarily divided into categories of professional skill, and in which he may be overwhelmed by highly technical reports from the professional officers. Political authority for changing policy rests with the party leadership for the city.

The problem goes to the heart of the inner area issue although its consequences are not confined geographically to that part of the city but are found in others, notably the outer council estates. Over-centralisation and departmental structures make for imperfectly fitting policies which may well fail to match, may not even recognise, the special needs of small areas and their variations from the average. They fail to give adequate recognition to the local impact of centrally determined policies and the ways in which different programmes interact locally. And these failings are at their worst in those parts of the inner city where conditions depart most seriously from the norm, amongst those who have fewest opportunities to improve their circumstances through choice of where to live, find a job and send their children to school. The remoteness of a centralised authority becomes a divergence of majority and minority values which local democratic processes seem unable to bridge.

But central government is even more remote. Its very centralism and departmental separatism, more extreme than in local government, prevents the proper perception of local issues which might sow the seeds of reform. The string of special and separate studies and projects of the last ten years would not have stemmed from a government able to take a comprehensive view of the issues involved. Nor, it could be argued, would reorganisation of local government and the trend towards corporatism have been allowed to take forms which reinforced a trend towards government by remote control.

The four programmes which we recommend thus present a real dichotomy of interest in this matter of style and attitudes in government. On the one hand, they specifically call for positive discrimination in favour of the areas of greatest need, whether they be social or economic, with priority given to the concentrations of deprivation within the inner areas. Such discrimination would require a redistribution of resources for which centralised authority and political commitment would be essential.

228

Conversely, the programmes equally specifically call for a change in attitudes within government. These changed attitudes should go beyond asking what are the problems of the inner areas and how can they be solved. They should also mean asking what are the strengths and attributes of the people of the inner area, what contribution they can make to Liverpool society, and what opportunities they need to be able to do so. They mean taking a more positive stand against discrimination by race or class. They mean a change in attitude from one which assumes that the people of the inner areas are simply to be supported through social and welfare services by ensuring that they do not fall below some datum of extreme poverty to one which gives much greater attention to changing peoples' circumstances fundamentally at the local level.

To achieve this degree of change at the local level would mean more than just the introduction of new programmes for, say, training or industrial development, but restyling the form and content of government to reflect the economic and social realities of the inner areas and the attitudes and aspirations of the people. It would mean planning the future of the inner city from the point of view of those living there, both now and in the future. Yet this change in attitude should not be equated with government taking an ever expanding responsibility for the maintenance, management and renewal of the physical, social, and economic fabric of the inner areas. Future intervention by central and local government in the affairs of inner areas should be based on an explicit recognition of the parts to be played by the people themselves, by private enterprise, and non-governmental bodies.

There are no easy ways of changing the attitudes which pervade both levels of government or of bridging the vast gap between governors and governed. But developments in the structure of government can be envisaged which might foster new attitudes in the long term. The basic requirement for the regeneration of the inner areas of our larger cities should be a total perception by government of the problems and a total approach to their solution.

A total approach can only be achieved by central and local government working together, though with clearly defined roles, to build an explicit and comprehensive understanding of the problems of inner areas and take concerted action for their solution, particularly in overcoming the historic divide between economic issues on the one hand and social and housing questions on the other. A total approach must have built into it machinery which is responsive to the needs of local communities and the people who live, work or invest in the inner city, encompassing its plurality of values and accepting that this must lead to variety in the ways in which government intervenes in the affairs of the inner area.

The task for central government

For central government the total approach would mean defining the broad aims of policy and redistributing resources. This must be a question which goes beyond the boundaries of Liverpool. Some of the problems are found elsewhere in Merseyside, though not on the same scale as in the city. The case of Glasgow is well known. London presents special problems. But other large provincial conurbations show many of the problems of inner Liverpool. Thus inner area policy for central government must embrace both the general direction of policy and a degree of responsibility for individual inner areas.

Central government departments until recently have pursued apparently separate policies in their approach to the inner areas. Some have operated through special projects, as described in chapter one (Departments of Education and Science, Environment and the Home Office); others through social policies (Department of Health and Social Security); or through concern with housing and local government finance (Department of the Environment, again). But the inner area perspective has been missing from two key departments. The Department of Industry has operated regionally and for the Merseyside Special Development Area, giving only recent and sporadic attention to the problems of the inner city. The Department of Employment has used so-called travel to work areas for collection and analysis of data, the Liverpool Exchanges Area in the case of Liverpool which extends beyond the city to include Kirkby. The weaknesses of this fragmentation have become clear as each special project in turn demonstrated the interrelatedness of economic and social issues, of community, housing, and education questions.

Recently the Secretary of State for the Environment has been appointed to take special responsibility for urban affairs and to chair a cabinet committee to coordinate the work of all departments in this field. The total approach by central government is beginning to seem a real possibility, provided it does actually involve all relevant government departments including the Treasury. The total approach for central government should thus be to decide on the priority to be given to the inner areas at large; to ensure that the responsible departments work together to a common purpose, nationally and locally; and to establish the processes and machinery for selecting the areas for action, for channelling resources and for ensuring appropriate action at the local level. But it will be vital for central government not to direct the detailed content of programmes. Its basis for action would be rather through its evaluation of programmes devised locally for individual inner areas, though using its power to encourage local authorities where necessary to modify their programmes and priorities in accord with the principles of the total approach.

The selected inner areas should not be many if a real degree of discrimination is to be practicable and resources are not to be dissipated in small, ineffectual increments. They should be chosen quickly and using straightforward methods of selection. A possible basis for the list was given in chapter eleven which picked out fifty-two constituencies located chiefly in the inner areas of the larger metropolitan conurbations. The special feature distinguishing the inner city constituencies from the rest of the country was not solely their social and economic characteristics. It was that the concentrations of deprivation were sufficiently large in scale to characterise whole constituencies or even groups of constituencies; and that the constituencies comprised a large proportion of the parent local authorities.

230

If the Liverpool example provides an appropriate illustration, and the statistical evidence suggests that it does, the broad aims of inner area policies would be similar in other areas as those for the regeneration of inner Liverpool given in chapter eleven. But the content and emphasis in programmes would obviously vary from one conurbation to another, particularly in the case of inner London areas compared with those of the provincial cities.

Part of the total approach for central government should be to take a hard look at regional policies. Rather than reassess the new towns programme nationally in comparison with a national programme for inner areas, the balance between special initiatives should be examined for each region or conurbation where the main problems are concentrated, mostly the older, northern industrial areas. For Merseyside, for example, it would be necessary to review the balance of investment between its new towns, expanded towns, outer urban estates and the inner areas of Liverpool and Birkenhead; but also between industrial development, training programmes and job creation.

We consider the question of resource allocation later in the chapter. But, provided the number of eligible inner areas is comparatively small, and the criteria for inclusion kept clear, it should be possible for central government to adopt a total approach to inner areas with quite simple machinery, building on the regional offices for the local evaluation of individual programmes for specific inner areas, and conceivably developing the type of structure described in the Joint Approach to Social Policy for central control.[1]

The total approach for an inner area

The total approach in individual inner areas is more complex. It would need a concerted definition of aims and coordinated planning and action covering all four of the programmes described in chapter twelve. It would mean ensuring that inner area policies were related to other government programmes and seen in the context of other parts of the city and conurbation. It would mean taking positive action to apply the lessons gained through inner areas programmes.

The complexity arises from the number of organisations and departments likely to be involved, and will vary for different inner areas. In the case of Liverpool it would involve the City Council, the Merseyside County Council, statutory agencies and the executive departments of central government. In other conurbations (and conceivably on Merseyside, though not very likely) it could involve several district councils. In Greater Manchester, for instance, the conurbation's inner area includes both Manchester and Salford. We confine our illustration of the total approach at the local level to the case of inner Liverpool, though laying emphasis on general principles which might be of wider application rather than detailed proposals for the city.

(1) Central Policy Review Staff, *A Joint Framework for Social Policies* (HMSO 1975).

The criteria for the total approach at the local level thus become crucial. On the one hand priority should be given to those in greatest need through positive discrimination. On the other hand, the action taken must be more responsive to the needs and values of people in the inner areas. To some extent these aims are contradictory. Insofar as it implies a redistribution of resources, the former requires strong centralised control. The latter works in the opposite direction. It implies that local democracy should be able more effectively to represent the interests and attitudes of the inner area; that policies should be more clearly accountable to local communities; that executive control of local services should be as close as possible to the people or areas they are designed to serve.

A number of possible institutional arrangements can be envisaged for carrying out inner city policies, from creating an entirely new administration to carrying on with the present arrangements modified to the smallest extent. The question is which would be most likely to induce the degree of innovation which both programmes and the total approach itself call for; and which stands the greatest chance of being accepted.

One approach would be to set up a new inner area administration, in effect a new towns corporation for the inner city. This was an idea which had some credence several years ago, when inner city issues were seen as analogous to those of constructing a new town; a matter of building new houses and improving old ones; of laying out industrial estates and promoting the industrial assets of the area. It is true that an appointed body such as a public corporation would be appropriate for the work of physical construction. It would have the advantages of a clear geographical focus and a finite and specific responsibility for action. But it could not, any more than the new towns corporation can, take over the statutory functions of education and social services. It would be difficult to integrate its work with that of the local authority within which it would be embedded; matters such as allocation of council tenancies would become the subject of negotiation between autonomous authorities, seedbeds of future conflict. It would create a new bureaucracy which might well be even more remote and impersonal than the existing local authorities. Conversely, if it were made not an appointed, but an elected body, it would become in effect a third tier of local government adding to the already complex maze of responsibilities in a metropolitan county.

An alternative approach would be to rely entirely on the existing agencies, modified internally as little as possible whilst still attempting a total approach. The County Council, as now, would be responsible for highways, structure planning and industrial promotion. Its other services would have an impact on the inner areas, for instance, in engineering services contributing to environmental care. The City Council would retain its responsibility for local planning and development control and for industrial development, giving due regard to the inner city. It would in any case amend its housing policy to build in the claims of those at greatest disadvantage in the housing system. It would channel resources to the areas of greatest social need by creating new arrangements within the authority. The Manpower Services Commission would be responsible for the training programmes.

Such an approach would have a general weakness in spreading responsibility for the inner city too thinly on the ground. It would leave too many bodies with equal status responsible for different parts of the policy, relying on each to carry out its programme within an ill-defined and amorphous context. The stock answer to this would be to set up a joint committee to meet formally and coordinate the work of its constituent members. Coordination however is no substitute for direction and the relevant precedents indicate that joint committees are not the means for building lasting commitment to a social policy of the kind being recommended. But a possibly more serious weakness of this approach is that it would completely fail to tackle the incoherence and divided responsibility for the current programmes of industrial development. It would perpetuate the division of responsibility, and the overlap of functions, between city, county, Department of Industry, and National Enterprise Board. It could bring little guarantee of any real change in attitude or effort in creating economic development in the inner area.

Both of the approaches so far described hold few prospects of effective action even if they were able to make use of the additional resources. But closer examination of the respective strengths and weaknesses of each agency involved points the way forward. New arrangements for training and placement are already under way, with the Manpower Services Commission setting up a pilot reorganisation of its functions on Merseyside, decentralising responsibility from London and coordinating locally the work of the Training Services Agency, the Employment Services Agency and the Job Creation Programme. This forms a potentially effective means of carrying out our recommendations for improving the levels of skill on Merseyside, especially in its areas of high unemployment.

The programme for those most disadvantaged in the housing market clearly and solely is the responsibility of the City Council as local housing authority. There is no way that this action can be hived off from the general responsibility for housing policy in public and private sectors, even less so in view of the changes foreshadowed in housing finance.[1] The third programme, channelling resources to the areas of greatest social need, should also in theory be comparatively straightforward as the majority of the actual work and responsibility for identifying needs already lies with the City Council. Nevertheless, it would require substantial changes in decision-making and administration to satisfy what we regard as the essential requirements of decentralisation, delegation, and local control. The main instruments, a priority areas committee for the programme as a whole, something akin to ward committees and multi-service centres for particular areas, were described in chapter twelve.

The economic development programme presents the greatest difficulty. Some of the activities proposed are already carried out by the City and County Councils but not at the scale or in the manner we consider necessary. Others are carried out by the Department of Industry or the National Enterprise Board, though here it is less the scale of activity than the geographical perspective that is wrong. But

(1) Speech by the Secretary of State for the Environment to members of Birmingham City Council, 10 September 1976.

233

there are some activities which are not actually carried out at all and require an entirely new basis for their implementation; in particular economic development planning and fostering of small scale enterprise.

Economic development of the kind we propose in the past has not usually been the responsibility of local government beyond a limited amount of industrial promotion and certain elements of land use planning. In many respects it would be incompatible with standard council committee procedure. It can be argued, however, that local government reorganisation, in creating a new institutional framework and division of responsibilities between counties and districts in the metropolitan areas, may have changed this. The responsibilities of the new metropolitan county councils are strategic compared with the day to day actions of the district council. Economic development could be seen as a logical extension of structure planning. It could thus be argued that the new metropolitan counties would be able to bring to an economic development programme the necessary dynamism and concentration of effort. But we doubt that in practice any local authority would be able to work in a risk taking, entrepreneurial manner. On the other hand, central government has most of the disadvantages of local government and is even more remote. So, in the end, the answer would probably have to be a new agency; a semi-independent body, an economic development board, possibly set up by, and responsible to, the local authorities but relying for financial support on central government; and set up in such a way as to have executive control over its day to day activities.

Set up in this way, the four programmes could meet most of the requirements of a total approach. The Manpower Services Commission, in its new local office, would be responsible for the training programme. The City Council would adjust its housing policies in favour of the most disadvantaged and would set up its own internal machinery for channelling resources to those in greatest social need. And a new agency would be set up, possibly jointly by the City and County Councils, to promote industrial development in the areas of high unemployment.

But thus far, the approach differs very little from the alternative of relying entirely on the existing agencies outlined previously. What is missing is a basis for creating and sustaining the political and administrative commitment which the policy would require, permeating the actions of the responsible executive agencies and motivating them with a common purpose. It might be argued that this does not require institutional form for its expression; alternatively, that structures will not by themselves generate commitment. Nonetheless, the appropriate institutional structure could act as the focus for generating the commitment, and in any case there would be day to day problems of planning to be resolved, such as the allocation of priorities. The question is where should the institution be based?

The City Council clearly would have the widest set of tasks, the most experience of inner city problems and the greatest potential for grass roots contact with inner city communities. Yet their past failure to coordinate their own activities effectively does not bode well for taking on a further coordinating role. Their lack of experience in economic development suggests that they may not be effective in adjusting the classic imbalance between economic and housing and social policies. The same

234

strictures apply to the County Council which anyway would have a much smaller but highly significant role in the whole operation, for the county structure plan would clearly need to express the inner area policy as indeed the draft proposals and target statement already do.

On balance, and at the risk of remoteness, this would seem to be a role for the regional level of central government, particularly as it should in any case be involved in the evaluation by central government of the locally devised programme for inner areas. Regional offices would thus not only be involved in the various aspects of inner city regeneration programmes in their regions, they would also be informing Whitehall about the continuing balance between industrial location policy, new towns and so on throughout the region. This could be made to work as far as matters of coordination and planning are concerned, working for instance through the Economic Planning Board. It already has a strong interest in economic development which should ensure sufficient priority being given to industrial development and an awareness of economic reality, provided it focussed more clearly on the priority area and integrated the economic issues closely with housing and social programmes.

Whether political, as well as administrative, commitment could be fostered at the regional level of government is more arguable under present circumstances. Effectively, it could only be done by ministers taking the lead in a form of joint committee with local authority members. But the future of political accountability at the regional level of government will depend on the outcome of the national debate about devolution and its English dimension.

Resources for the inner area

Despite the priority we have given to attitudinal and organisational changes, it would be wrong to assume that resources for the inner area policies and the four programmes which we recommend could be met without a substantial increase in spending on inner area programmes and a redistribution of resources within the public sector. The total volume of the increment in resources, the net addition to public expenditure for the inner areas, is very difficult to estimate. It would depend on the general level of public expenditure permitted nationally and, within that, the degree of priority which might be accorded to the inner city. It would depend too on the rate and speed with which policies were pursued, or indeed the rate at which public expenditure for the inner areas could in practice be increased. The rate of take up of public resources by the private sector would also be important as much of the public expenditure would be designed to stimulate private investment and supplement private incomes through regional grants, housing improvement grants and various social security and welfare benefits. In the end, the volume of public expenditure would depend on the priority given to the programmes, the response by the private sector and the capability of the local agencies in carrying out the programmes.

The total volume of resources could be considerable. We have, for instance, prepared a rough estimate of the cost of implementing our recommendations for economic development, and raising levels of skill, the first two programmes.[1] The estimate assumes that rapid progress is made in implementing the programmes at the scale indicated in our report on Economic Development and summarised in chapter twelve of this report, working towards a reduction in levels of unemployment and increasing levels of skill in the inner area to rates more comparable with the county as a whole. The estimate shows a net additional annual expenditure of about fifteen million pounds of which about three quarters would be on the training programmes and the rest on industrial development. The estimate excludes the take up of selective financial assistance to firms, and any redistribution of resources currently being spent within Merseyside. The actual level of expenditure would depend too on matching private investment occurring. The figure is substantial but must be seen in the context of possible benefits. These would include a reduction in unemployment and welfare payments, currently at a level many times the estimated expenditure; the comparable opportunity cost of holding land vacant; and the returns accruing through having more trained labour whether it be deployed locally or moving away from Liverpool.

The most vital point about resources however is not the total volume which might be required but comparing that figure with the financial capabilities of the local authority. Any increase in expenditure by the City of Liverpool beyond its present level would present real difficulty.

The Merseyside County Council has recently prepared its report of survey on financial resources for the structure plan.[2] It shows that, compared with the rest of Great Britain, Merseyside in general and Liverpool in particular have below average rateable bases and above average rate levies, giving an inherent lack of buoyancy in the capacity to raise resources locally. The subsequent room for manoeuvre in the allocation of expenditure is further reduced by the extent to which the former county boroughs financed capital expenditure from loans. Merseyside's debt per capita is twenty five percent greater than the national average and the consequent loan charges became the first call on resources. The situation is aggravated too by the declining population. Sixty nine percent of relevant expenditure in Liverpool and Merseyside as a whole comes through government grants, the vast majority through the rate support grant. But the County Treasurer estimates that for each person who leaves Merseyside, the area loses around two hundred and twenty pounds grant aid by way of the needs and resources elements (particularly the latter) in the rate support grant. The per capita loss from Liverpool is even greater, at two hundred and thirty four pounds. The population of the city is currently declining by about thirteen thousand people annually, an additional

(1) For further details, see IAS Liverpool, *Economic Development of the Inner Area* (Department of the Environment 1977). Merseyside County Council has prepared a roughly similar estimate for the whole of the county but including selective financial assistance to firms, showing a net additional public sector investment of four hundred million pounds over ten years. See *Targets for Merseyside for the 1980s*, Report of the County Planning Officer, 17 December 1976.

(2) *Merseyside Structure Plan: Draft Report of Survey, Financial Resources* (August 1976), and *Report by The County Treasurer*, 17 December 1976 (Merseyside County Council).

loss of grant aid of about three million pounds. But the loss of population does not only reduce the amount of grant. It means too that the increasing burden of local authority expenditure has to be met by fewer people.

Regeneration of Liverpool's inner area will therefore depend on central government redistributing resources to selected inner areas by a clear system of priorities. But it should use the power this creates to foster significant changes in the ways in which local authorities and others approach the task of regeneration. It would therefore be necessary for government to ensure that the additional resources are used for the benefit of the inner areas and not either subsumed in general local authority expenditure or used, as it were, to release resources for use in other parts of the city. The additional resources would thus clearly have to be tied to existing inner area spending programmes. But equally they cannot be treated simply as a topping up of current expenditure in the inner city. Extra money should not be made available for council housing management in the inner area for instance unless there is some guarantee that it would be used, together with the current expenditure, to develop new methods and attitudes in housing management.

So one principle must be a clear system of accountability which includes existing expenditure on inner city programmes, as well as the extra resources provided. Similar methods to those developed for area resource analysis would be of assistance in this. But to maximize local control over spending, action by central government should be restricted to responding to claims for resources devised locally for individual inner areas. This suggests the extra resources should take the form of specific grants for individual inner areas, based on locally generated programmes, rather than a general grant based on some formula of need, as in the rate support grant.

The criteria for success

The four programmes described in chapter twelve are a necessary set of measures for the regeneration of inner Liverpool. Each is of equal importance, interacting as they do in the achievement of the aims of inner area policy. But whatever measures are taken will come after a long period of neglect and at a time of severe cuts in public expenditure and a low level of industrial investment. Results will take time to materialise. But the aims of policy should not be confused with the achievement of specific targets such as a particular population for the inner area, or a predetermined social mix.

The real index of achievement should be a clearly discernable and significant change in the long term trends which describes the quality of life in the inner area and particularly in the areas of greatest social need. Indicators of such change would include the rate of investment in private industry and the rate of unemployment, particularly among the groups at greatest risk of irregular work and loss of jobs. It would include the level of skill in the resident work force and of educational achievement among the wider population. In the field of housing they might include the take up of improvement grants, the time taken to complete the repairs to council houses, the demand for council tenancies in the inner city, or the investment by the private sector in new housing.

The list of possible indicators is long and indeed the most important are not measurable at all. The aims of inner area policy are very general and in one sense amount to no more than that the residents of the inner city should share in the opportunities for secure, well-paid work, a home and a decent environment to the same degree as people living in the more favoured parts of the city. Success depends on the degree to which confidence in the future of the inner city can be built and sustained and respect engendered for the values of its residents. But there are four crucial specific issues which need discussion if an effective evaluation is to be made. These are the level of employment in the inner city, the total population, the concentrations of vulnerable groups of people at risk and the allocation of resources to the area.

Opportunities for employment of a kind appropriate to the needs of inner city residents and easily accessible to where they live are of vital importance. The number of suitable jobs has been falling more rapidly than the population seeking them for many years. Successful training programmes, improved and cheaper public transport to the employment centres on Merseyside, further reductions in population (if they were not confined to the skilled and successful) might all lessen the gap between the supply and demand for jobs. But for many inner city residents, local opportunities for work will continue to be the only answer. Thus some increase in manual employment in industry and services will be essential.

The total future population of inner Liverpool is an imponderable question. Population has been falling for decades as a result of planned dispersal and voluntary movement to the new suburbs. The only movement into the inner city has been by those for whom private rented housing is the only type available, or the small numbers of young professional people, or students for whom the inner city is a favoured location for one period of their lives.

Conceivably the population might have fallen even faster if more inner city residents had been able to choose where to live. But it might have been less if opportunities for work and the quality of housing and the environment had been better. Now that the major clearance programmes have ended it is conceivable that the population of the inner city will, for the time being, stabilize at about its present level, particularly if there are signs of a real improvement in the quality of its environment and opportunities for work. But in the longer term, more serious questions will once more need to be asked. The private housing stock is old and improvements can at best be a temporary measure; there are limits to how far improvement can extend the life of the property. Equally, much of the council housing is aging, cannot easily be adapted, and will one day need to be replaced. Renewal in the longer term will very likely result in a resumed loss of population, depending on the changing attitudes to density and life style.

One of the defining characteristics of the inner area, and the basis for an inner area policy, is the concentrations within it of people who risk poverty or some form

238

of stress. Inevitably, their poverty results from their status in society, from their inability to gain well paid and secure employment and to make provision for the future. There is evidence of a strong and growing polarisation between the high status areas of the city and the rest. So far this polarisation most strongly affects the inner city where there is a residue of cheap housing and where the loss of opportunities for work has been greatest. But concentrations of deprivation have recently appeared in some of the outer council estates. The question for the future is whether this social polarisation will intensify, or whether as a result of inner area policies the concentration of deprivation will be dispersed, and those at risk become more widely scattered in other parts of the city.

Our recommendations are designed to tackle the conditions which lead to the concentrations of deprivation contained within the inner city, the worst social and economic conditions currently to be found within Liverpool or Merseyside. This is one reason for giving them high priority. Furthermore, the accumulated disadvantage which comes from living in their worst concentrations is shared by all their residents, adding a further dimension to the personal poverty and deprivation experienced by a significant minority. One outcome of the inner area policy should therefore be a reduction in the degree of social polarisation between the inner area and the rest of the city. But it will be essential to ensure that the concentrations of poverty are not dispersed simply by forcing poorer families to move as their existing houses are improved, to the next ring of inner suburbs or to council estates elsewhere in the city. This, too often, has been the pattern in the past, its results to be seen particularly in the growing concentrations of deprivation in certain of the outer council estates. Thus area-based policies designed to remove the conditions leading to concentrations of deprivation, initially in the inner areas and later in other parts of the city, should be seen as but one element of more general policies for tackling poverty in our society.

In our report, we have inevitably focussed on the problems of the inner areas, the stigma attached to certain districts within the inner city, their poverty and alienation, the failures of past policies. These are the measure of change which is required in policies and attitudes. But we have been at pains to stress that the problems are only one side of life, even in the worst areas. The other side is shown in the diversity of social circumstances, the strength of many of the communities, their location close to the centre of a large conurbation, the number of people still living in the inner city and the large stock of housing which they offer.

Visions for the future of the inner areas must be to build on their good features, through the programmes which we recommend. The people of all sections in the inner city must be able, in the future, to live there through choice and not because no alternative is available. They must be able to live in reasonable housing and a cared-for environment with good opportunities for the education and training of their children. Private investment must be brought back into the inner city, whether it be in sustaining current levels of employment and creating new jobs, or in improving the private stock of housing.

But a strong element in the vision must be a change in the style and attitudes of government. We have spelt out the problem. The redistribution of resources to the areas of greatest social need will depend on the creation of a strong, central commitment to the aims of inner area policy. But ensuring that programmes are identified and services provided with sensitivity to match the diverse needs of such areas will depend on a considerable measure of decentralisation and local control. The real priority for an inner areas policy both nationally and locally must be to build and sustain a political and administrative commitment to the reconciliation of these two requirements. Building that requirement will require changes in attitudes within government and the creation of appropriate institutions for their expression.

We do not suggest that any of these measures or changes of approach will be easy or quick to implement. We are all too conscious of the fact that criticism without responsibility is a relatively simple activity to be indulged in with care and circumspection. Nevertheless, we have tried over the past four years to understand at least some of the agonising problems that face those who are charged with the duty of helping those who are less able to help themselves. We have not feared to point out some of the mistakes which we believe have been made, but we also realise that hindsight can be a gift of great value. We can now only hope that our work, sincerely carried out and presented, can make some contribution to the betterment of the conditions of life of a great many people in this country.

Printed in England for Her Majesty's Stationery Office
by Bemrose & Sons Ltd., Wayzgoose Drive, Derby

Dd 587492 K28 6/77